JANE AUSTEN'S COUNTRY LIFE

JANE AUSTEN'S

COUNTRY LIFE

*Uncovering the rural backdrop to
her life, her letters and her novels*

DEIRDRE LE FAYE

F

FRANCES LINCOLN LIMITED
PUBLISHERS

Frances Lincoln Ltd
74–77 White Lion Street
London
N1 9PF
www.franceslincoln.com

HALF TITLE *Vignette from map of Knight estates
in Hampshire, by Henry Hogben, 1771.*

TITLE PAGE The Country round Dixton Manor
(detail), oil on canvas, English School, c.1725.

CONTENTS

✥ ✥

INTRODUCTION

T ODAY IN THE TWENTY-FIRST CENTURY there must be dozens of works of literary criticism studying Jane Austen's six famous novels and, in addition, there must be at least another dozen modern biographies discussing her short uneventful life, all of which endeavour to pinpoint the source of the genius that enabled her to compose these novels, paradoxically far more popular now than when they were first published two hundred years ago. It has become well known that her father was a Church of England clergyman, rector of the two little adjoining Hampshire parishes of Steventon and Deane, and that her elder brother Edward was adopted by wealthy cousins and became a large landowner, holding the three estates of Godmersham in Kent, and Steventon and Chawton in Hampshire. It is equally well known that her brothers Francis and Charles served in the Royal Navy during the French Revolutionary and Napoleonic Wars and both rose to the rank of admiral. Much has already been written regarding Jane's visits to London, her urban life in Southampton and Bath – especially the latter city, as it figures so largely as a location for both *Northanger Abbey* and *Persuasion* – and her holidays in the West Country, together with the family legend of an abortive romance at one of the seaside resorts there. It is perhaps less well known that Jane never crossed the Channel to travel on the Continent, and that her journeyings took her no further afield than from the Isle of Wight in the south to Staffordshire in the north, or from Kent in the east to Wales in the west.

Jane Austen, *steel engraving made in 1869 as frontispiece for her nephew's* A Memoir of Jane Austen, *based on Cassandra's portrait (see page 59).*

7

However, it has not yet been specifically noticed that of Jane's brief life span of forty-one years, three-quarters of this – almost exactly thirty-three years – was spent in the Hampshire countryside: first of all from her birth in 1775 until 1801, when she was growing up in the isolated hamlet of Steventon and learning at first hand about the never-ending seasonal round of farming which provided both food and income for its inhabitants; and then from 1809 until her death in 1817 in the larger village of Chawton close to the bustling little town of Alton, where she could participate in the wider life of brother Edward's mansion there – known to the family as the Great House – and its surrounding estate. Her niece Anna recalled in later years that Jane loved the country, and her delight in natural scenery was such that she would sometimes say she thought it must form one of the joys of heaven. This first-hand knowledge of country life underpins her writings and gives the time-frame against which she constructs her plots; she was not only a clergyman's daughter, but a farmer's daughter as well, and the following chapters will enlarge upon this rural background in order to complement the studies already published regarding the clerical and naval aspects of her family life.

CHAPTER 1
HAMPSHIRE

W HEN JANE AUSTEN WAS BORN IN 1775, the English countryside, even in the rich and populous county of Hampshire, was
a great deal wilder and rougher than it is now. For centuries
past farming had been carried out on the 'open-field' system, whereby the
land belonging to each village or parish was divided into two or three very
large unfenced areas of ploughland, each containing a different arable
crop, these areas being in turn divided into smaller strips or blocks, which
were cultivated by the individual cottagers. In appearance, these open or
'common-fields' would have looked something like the patchwork of
modern allotments, though the strips would have been larger, covering about half an acre apiece. The crops were usually wheat for finest
quality bread, barley and rye for coarser and cheaper breads – also some
barley would be malted and brewed to make beer – oats to feed livestock, and peas, beans and turnips for men and animals alike. In addition
to these open fields, which were grazed and manured by sheep flocks
after the cereal crops had been harvested, there would be meadows to
produce hay for winter fodder; and beyond the fields and meadows and
along roadsides was the 'waste' or common land, where the villagers
could graze their rough scrawny beasts, pick berries, nuts and mushrooms in season, cut furze and dig peat for fuel; and finally woodland,
not wild but managed to provide the slow-growing large timbers necessary for building houses or ships, with the smaller trees and branches
– 'underwood' – being cut more frequently for all other agricultural
and domestic purposes, as well as providing acorns and beech-mast to

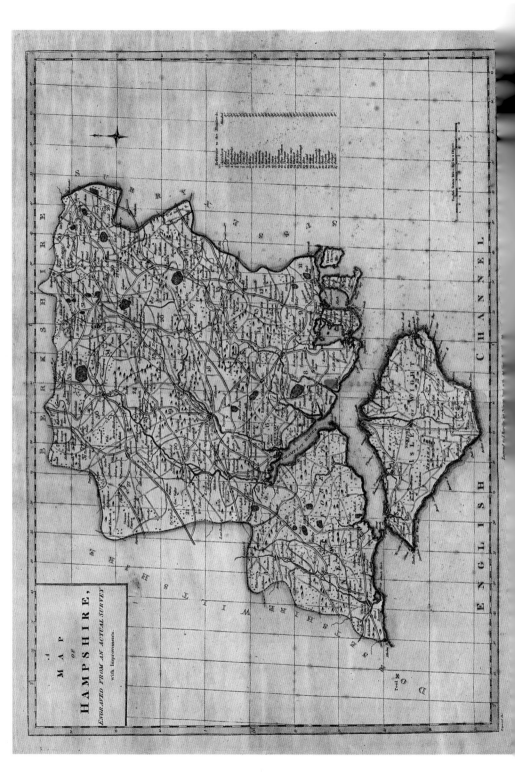

A
M A P
OF
HAMPSHIRE,
ENGRAVED FROM AN ACTUAL SURVEY
with Improvements.

feed free-ranging pigs in the autumn before they were killed and salted down for winter meat supplies. This open-field system, hardly more than subsistence farming, usually provided enough crops to feed the villagers and their livestock and leave some over for sale in the nearest town, though the fickleness of the English climate often resulted in poor harvests, semi-starvation for the villagers, and the slaughter of livestock for which no winter fodder was available.

During the eighteenth century, as the population increased, landowners gradually became discontented with the open-field system, realizing that the cultivation of such small individual plots scattered throughout the common-fields was wasteful of time and effort, and prevented any increased production or modernization of farming techniques. The idea therefore of 'enclosure' emerged, meaning that the 'waste' and the small strips of the common-fields were all joined together and then formally enclosed by hedges or fences to make larger and more compact areas of land, which in turn meant the individual farmer was better able to plan the rotation of his crops, could make use of newly invented machinery to improve their yields, and could undertake selective breeding to improve his livestock. The Knight family, who had owned the Steventon estate for generations, and their neighbours the Harwoods and Bramstons at Deane and Oakley, were well aware of the benefits of enclosure, and these estates had been laid out in field systems that survive this day. By the time the Austen family came to Steventon, the hedges were no longer thin lines of newly planted quickset, but had grown into hedgerows – borders of copse wood and timber, often wide enough to contain within them winding footpaths or rough cart tracks, and providing shelter for primroses, anemones and hyacinths, the wild flowers of early spring.

When we think nowadays of 'the countryside', the image that comes to mind – for the south of England at least – is of large well-tended fields, divided from each other by these planted hedgerows, some of which perhaps by now have been widened and trimmed into proper lanes while

Map of Hampshire, *hand-coloured engraving by Haywood, published by John Harrison, 1788.*

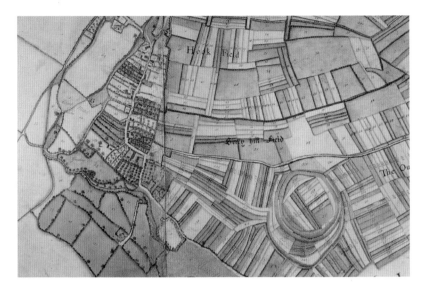

Detail from a map of Upper Clatford Manor, near Andover in Hampshire, *by John Reynolds (1733), showing strip cultivation around the village and the Bury Hill Iron Age hill fort.*

others remain as sheltered footpaths. Some of the fields will be grassy and grazed by herds of pedigree cows and sheep, with open streams still meandering through to provide water for the beasts; others, when not freshly ploughed, will show the shades of green and yellow of a wider variety of crops than were known to our ancestors. This present-day countryside is the culmination of the process of enclosure, which went on for a century, from 1750–1850. In *Sense and Sensibility,* which Jane Austen wrote in the late 1790s, the Middleton family in Devonshire have already enclosed their Barton estate and created a farm at the edge of High-church Down, while genial Sir John has laid out new plantations of trees at Barton-Cross and Abbeyland. We also see enclosure in action, when the mean-minded John Dashwood, who has only recently inherited the Norland Park estate in Sussex and is trying to avoid giving any financial support to his widowed stepmother and half-sisters by claiming his own income is too limited, solemnly tells Elinor:

The inclosure of Norland Common, now carrying on, is a most serious drain. And then I have made a little purchase within this half year; East Kingham Farm, you must remember the place, where old Gibson used to live. The land was so very desirable for me in every respect, so immediately adjoining my own property, that I felt it my duty to buy it. I could not have answered it to my conscience to let it fall into any other hands. A man must pay for his convenience; and it *has* cost me a vast deal of money.

At this time the process of enclosure was still very much under public discussion, since it deprived the rural poor of the use of common land; hence Henry Tilney's youthfully pedantic lecture to his sister and Catherine Morland during their walk on Beechen Cliff above Bath, regarding 'forests, the inclosure of them, waste lands, crown lands and government', which led him on to politics in general, 'and from politics, it was an easy step to silence' – for which perhaps the girls were thankful.

In *Emma*, written twenty years later, there are references which show that the Donwell Abbey estate, near Richmond in Surrey, has been enclosed for some time past, and is presently run as two farms. The large Abbey Mill Farm is tenanted by the efficient young Robert Martin, while Mr Knightley keeps in hand the home-farm and manages it himself. He can therefore tell his brother John 'what every field was to bear next year . . . the plan of a drain, the change of a fence, the felling of a tree, and the destination of every acre for wheat, turnips, or spring corn'; he also has an 'idea of moving the path to Langham, of turning it more to the right that it may not cut through the home meadows' – but will not do this 'if it were to be the means of inconvenience to the Highbury people'. The village of Highbury is part of the Donwell Abbey property, and Mr Knightley is as always considerate of other people's feelings. On the other side of Highbury, in contrast, the chief landowners are the Gilberts of Clayton Park, 'a proper unobjectionable country family', but who are nevertheless old-fashioned and unenterprising, since there is still a 'bleak common-field' outside the village, and the road passing this field and leading to Mr Weston's adjoining small estate is liable to become impassable in snowy weather. It is probably this same road which, further on, has 'a broader patch of greensward by the side' – that is, 'waste' – giving space for the gipsies to camp, who then so frighten Harriet Smith and her friend Miss Bickerton with their noisy and threatening demands for money.

Hampshire is a large county, and its southern boundary is the English Channel, with the two main coastal settlements of Portsmouth and Southampton lying close to each other. In Jane Austen's time Portsmouth was a garrison town as well as the traditional home of the Royal Navy, and Fanny Price, the heroine of *Mansfield Park*, lives there in her child-hood. Southampton was the ancient trading port and commercial hub, which by the eighteenth century was trying to reinvent itself as a genteel city of newly built smart terraces and landscaped promenades, complete with the civilized requirements of assembly rooms, libraries and elegant shops, and surrounded by a ring of country villas built by wealthy mer-chants. However, Jane had lived in Southampton for a few months in her childhood, and when she was a teenager and wrote her comic short story 'Love and Freindship' in 1790, she recalled with mockery 'the stinking fish of Southampton', as she remembered the fishermen's catches laid out on the quayside. In her widowhood Mrs Austen, with Jane and Cassandra, lived in Southampton for about three years, from the autumn of 1806 until they moved to Chawton in the summer of 1809; and from the garden of their rented house in Castle Square they could see the Isle of Wight – '*the Island*', as little Fanny Price calls it, much to her Bertram cousins' jeering amusement – 'as if there were no other island in the world'.

To the west of Southampton is the New Forest, whose history belies its name; it had been 'New' in 1080, when William the Conqueror, the first Norman king of England, declared that some 200 square miles of heath and woodland were to become a royal forest, for his private use and enjoyment – mainly the hunting of deer, which provided both sport and food for himself and his courtiers. In later centuries the New Forest was legally declared common-land, and the inhabitants acquired spe-cial rights for grazing their ponies and pigs, while its oak trees became a source of timber for the Royal Navy. From 1777 to 1804 the Revd William

Gilpin was vicar of Boldre, a Forest village only a few miles away from Southampton, and while there wrote several books praising what he called the 'picturesque' qualities of rough untamed landscapes – 'that kind of beauty that is agreeable in a picture' – illustrated by his own aquatint engravings. His books became very popular, and soon tourists in search of the 'picturesque' views he recommended were going to the Forest to admire the variety of its wild scenery – changing from thick clumps and avenues of very old oak and beech trees, threaded through by peaty brown streams which created moors and bogs in the lower-lying parts, with tangled patches of dark yew trees and holly bushes bound together by honeysuckles, to scattered groups of tall windblown pine trees above sandy tracks criss-crossing through the purple heathland and golden gorse bushes. One young lady, visiting Lyndhurst in the summer of 1810 and walking or driving about the neighbourhood with her family every day, rhapsodized constantly in her journal about the

> ... scenery in all its charms ... those delightful groves of tall beech trees so frequent in the forest. ... After tea Mama & I strolled out by owl-light till 8 o'clock ... the sky, tinted by the rays of the setting sun, & the glow on the surrounding forest scenery, together with the stillness & beauty of the Evening, would have formed a landscape for Claude Lorraine ... as we entered the Forest the setting sun threw its departing rays on the luxuriant foliage & the pale moon soon succeeded it & shed its silvery beams over the landscape ...

In *Sense and Sensibility* the down-to-earth Edward Ferrars teases romantic Marianne Dashwood by declaring: 'I like a fine prospect, but not on picturesque principles. I do not like crooked, twisted, blasted trees. I admire them much more if they are tall, straight and flourishing. I do not like ruined, tattered cottages. I am not fond of nettles, or thistles, or heath blossoms.' There is no documentary evidence that Jane ever visited Boldre, but as her brother Henry said in his 'Biographical Notice' that 'At a very early age she was enamoured of Gilpin on the Picturesque; and she seldom changed her opinions either on books or men', it seems very likely that she would have taken the opportunity to go there while she was living so close.

On the east of Southampton are the chalk uplands of the South Downs, which continue on into the neighbouring county of Sussex and provide short dry turf ideal for sheep to graze. These gradually change into the sandy wastelands of the north east corner of Hampshire, similar to those of the New Forest, with heathland stretching from Aldershot to Hartfordbridge Flats.

Further inland, in the low-lying green water meadows of the River Itchen, is Winchester, the former capital of England, with its ancient cathedral and the famous boys' school, Winchester College, close by. During Jane's lifetime many of her nephews were educated at the college, and the cathedral has now added to its renown by becoming her last resting place.

Although Jane and all her siblings were born in Hampshire, neither her father the Revd George Austen, nor her mother, Cassandra Leigh, had any previous connection with the county. George's ancestors had been living in West Kent, around Tonbridge and Sevenoaks, for at least two centuries, and had flourished as clothiers – that is, middlemen who bought up wool from the local sheep farmers, organized its spinning and weaving into cloth as a cottage industry, and then sold on the cloth to wholesale merchants – and had prospered sufficiently to acquire two manors, Broadford and Grovehurst, near Horsmonden. George, though, was the orphaned son of a younger son, and as such not likely to inherit these family estates. Instead, his uncle Francis Austen, a rich solicitor in Sevenoaks, saw to it that he had a good education at Tonbridge School, from where he gained scholarships to St John's College in Oxford, and in due course became a clergyman. A distant Kentish cousin, Mr Thomas Knight of Godmersham, then presented George to the living of his Hampshire estate of Steventon, and with this assured position and income, George was able to think of marriage. It was probably while he was in Oxford that he had met Cassandra Leigh, the niece of the Revd Dr Theophilus Leigh, Master of Balliol College, and they became engaged in 1763. Cassandra had grown up in Harpsden, a village close to Henley-on-Thames in Oxfordshire, where her father Revd Thomas Leigh was the rector; and when she visited Steventon for the first time, just before her marriage, she thought it an unattractive place when compared to the Oxfordshire scenery of wooded hillsides rising above the rich valleys of the wide River Thames. However, for the first few years after their marriage in 1764, the young couple had to rent the rectory in the neighbouring village of Deane, while George carried out repairs to the ramshackle old rectory at Steventon, some two miles away. Their first three children, James, George and Edward, were born at Deane, and the family did not move to Steventon until the summer of 1768.

Steventon and Deane

Steventon and Deane were then very small villages, hardly more than hamlets, hidden in the chalk hills in the north-east corner of Hampshire, and even today they are still small and off the beaten track. Deane had only about 130 inhabitants of 23 houses, even though it was close to one of the main coaching routes from London to the west of England; the Deane Gate Inn, situated at the turnpike gate which closed off the village street from the main road, was the stop for these coaches. It was probably also the 'post-box' for the Austens' letters, since Mr Austen would be riding regularly about the parish in the course of his clerical duties and so could drop off and collect them without any extra difficulty. In Jane's very first sur-viving letter, that of 9–10 January 1796, she tells Cassandra that 'We

The Deane Gate Inn, *drawing by Ellen Hill,* c.*1900.*

left Warren at Dean Gate, in our way home last night, and he is now on his road to town [that is, London]'; and almost exactly two years later, in January 1798, Charles Austen 'attempted to go to town last night, and got as far on his road thither as Dean Gate; but both the coaches were full, and we had the pleasure of seeing him back again.' Deane rectory stood on a corner of the village street, facing the decrepit little All Saints church and the handsome red brick manor house, home of the Harwood family for several generations past. When Mr and Mrs Austen moved in, the rectory was described in advertisements as a 'neat brick dwelling house', comprising four living rooms and four bedrooms, together with all necessary store rooms and servants' quarters and stabling for six horses; but later on, in the nineteenth century, their descendants called it 'a low damp place with small inconvenient rooms, and scarcely two on the same level'. Indeed, only a few months before Mr and Mrs Austen took up residence in April 1764, the preceding very wet autumn and winter had so saturated the land that the villagers' wells were overflowing and a stream had sprung up and was running through the rectory garden. By 1810, Mr Austen's successor as rector, Revd John Smith, gave as his excuse for non-residence in the parish the 'very delicate state of his wife's health, and the parsonage house being so old and so remarkably damp' – though he nevertheless considered the house quite suitable for the new curate, Revd Arthur Hammond. Twenty years later, Mr Smith was still refusing to live at Deane, for the same reasons, and the house was eventually demolished during the 1830s.

Steventon was a rather more populous village than Deane, with about 150 inhabitants and 20 houses. This figure included the Digweed family, who rented the manor house and most of the land in the parish from Mr Knight of Godmersham, and Mr Austen's own family in the rectory. St Nicholas's church, and the manor house with its farmyard opposite, were both situated in some isolation at the top of a slight hillside, and the rectory stood in the shallow valley below, half a mile away. It was surrounded by sloping meadows dotted with elm, chestnut and spruce fir trees, at the end of a small village of about fourteen cottages scattered along either side of the lane which linked the Austens to Deane in one direction and to North Waltham in the other. As at Deane, there was no village stream – the

Steventon Rectory, *wood engraving by George Pearson (1869), based on an Austen family drawing.*

Steventon cottagers had to rely upon wells for their water supply, and the farmers had to dig ponds to provide water for livestock. The rectory was also an old building, and when the Austens moved in its walls were a patchwork of timber-framed brick panels and weather-tiled lath and plaster, under a red tiled gabled roof. Over the years Mr Austen gradually enlarged and improved the house, and eventually it had five rooms on the ground floor, seven bedrooms and three attics above. He could not afford to rebuild it entirely, and later in the nineteenth century his grandson recalled that 'the rooms were finished with less elegance than would now be found in the most ordinary dwellings. No cornice marked the junction of wall and ceiling; while the beams which supported the upper floors projected into the rooms below in all their naked simplicity, covered only by a coat of paint or whitewash.' The front door was on the north side of the house, and opened straight into an entrance or common parlour, where Mrs Austen sat to do her sewing in clear light, making and repairing the family's clothes. On the left side of the front door was the dining parlour or sitting room, and on the

Alderney cows: The Victoria Cow 'Buffie', *oil on canvas, by Thomas Sidney Cooper (1848).*

other was the main kitchen; behind these rooms on the south side were Mr Austen's study, overlooking the garden, and the back kitchen which opened out on the west side of the house.

Now that Mr Austen and his young family were settled in their own home, he and his wife started to create the busy routine that would continue for the next thirty years. George was a most conscientious parish priest, hardly ever taking time off from his clerical duties to travel to London or Kent to see his relations, and in addition was a practical and enterprising farmer. Steventon is situated upon light heathland, very suitable for grazing sheep and growing cereals – wheat, oats and barley – with peas and clover as alternative crops, and a few cattle to provide beef and milk. From his Kentish cousins, the Knights, Mr Austen rented Cheesedown Farm, in the north of the parish, amounting to 195 acres, and later on was able to take over another 57 acres lying in Deane parish. These lands he farmed with the assistance of his trustworthy chief labourer John Bond, whose name occurs frequently in Jane's letters, and who seems to have been as devoted a servant to Mr Austen as William Larkins is to Mr Knightley in

Emma. Pigs were kept at Cheesedown, and on the downland around the village grazed the hundreds of sheep owned by Mr Austen and his neighbours the Digweeds. A visitor to Hampshire in 1792 commented: 'There is something pleasing and pastoral in the scenery hereabouts. Broken ground, green valleys, sheep-clad knolls, and gentle hills covered with wood, and openings through the boles of trees into the neighbouring open country, have a very delightful effect here, especially in spring.'

Mrs Austen, for her part, already mother to three little boys, went on to have another five children at Steventon – Henry, Cassandra, Francis, Jane and Charles – as well as being surrogate mother to the teenage boys whom Mr Austen took into the family home as a third source of income, tutoring them for entry to Oxford colleges. She also supervised the walled gardens on the south side of the rectory, which were bounded by a straight row of spruce firs, and a terrace walk of turf; probably these firs provided the wherewithal for brewing spruce beer, a drink which the Austens enjoyed and which Jane later on mentions in *Emma.* It is made by boiling the tips and twigs of spruce until they start to disintegrate, then skimming them off and adding molasses to the remaining liquid; once cool, yeast is added and the brew allowed to ferment for a few days, resulting in a pleasant drink which both smells and tastes like beer. Flowers, strawberries, cucumbers, vegetables and soft fruit trees were all grown together in the gardens, and bees kept to provide honey, wax and mead; potatoes were still something of a novelty, and it was remembered in the family that when Mrs Austen advised the wife of one of the villagers to plant them in her own garden, the latter replied, 'No, no, they are very well for you gentry, but they must be terribly *costly to rear.*' And as if these occupations were not enough, Mrs Austen had her own little dairy farm and chicken run in the field on the west side of the rectory, to provide milk, meat and eggs for her household. Perhaps it was these memories of the Steventon rectory farmyard and the Digweeds' larger farmyard higher up the hill, which in later years led Jane to place the parsonage at Mansfield Park in a very similar setting, as Mary Crawford comments: 'I cannot look out of my dressing-closet without seeing one farm yard, nor walk in the shrubbery without passing another . . .'

A few letters survive, written by Mrs Austen in the early years of her married life to her sister-in-law Mrs Walter in Kent (wife of Mr Austen's elder half-brother William-Hampson Walter), which show that she was as good a farmer as her husband:

> *26 August 1770:* What Luck we shall have with those sort of Cows I can't say. My little Alderney one turns out tolerably well, and makes more Butter than we use, and I have just bought another of the same sort, but as her Calf is but just gone, can not say what she will be good for yet.

> *6 June 1773:* We will not give up the hopes of seeing you both at Steventon before the Summer is over; Mr Austen wants to shew his Brother his Lands & his Cattle & many other matters; and I want to shew you my Henry & my Cassy, who are both reckoned fine Children. . . . I have got a nice Dairy fitted up, and am now worth a Bull & Six Cows, and you would laugh to see them; for they are not much bigger than Jack-asses – and here I have got Turkies, & Ducks & Chicken . . .

In 1775 rain fell almost incessantly until the middle of March, but it was followed by a dry warm summer, which led to an abundant harvest – though there was rain again in July, as Mrs Austen told Mrs Walter:

> *20 August 1775:* The Wheat promises to be very good this year, but we have had a most sad wet time for getting it in, however we got the last Load in yesterday, just four weeks after we first began Reaping. I am afraid the weather is not likely to mend for it Rains very much to-day, and we want dry weather for our Peas and Oats, I don't hear of any Barley ripe yet, so am afraid it will be very late before Harvest is over. I was in hopes I should have seen you in Hampshire this Summer, but it is now getting so late in the year that I suppose I must not think of it . . .

Mrs Austen was already pregnant when she wrote this letter in August to Mrs Walter, and Jane was born in the early hours of Saturday 16 December 1775. The next morning it was Mr Austen's turn to write to the Walters, when he announced her birth – though he was perhaps more interested to pass on farming news than that of the arrival of a seventh child:

> You have doubtless been for some time in expectation of hear-
> ing from Hampshire, and perhaps wondered a little we were
> in our old age grown such bad reckoners but so it was, for
> Cassy certainly expected to have been brought to bed a month
> ago: however last night the time came, and without a great
> deal of warning, everything was soon happily over. We have
> now another girl, a present plaything for her sister Cassy and
> a future companion. She is to be Jenny, and seems to me as if
> she would be as like Henry, as Cassy is to Neddy. Your sister
> thank God is pure well after it. . . . Let my brother know his
> friend Mr Evelyn is going to treat us with a ploughing match in
> this neighbourhood on next Tuesday, if the present frost does
> not continue and prevent it, Kent against Hants for a rump of
> beef; he sends for his own ploughman from St Clair. Does my
> brother know a Mr Collis, he says he is very well acquainted
> with him, he visited me to buy some oats for Evelyn's hunters.

However, the 'present frost' did continue, for the winter of 1775–6 was unusually cold over most of Europe, including Britain. Another Hampshire clergyman, the Revd Gilbert White of Selborne, a village about fifteen miles from Steventon, recorded in his naturalist's diary that a blizzard started on 7 January and continued on and off until 12 January, by which time

> . . . a prodigious mass overwhelmed all the works of men, drift-
> ing over the tops of the gates and filling the hollow lanes. . . .
> The poultry dared not to stir out of their roosting-places, for
> cocks and hens are so dazzled and confounded by the glare of
> snow that they would soon perish without assistance . . . From

Steventon Cottages (now demolished), *an Austen family drawing*, c.*1810*.

the 14th the snow continued to increase and began to stop the road waggons and coaches, which could no longer keep on their regular stages and especially on the western roads, where the fall appears to have been deeper than in the south.

In Kent, a colder part of southern England than Hampshire, it was recorded that streets in Canterbury were impassable for horses and carriages, and that no mail had been received from London for several days past, while it was only the most extreme necessity for want of provisions which led in some places to villagers co-operating in digging tunnels through the snow, as in coal mines and chalk pits. Although the sun shone on the 20th, it was too cold to thaw, and during the last few days of the month the temperature dropped ever lower and lower until it sank well below the freezing point of water, perhaps as low as 27 degrees Fahrenheit

Interior of a cottage at Oare, Somerset, *drawing by W.W. Wheatley, 1849.*

– 'the cold was so penetrating that it occasioned ice in warm chambers and under beds [that is, the urine froze in the chamber-pots]; and in the day the wind was so keen that persons of robust constitutions could scarcely endure to face it.'

The thaw finally started on 1 February, but March was still frosty; so it is hardly surprising that, after being baptized by her father as soon as she was born, Jane was not taken out for her public christening in church until Good Friday, 5 April. It was Mrs Austen's custom to nurse her babies herself for their first three months of life, then wean them and put them out to be dry-nursed by one of the Steventon cottage families for a year or so, until they were able to talk and run about and were clean enough to be brought back into the rectory household. It was therefore probably soon after her christening that Jane in her turn was handed over to foster parents; and it would seem that it was the extended Littleworth family, some of whom lived at Cheesedown Farm and others in a cottage beside the lane just below the rectory, whom the Austens had chosen to look after their babies. Different members of this group are often mentioned in Jane's letters, and in 1789, at the age of fourteen, Jane herself stood godmother to one of their children, Eliza-Jane Littleworth. This fostering was in no way an abandonment of the baby, for the Austen parents would visit it daily and it was also often brought to see them in the rectory. Jane's eldest brother James remembered in later life that he used to call his foster mother 'Movie', and her third brother, Edward Knight, remembered that his playmate in infancy had been one of their young daughters, Elizabeth ('Bet') Littleworth.

As Jane grew up she would gradually learn her way about Steventon. The Littleworths and their neighbours lived on each side of the village street in whitewashed cottages with thatched roofs, which had grape vines and woodbine clinging to their cob walls [a mixture of clay and straw] and beans,

Work and Play in the Kitchen, *watercolour by Thomas Heaphy (1775-1835)*.

potatoes and coleworts [vegetable greens which do not heart, or cabbage plants before they heart] growing in their gardens. The cottage wives sat at home, in summer out on their doorsteps in the sunlight, spinning flax and wool. The rectory was halfway between the village street and the crest of the rising ground upon which stood St Nicholas's church and the old rambling Elizabethan stone-built manor house opposite, home of the Digweed family of tenant farmers, with all its barns, stables and granaries dotted around behind it. The Digweeds had five sons – John, Harry, James, William and Francis – all much of an age with the Austen children, and who must therefore have been their earliest playmates; and Jane was undoubtedly speaking from experience when she wrote that the ten-year-old Catherine Morland, the future heroine of *Northanger Abbey*, was 'noisy and wild, hated confinement and cleanliness, and loved nothing so well in the world as rolling down the green slope at the back of the house'.

Still further away from the village street there were fields enclosed by newly planted green thorn hedges, small copses with oak, elm, ash, maple and sycamore trees, and then many acres of rough downland where flocks of sheep roamed freely. In those days it was the custom for each flock to have as its leader an old castrated male, known as a 'bell-wether' because a small iron bell was hung round his neck which tinkled with every movement; hence even when out of sight an experienced shepherd would listen for the bell to know where his sheep were, and any sudden alteration in its gentle tinkling would alert him to the fact that something was frightening the animals and making them run about wildly. Jane would have grown up with the constant background noises of tinkling sheep-bells and the bleating of sheep and lambs, the songs of pewits and larks on the hillsides and the cooing of pigeons in the woodlands, as well as the nearer noises and smells of the pigs at Cheesedown Farm and the cows and poultry in her mother's little domestic farmyard.

Southwards from Steventon lay the village of North Waltham, where the rector, Revd Charles Cottrell, did not reside; he had rented out the rectory to a local farmer, with the obligation in the lease that two rooms were to be set aside in which a curate could lodge. There was no resident squire or other landowner, and hence no gentleman's family whom the Austens could visit as social equals. Beyond North Waltham the road became known as Popham Lane, and led to a junction where the coach road from Salisbury to London met that from Southampton to London. Here stood – and still stands – the Wheatsheaf Inn, a well-known landmark and meeting place – the Georgian equivalent of a modern-day service station on a motorway – being described by one inveterate traveller as a most excellent inn, which in 1794 could muster thirty-nine post-horses for hire, as well as four post-chaises. It does not seem, however, that the Austens normally travelled this way, but preferred to catch the London coach on the alternative route that stopped at the Deane Gate Inn. On the other side of the coach road and further to the east was the village of Dummer, home of the thirteen-strong Terry family, whom Jane often met at dances in later years.

Walking on northwards from Steventon Jane would have become accustomed to visiting one of the local squires, John Harwood and his family, in their manor house opposite her parents' original home of Deane rectory. The Harwoods had owned lands in Deane parish for several generations, and had improved their estate by enclosing it in 1773, with the co-operation of their nearest neighbours, the Austens and the Bramstons. There were three Harwood sons – John, Earle and Charles – so here were yet more boys to join with the Digweeds and Jane's brothers in playing cricket and baseball, riding on horseback and running about the countryside. Whether Jane and Cassandra took part in these boys' games is not known; but certainly Jane wrote later on that Catherine Morland did so when she was in her early teens, before she entered into training for the part of the heroine of *Northanger Abbey*.

Oakley and Ashe

Adjacent to the Harwoods' lands on the east side of Steventon Lane were those of Mr and Mrs Wither Bramston of Oakley Hall, and as Jane and Cassandra grew up they often walked there – in 1799 Jane referred to Mrs Bramston as being very civil, kind and noisy. The Bramstons were a youngish couple, but childless, and Mrs Bramston filled in her days by reading novels, tending her flower garden, doing embroidery and experimenting with other ladylike handicrafts, as well as scribbling rather incoherent letters to her kinswoman Mrs Hicks Beach in Gloucestershire. Mr Bramston was a good amateur architect and largely rebuilt Oakley Hall in 1792, as well as planning new cottages for his tenants and, in 1818, building a completely new smart church at Deane to replace the tiny decrepit one in which Mr Austen served. He took a keen interest in local politics, and also prided himself upon his home-brewing. In 1800 Jane told Cassandra: 'At Oakley Hall we did a great deal – eat some sandwiches all over mustard, admired Mr Bramston's Porter & Mrs Bramston's Transparencies, & gained a promise from the latter of two roots of hearts-ease, one all yellow & the other all purple, for you.' Porter was a strong dark brown bitter beer, brewed from malt which had been charred or browned and thought to be very nourishing, and was supposed to have acquired its name from being the favourite drink of that class of labourers who earned their living as deliverymen, carrying goods and parcels on foot across towns and cities. When Willoughby is driving wildly from London to Devonshire to see the Dashwoods again, he stops briefly at Marlborough to gulp a pint of porter. Transparencies were pictures painted in watercolour on fine fabric, usually linen, which were then stuck against the glass of a window so that light could shine through them and add brilliance to the drawing. It was perhaps Mrs Bramston's artistic efforts in this direction which Jane remembered and brought into the school room at Mansfield Park, where the Bertram sisters had painted '. . . three transparencies, made in a rage for transparencies, for the three lower panes of one window, where Tintern Abbey held its station between a cave in Italy, and a moonlight lake in Cumberland . . .' Mrs Bramston was much pleased when she read the book, and thought that Lady Bertram was very like herself, saying that she preferred it to either *Sense and Sensibility* or *Pride and Prejudice* – but added humbly that this might be due to her want of taste, because she did not understand wit.

To the west of the lane running from Steventon to Deane was the village of Ashe, rather bigger than Deane and Steventon, where the aged Revd Dr Richard Russell had been rector ever since 1729. When he died in the spring of 1783 the new rector was the Revd George Lefroy, who arrived in the parish with his wife and two young children, Jemima-Lucy and George junior, their family increasing as the years passed. The Lefroys were much better off than the Austens, and were able to rebuild the rectory into a handsome red brick Georgian house that had 'charming views of the meadows, fields and woods'; its living rooms were hung with family pictures 'as elegantly executed as any in the kingdom', and were large enough to provide the space for family dances as their children grew up. In one of Jane Austen's earliest surviving letters, written in January 1796, she tells Cassandra about a ball on 8 January in one of the neighbouring mansions, when she danced and flirted with the rector's Irish nephew, Tom Lefroy: 'Imagine to yourself everything most profligate and shocking in the way of dancing and sitting down together', and adding that she intended to flirt again with Tom when the Lefroys held their own dance on 15 January. The rector's wife, who was known respectfully in the neighbourhood as 'Madam' Lefroy, was not interested in farming and gardening as was Mrs Austen, but instead busied herself by teaching the Ashe village children to read and write, and also trained the girls in straw plait work, as another form of profitable cottage industry. She was so successful in this respect that a scholarly gentleman, collecting information on local history more than twenty years later, could write: 'In this part of Hampshire the females are much employed in the braiding or platting of straw for hats and bonnets. This they perform with much felicity and neatness and in every respect equal to the celebrated manufacture of these articles at Dunstable.' Unlike spinning, where the worker – the 'spinster' – had to stay at home in front of her spinning wheel, the straw-plait worker did not need to sit down to plait the straws, and even while her hands were busily employed could still walk out to meet other girls in the village street or on the village green; some clergymen therefore disapproved of this type of work, saying it encouraged girls to go 'gadding and gossiping about the village' – but Madam Lefroy evidently did not share this pursed-lipped attitude. Apart from the Lefroys at the rectory, the manor house Ashe Park was owned by the Portal family and tenanted by Mr James Holder, wealthy from the proceeds of his West Indian estates, but a rather dull bachelor given, as Jane said, to making 'infamous puns' whenever he held small dinner parties.

St Mary's Church, Overton, *drawing by Inigoe Millard, 1785. Court House is next door to the church.*

Overton, Basingstoke and Odiham

Overton was about one mile from Ashe and three miles from Steventon, and the mail coach running between London and Exeter passed through it twice a day, hence the New Inn was also the post office and all Jane's letters written from Steventon bear the Overton postmark. The little trout stream that rose from marshy ground at Ashe was large enough, by the time it reached Overton, to drive three corn mills and a large silk milk that was the pride of the town. With about a thousand inhabitants, Overton could support a number of tradesmen, and in addition four fairs in the year were held in Winchester Street, the wide main thoroughfare, all principally for the sale of sheep and lambs – it was estimated that there were 4,000 sheep in the parish. However, despite this apparent agricultural prosperity, visitors were unimpressed by the town – one tourist calling it little and dirty,

31

and another family describing it as ugly with nasty shabby houses. Jane's eldest brother James became curate of Overton in 1790, and lived at first in the very small vicarage; it was so small, indeed, that when his successor the Revd William Harrison and his wife were living there in 1803, they had no spare bedroom and so had themselves to sleep out elsewhere in the town when their friends the Mackie family came for an overnight visit. Like Mrs Austen, the Harrisons put their garden to good use, as young Sophy Mackie noticed: 'The house has a green in the front, of which they have made quite a farm yard, as all the hens & chickens are there.' After James Austen married Anne Mathew in the spring of 1792, the young couple lived for a few months in Court House before moving to Deane parsonage later on in that year. Court House was next door to the church and very much larger than the vicarage, having six bedrooms and three large living rooms or parlours.

The Austens would obviously have visited James while he was living in Overton, whether at the vicarage or at Court House, but otherwise it seems they had little contact with the town – perhaps they too thought it was small, dirty and shabby. There were no dressmakers, haberdashers or milliners amongst the tradesmen there to warrant any calls by Mrs Austen and her daughters, and only one mercer [a dealer in textiles, especially woollen, and associated small wares]. He may, however, have been the base supplier of the pedlars who roamed around the surrounding countryside with bulging backpacks to carry out doorstep sales at isolated cottages. They were known as 'scotchmen' because when dealing with illiterate customers the only way accounts could be kept was by 'scotching' or cutting notches on tally-sticks. One of these certainly used to call at Steventon rectory, for Jane wrote to Cassandra in November 1798:

> The Overton Scotchman has been kind enough to rid me of some of my money, in exchange for six shifts and four pair of stockings. The Irish [that is, the linen, enough to cut up into six shifts] is not so fine as I should like it; but as I gave as much money for it as I intended, I have no reason to complain. It cost me 3s.6d. per yard [17½p in modern currency]. It is rather finer, however, than our last, and not so harsh a cloth.

Jane and Cassandra seem to have used most of the linen to make shifts for themselves, but in a later letter Jane records that the four pairs of stockings were given as Christmas presents to some of the Steventon village wives. There was also another pedlar who made regular visits to the rectory, and in October 1798 he called when the sisters were away: 'The Lace Man was here only a few days ago; how unfortunate for both of us that he came so soon!'

Basingstoke, about eight miles to the north-east of Steventon, was the Austens' local metropolis, supporting a wide variety of shops and tradesmen; with a population of about two thousand and still increasing, it was twice the size of Overton and far busier, since it had grown up at the junction of five major roads along which Royal Mail coaches, stage coaches and lumbering goods waggons made regular journeys between London and the south and west of England, and the journey from Basingstoke to London took only six hours. In 1791 a contemporary gazetteer could describe the district as being 'rich in pasture, and sprinkled with fine houses, and a brook runs by the town, which has plenty of trout. Many thousand acres of the adjoining downs have been lately enclosed, and now produce abundant crops of all kinds of grain.' The Austens would see this improvement in agriculture as they drove in on their shopping expeditions, or to call on their friend Mrs Russell at Goldings Park on the London Road side of the town; and no doubt Mr Austen would comment approvingly upon the benefits Basingstoke would gain from the increase in employment as well as in the production of one of the necessary staples of life. There was also a racecourse on Basingstoke Down, with races being held on two days early in October, followed by a ball on the second night for the nobility and gentry who had come to watch the sport. It does not seem that Jane ever attended these races, but in later years her brother James and his family certainly did, and in the very wet October of 1813 Jane commented to Cassandra: 'Poor Basingstoke Races! – there seem to have been two particularly wretched days on purpose for them . . .'

The town hall stood in the market place; it was supported upon pillars and so provided shelter for open stalls set up beneath it on market days, and the large rooms above were used for civic meetings and assembly balls – these latter were held on Thursdays, once a month from October to March, and in her letters Jane often mentions attending them, providing her with scenes which she could reproduce when writing *Pride and Prejudice*. There were sixteen inns in the town, of which the Maidenhead and the Crown were considered to be the best – Thomas Robbins of the Crown being also Post Master for the town – while the Angel claimed to be the biggest, with stabling for nearly a hundred horses, needed to service some of the many coaches which passed through daily; it also had a small ballroom built over the stables at the rear of the yard, and here again this provided Jane with the setting for the ball at the Crown in Emma's Highbury. A corn market was held every Wednesday, and there were four big fairs during the summer months, two for sheep and two for cattle, as well as a hiring fair on 10 October when farm workers could take the opportunity of changing their employment. The workers would stand in the market place waiting to be approached by would-be employers, and identified themselves by tokens of their trade: a shepherd would have a twist of wool pinned to his smock, a dairyman or dairymaid a tuft of cow hairs, and a carter would carry his long whip, while maidservants might carry a mop or a pail.

The Lyford family of surgeons and doctors lived at No. 1 New Street, Basingstoke, and are frequently mentioned in Jane's letters, partly as personal friends of the Austens and partly because Mrs Austen often consulted John Lyford senior in his professional capacity – on 26 October 1798 he prescribed '12 drops of Laudanum when she went to Bed, as a Composer' and highly approved of her recipes for dandelion tea, which she was to drink to cure 'a sluggish state of the liver'. Several of the Basingstoke shopkeepers also appear in Jane's letters, especially, of course, those whose stock-in-trade would appeal to female customers. On this same day in October 1798, Jane went to one of the haberdashers in the town, and told Cassandra:

> While my Mother & Mr Lyford were together, I went to Mrs Ryders, & bought what I intended to buy, but not in much perfection. There were no narrow Braces for Children, & scarcely any netting silk; but Miss Wood as usual is going to Town very soon, & will lay in a fresh stock. I gave 2s/3d a yard [about 11p in modern currency] for my flannel, & I

Engraving of the old Town Hall and Assembly Rooms in Basingstoke market place (demolished in the 1830s).

fancy it is not very good; but it is so disgraceful & contemptible an article in itself, that its being comparatively good or bad is of little importance.

Mrs Ryder died two years later, and Jane then wrote sardonically to Cassandra: 'The Neighbourhood have quite recovered the death of Mrs Ryder – so much so, that I think they are rather rejoiced at it now; her Things were so very dear! – & Mrs Rogers is to be all that is desirable. Not even Death itself can fix the friendship of the World.'

Mrs Ann Davies was a linen-draper, and perhaps something of a martinet

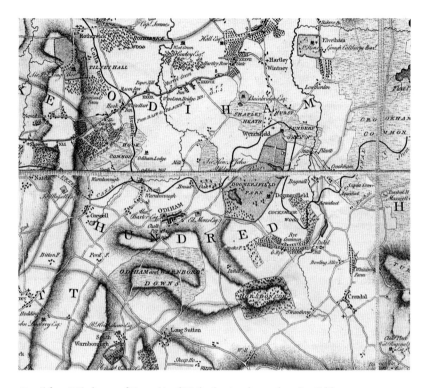

Detail from Milne's map of Hampshire (1791), showing the canal passing Odiham.

in her dealings with the public, since according to Jane she 'frightened' young Charles Austen into buying a piece of Irish linen in January 1799 when they were shopping in Basingstoke together, which his sisters would then make up into shirts for him. A more amiable businesswoman was Mrs Mary Martin, landlady of the Maidenhead inn, who had been in the habit of organizing the monthly assembly balls in the Town Hall, until this task passed to William Wilson of the Crown inn, who became landlord of the Maidenhead as well. Instead, Mrs Martin took over the haberdashery and millinery business of John Chambers, and also started a lending library in December 1798, as Jane wrote: 'I have received a very civil note from Mrs

Martin requesting my name as a Subscriber to her Library which opens the 14th of January . . . Mrs Martin tells us that her Collection is not to consist only of Novels, but of every kind of Literature . . .' but the inhabitants of Basingstoke were perhaps not sufficiently intellectual to appreciate such works, for by October 1800 she had become bankrupt: 'Our whole Neighbourhood is at present very busy grieving over poor Mrs Martin, who has totally failed in her business, & had very lately an execution in her house' – that is, the bailiffs had entered to assess the value of her possessions with a view to paying off her debtors' claims.

John Ring, by trade an auctioneer, house furnisher, cabinet-maker and upholsterer, and five times Mayor of Basingstoke, lived in Lower Church Street, and both Mr Austen and James Austen were his clients, as his account books show. When James and his first wife Anne Mathew moved into Deane parsonage in 1792, they spent £200 on completely fitting out and furnishing the house, right down to the pots, pans and scrubbing brushes used in the kitchen. In January 1794 Mr Austen bought two new four-poster beds for Jane and Cassandra, and then in early December that year he ordered a small mahogany writing box to be made, costing 12 shillings [60p in modern currency]; this was probably a present to Jane for her nineteenth birthday on 16 December, and upon it all her letters and novels were subsequently written. The box went with her when she travelled, and on one occasion was very nearly lost. In October 1798 Jane and her parents were staying overnight at the Bull & George inn at Dartford in Kent, and 'it was discovered that my writing and dressing boxes had been by accident put into a chaise which was just packing off as we came in, and were driven away towards Gravesend in their way to the West Indies . . . in my writing box was all my worldly wealth, 7£ . . .' but the innkeeper sent a man and horse after the chaise, the box was safely retrieved, '. . . and in half an hour's time I had the pleasure of being as rich as ever'.

Some seven miles to the east of Basingstoke was another little town, Odiham, about the same size as Overton but far more elegant, with the remains of an ancient royal castle and palace to prove its importance in antiquity, while several turnpike roads and a newly made canal linking its trade to both Basingstoke and London proved its modern enterprise. Odiham is not mentioned in Jane's surviving letters, but it must have been quite well known to her, since Mr Austen was one of the group of local gentry who had been involved in the planning of the route of the canal as it passed by the town, and several of the families whom she met at the Basingstoke assembly balls lived in the vicinity. In addition, for a few years at the end of the eighteenth century Odiham suddenly became a centre of agricultural study and research for, presumably at the instigation of its first president, Lord Rivers, the Odiham Society of Agriculture and Industry held its first meeting at the George Inn, Odiham, on 16 May 1783. In the florid style of the time, it published what we would now call its mission statement:

> The principal objects of the Society's attention are: to excite, by premiums and otherwise, a spirit of emulation among ploughmen; to encourage a spirit of industry and sobriety among poor labourers and cottagers; to encourage the poor female part of society in spinning worsted; to promote the knowledge of agriculture, by encouraging experiments on those subjects which are of the most importance to it, by distributing rewards to such persons as shall raise the largest and best crops of natural and artificial grasses ['natural' meant grass already growing in the district, while 'artificial' meant using for comparison different varieties of grass seed brought in from other parts of the country, such as timothy, silver hair, burnet, fine bent], and the several species of grain, on any given quantity of ground; to encourage the improvement of waste lands by inclosing, draining, manuring, raising quick-hedges, plantation, and by the introduction of various kinds of vegetable food for cattle; to induce those, whom it may most concern, to provide for the health of horses, cows, and sheep, better than has hitherto been done; to promote all improvements in the various implements belonging to the farmer, and introduce such new ones as the experience of other counties has proved more valuable than those generally in use; to promote the interests of agriculture by premiums

for reducing the expences of agriculture and for keeping regular accounts and minutes of the proceedings, expences, and profits, in the different departments of farming business; to provide for the better education of the lower ranks of people, by some appropriate course of elementary instruction at schools, and by rewarding the diligence and improvement of scholars at parochial schools; and, as a necessary part of such education, to encourage and assist the establishment of Sunday-schools.

There were originally forty-seven members, drawn from 'Gentlemen of Rank, Fortune and Ingenuity', plus some 'intelligent farmers', and on 29 August 1785 the main local newspaper, the *Reading Mercury*, published a list of new subscribers, which included Jane's father. But perhaps its remit was too wide, for the Society was in fact wound up in the late 1790s; nevertheless its interest in improving the health of horses, cows and sheep left a lasting legacy in the creation of the present Royal Veterinary College in London. In addition to joining the Odiham Society, in 1785 Mr Austen also subscribed to *The Annals of Agriculture*, along with the Revd Mr Lefroy of Ashe and Mr Bramston of Oakley Hall. This was a newly founded periodical, which was intended to put before the public the views and experience of the foremost agriculturalists, hence there must have been much discussion at Steventon rectory of both the Society's aims and the content of the *Annals*. When Jane came to write *Emma*, years later, she shows us little Harriet Smith, awestruck at the intelligence of her admirer, young Robert Martin, the tenant of Mr Knightley's Abbey Mill Farm, proudly saying: 'He reads the Agricultural Reports and some other books, that lay in one of the window seats – but he reads all *them* to himself. But sometimes of an evening, before we went to cards, he would read something aloud out of the Elegant Extracts – very entertaining.'

These Hampshire towns and villages marked the boundaries of Jane's world for the first twenty-five years of her life, apart from brief sorties to Oxford and Reading in childhood, and then visits to her brother Edward in Kent once she had entered her teens.

Fig. 55.

Published as the Act directs June 1 1795, by N. Heideloff, at the Gallery of Fashion Nº 90. Wardour Street.

CHAPTER 2
LIFE AT STEVENTON RECTORY

I N AN AGE WHERE THERE ARE NOW 460 CARS to every thousand residents of the United Kingdom, we have forgotten that in Jane Austen's time the only means of transport was literally by *live* horse-power, and also that in the countryside bad roads could render travel, especially in winter, almost impossible. When the Revd George Austen moved his young family from Deane to Steventon in the summer of 1768, the lane between the villages was a mere cart-track, so cut up by ruts that no light carriage could be used, and Mrs Austen made the short journey lying on a feather bed placed on top of other soft items in the heavy farm waggon which was packed with their household goods. For those who could afford it, and on such special occasions as weddings and funerals, it was not unusual to set men to work with shovels and pickaxes to fill up the ruts and holes in lanes seldom used by carriages. Each parish was responsible for the stretch of the roads that passed through it, and some worthy inhabitant was appointed to act as 'surveyor' and to do his best to see that repairs were carried out. In Jane's unfinished novel *The Watsons*, written probably in 1804, the disagreeable lawyer Robert Watson, who has travelled a few miles across Surrey from Croydon to the village of Stanton near Dorking to call upon his ailing father, grumbles upon arrival: 'Your road through the village is infamous, worse than ever it was. By heaven! I would endite it [start a lawsuit] if I lived near you. Who is surveyor now?'

A lady going out on horseback in riding dress, *from Nikolaus Heideloff's* Gallery of Fashion, *Vol. II, June 1795.*

Even as late as 1819, the rich old Mrs Harriet Brocas, who owned one stately home, Beaurepaire at Bramley in Hampshire – only a few miles to the north of Steventon – and another, Wokefield Park just over the county boundary at Mortimer in Berkshire, had to use a four-horse carriage when travelling between them, and it took her the best part of a day to make the journey of less than ten miles, with two men walking by the side carrying poles with which to help the wheels out of the deep ruts.

However, Mr Austen must have persuaded his neighbours and parishioners to spend money on improving the Deane–Steventon lane, because by about 1780 it had become fit for light carriages; the earliest family reminiscence of Jane is that when she was about six or seven, she and her youngest brother, little Charles then aged about three, ran away one summer evening to meet their father bringing home Cassandra from a visit to Bath in a chaise hired for the purpose. Perhaps Jane remembered this childhood escapade when she wrote *Northanger Abbey* in 1798, and described how Catherine Morland returned to her isolated home in the Wiltshire countryside, travelling like-wise in a hired post-chaise: 'The chaise of a traveller being a rare sight in Fullerton, the whole family were immediately at the window; and to have it stop at the sweep-gate was a pleasure to brighten every eye and occupy every fancy . . .' – a rare sight indeed, since their only neighbours, the Allens, lived a quarter of a mile away. The isolation of rural life is noticed again in *The Watsons* in very similar terms, when an unexpected visitor arrives in the even-ing: 'A sound like a distant carriage was at this moment caught; everybody listened, it became more decided; it certainly drew nearer. It was an unusual sound in Stanton at any time of the day, for the village was on no very public road, and contained no gentleman's family but the rector's' – a description that could equally well apply to Steventon itself.

In *Sense and Sensibility* Mrs Jennings comments on the joys of Delaford, Colonel Brandon's house in Dorset: '. . . a nice old fashioned place, full of comforts and conveniences . . . it is close to the church, and only a quarter of a mile from the turnpike-road, so 'tis never dull, for if you only go and sit up in an old yew arbour behind the house, you may see all the carriages that pass along. . . . A butcher hard by in the village, and the parsonage-house within a stone's throw' – so in her opinion it is not at all isolated. The Bertram family

A post chaise, *from W.H. Pyne's* Microcosm, *1805.*

at Mansfield Park in Northamptonshire, and the conceited Elliots at Kellynch Hall in Somerset, are isolated within the grounds of their respective mansions but are rich enough to own carriages and drive out to neighbouring towns. In Surrey, Emma's house Hartfield is on the outskirts of Highbury, which is said to be a 'large and populous village almost amounting to a town', so that she is able to walk to the shops in the High Street without difficulty; while in *Pride and Prejudice* the Bennets live at Meryton in Hertfordshire, some twenty miles to the north of London, and Mrs Bennet cries proudly: 'I believe there are few neighbourhoods larger. I know we dine with four and twenty families.' In these last two cases it is the influence of London which increases the population of the surrounding towns and villages, and which ensures that the roads are kept in better condition – though even then, the 'near way' from Highbury to Hartfield can become 'floated' in heavy rain, and Robert Martin kindly advises Harriet Smith to 'go round by Mr Cole's stables' instead, when he meets her unexpectedly in Mrs Ford's shop in the High Street.

As far as the Austens were concerned, for the first few years of their life in Steventon their social circle must have been largely confined to those neighbours within walking distance – the Digweeds, Harwoods, Bramstons, Russells, Lefroys and Holders – or perhaps now and then calls further afield made possible by the hire of a post-chaise from the Wheatsheaf Inn in Popham Lane, varied only by occasional visits from relations. Mr Austen's sister-in-law Mrs Walter and her little daughter Phylly came to stay for a few weeks in the summer of 1770, but thereafter for many years Mr Austen had to augment his income by taking in pupils, and all available beds in Steventon parsonage were filled by them. It was only when these boys went home for

Christmas or summer holidays that other members of the Austen family could be invited to visit – Mr Austen's sister Mrs Hancock and her daughter Eliza de Feuillide, or Mrs Austen's niece and nephew Jane and Edward Cooper. Jane and her siblings therefore had to find their own outdoor pastimes and make their own indoor amusements. As there was no stream at Steventon, there could be no fishing, swimming or rowing, but in the summer there would be ball games and in winter the boys all went out to follow the foxhounds, on any pony or donkey they could borrow, or failing that on foot. Jane's fifth brother Frank somehow managed to buy a chestnut pony for £1.11s.6d. [£1.57½p in modern currency], which he kept for two years, jumping everything the pony could get its nose over, and then sold it for £2.12s.6d. [£2.62½p]; and Mrs Austen cut up an old red dress of hers to make him a jacket and breeches to wear in the hunting field.

Mr Austen would of course have a riding horse of his own to enable him to move easily round his parishes fulfilling his clerical duties and overseeing the progress of his farm; and probably another couple of horses were kept later on for his elder sons to use; but it does not seem that either Jane or Cassandra was taught to ride. In *Pride and Prejudice* Jane Bennet rides, which enables Mrs Bennet to send her off in wet weather to visit Netherfield Park and thereby catch the cold which conveniently necessitates her staying on for several days so that Mr Bingley can fall in love with her; but when Elizabeth wants to go to see her the Bennet family carriage is not available because the horses are wanted on the farm, 'and as she was no horse-woman, walking was her only alternative' – much to the scorn of Mr Bingley's sisters. At Mansfield Park the rich Miss Bertrams each have a horse, and at Sir Thomas's command even timorous Fanny is taught to ride on the 'old grey poney' in her childhood, despite her fears: 'Ah! cousin, when I remember how much I used to dread riding, what terrors it gave me to hear it talked of as likely to do me good . . .'. Later on Edmund Bertram has the kindness to acquire a mare quiet enough for Fanny to ride; but when the town-bred Mary Crawford comes to stay with her sister Mrs Grant at Mansfield parsonage, he starts teaching her to ride on this same mare, much to Fanny's chagrin. The Dashwood sisters have probably had horses of their own during their earlier, richer life at Norland, since Marianne is prepared to accept the gift of a horse from Willoughby; and Catherine Morland certainly learns to ride in a scrambling sort of way in the course of joining in boys' games with all her brothers, romping around the Fullerton countryside. When Frank Churchill comes to Highbury for the first time, he enquires of Emma: 'Was she a horse-woman? – Pleasant rides? – Pleasant walks?' but we do not hear her replies; and in view of Mr Woodhouse's constant nervous terrors, it is unlikely he would have permitted her to learn. There is no hint that Anne Elliot rides, and it is doubtful that Sir Walter would have wanted to spend money on a horse for his unloved younger daughter, unless for the sake of his own conceit and appearance in the eyes of the world.

After a few years, probably in 1784, Mr Austen was able to purchase his own carriage, which was a chariot, a light four-wheeled vehicle providing accommodation for three passengers; it was drawn by a pair of horses, with a coach-box upon which the driver was seated. As Jane and Cassandra were growing up, and their mother correspondingly ageing, a carriage would become a necessity for them to travel about together for shopping expeditions to Basingstoke, and attendance at assembly balls and other social functions in the neighbourhood – although perhaps sometimes these trips had to be fore-gone if the horses were unavailable, as in Elizabeth Bennet's case. The chariot remained in use until 1798, when an increase in taxation obliged Mr Austen to 'lay it up' – or, as we would now say, 'mothball' it – until it was finally sold off when the family left Steventon in 1801. During these last few years, Jane and Cassandra had to rely upon lifts from their obliging neighbours when they wished to attend private or public balls. In January 1799 Jane wrote: 'Mrs Bramston's little moveable apartment was tolerably filled last night by her-self, Mrs H. Blackstone, her two daughters & me' – and in November 1800: 'Did you think of our Ball on Thursday evening, & did you suppose me at it? – You might very safely, for there I was. – On Wednesday morning it was settled that Mrs Harwood, Mary & I should go together, & shortly afterwards a very civil note of invitation for me came from Mrs Bramston, who wrote I believe as soon as she knew of the Ball. I might likewise have gone with Mrs Lefroy, & therefore with three methods of going, I must have been more at the Ball than anybody else.'

Another way in which neighbours and their servants could be obliging was in the transmission of messages, letters and parcels – everybody carried messages in those days, to save the recipient time and money. The travelling pedlar, the carter, the butcher's boy on his fast-trotting pony: each bore an invisible packet of reminders and requests, which were paid for with rabbits and apples and chitterlings [small sausages akin to modern chipolatas]. Mrs Dashwood's servant Thomas was taking a message from Sir John Middleton's servant Sally at Barton Park to her brother who was one of the post-boys at the New London Inn in Exeter, when he met there the just-married Lucy Steele and Robert Ferrars on their way to Dawlish, and takes back to the Dashwoods Lucy's malicious message deliberately calculated to hurt Elinor. Miss Watson tells her youngest sister: 'I have begun my letter, Jack Stokes is to call for it tomorrow, for his uncle is going within a mile of Guilford the next day –' Mrs Elton, anxious to boast of her newly acquired marital status and prosperity as the vicar's wife and employer of several servants, tells Jane Fairfax that she is not to go to the Highbury post office herself to collect letters: 'The man who fetches our letters every morning (one of our men, I forget his name) shall inquire for yours too and bring them to you.' And when Mary Crawford had arranged for her harp to be sent from London to Mansfield Park, she tells Edmund:

> I have tidings of my harp at last. I am assured that it is safe at Northampton; and there it has probably been these ten days, in spite of the solemn assurances we have so often received to the contrary. . . . The truth is, that our inquiries were too direct; we sent a servant, we went ourselves; this will not do seventy miles from London – but this morning we heard of it in the right way. It was seen by some farmer, and he told the miller, and the miller told the butcher, and the butcher's son-in-law left word at the shop.

Indoors at the rectory Jane and her siblings would receive their earliest lessons from their parents. It was taken for granted that it was a mother's task to teach her children to read, and thereafter teaching was probably shared between Mr and Mrs Austen very much in the manner of Catherine Morland's schoolroom tasks: 'Writing and accounts [arithmetic] she was taught by her father;

French by her mother . . .'
as well as learning by heart
two popular moral poems:
'The Beggar's Petition'
and 'The Hare and Many
Friends'. The first urged its
readers to show compas-
sion towards the aged poor,
and the second pointed out
the difference between
true and false friendships.
A few of Jane's childhood
books still survive: the earliest is a little fairy tale,
*The History of Goody Two
Shoes*, followed soon after
by *Fables choisies* and *L'ami
des enfants*, which are elementary French textbooks.
Once the children were lit-
erate, their lessons would

Butcher-boy, *from W.H. Pyne's* British Costumes, *1805.*

diverge according to their sex: Mr Austen taught his sons Latin and Greek
with a view to entering and obtaining a degree from Oxford or Cambridge
universities, without which no gentleman could hope to make a satisfactory career. He started taking pupils in 1773, both to add to his income and
to provide competition for his sons in their studies, hence throughout Jane's
childhood several other 'great boys' came and went, sharing rectory life with
herself and her brothers, and some of them became lifelong friends. Girls
were not supposed to learn Latin, but Jane evidently listened to her father and
the boys as they discussed their lessons, and so was able to bring Latin tags and
classical allusions into her letters in later life.

Mrs Austen taught her daughters to sew and embroider, so that in adult
life they could make and mend their own clothes, as well as the innumerable
baby clothes that would inevitably soon become necessary if they married. She

would also instruct them in household management and all domestic duties, using perhaps volumes such as Mrs Eliza Smith's very popular *The Compleat Housewife: or, Accomplish'd Gentlewoman's Companion*, first published in 1727 and constantly reprinted thereafter. Its title page promised 'A Collection of upwards of Six Hundred of the most approved Receipts in Cookery, Cakes, Pastry, Creams, Confectionary, Jellies, Preserving, Made Wines, Pickles, Cordials', together with 'A Collection of above Three Hundred Family Receipts of Medicines . . . never before made publick; fit either for private Families, or such publick-spirited Gentlewomen as would be beneficent to their poor Neighbours' – and so very appropriate for a parson's wife, who would be expected to care for the bodies of her husband's parishioners while he was caring for their souls. Mrs Austen might well also have had a copy of the more modern (1780) and down-to-earth, anonymously written, *The Farmer's Wife, or, Complete Country Housewife*, which dealt with the rearing of poultry and pigs, bee-keeping, dairy work, brewing beer and ale, cider, perry, mead and English wines, pickling and preserving vegetables and fruit. The pig was the most useful animal for a cottager or small farmer to keep, since apart from its joints being eaten fresh as soon as killed, the rest of its meat could be pickled, salted, cured into hams, smoked into bacon, and all remaining scraps chopped up into brawn, black puddings, sausages and chitterlings. Bread, suet puddings, cabbage and bacon were the staple foods of the countryman, and pigs and farm workers came to be so associated in the popular mind, that the urban insult for a countryman was to call him a 'chawbacon'. In January 1791 William Rolfe, one of Mr Austen's parishioners at Deane, was mentioned in the local county newspaper, the *Reading Mercury*, for having grown an enormous cabbage, which 'measures five feet in circumference in the solid part, and weighs upwards of 32 lbs'.

Food in the Steventon rectory was good, plain and solid – roast, boiled or stewed meat, and frequent suet puddings, either plain or savoury, which often took the place of potatoes in the diet at that time. The Austens were almost self-sufficient with their home-produced veal, mutton, pork, poultry, vegetables, cereals, dairy produce and orchard fruit, having to buy only such groceries as tea, coffee, sugar, rice and currants. They were perhaps able to buy river trout and other freshwater fish in Basingstoke, and they might also have bought in specialised types of cheeses such as the Cheddar from Somerset, or the Stilton from Leicestershire and the North Wiltshire from the dairy country between Swindon and Cirencester, which Mr Elton greedily remembers from last night's dinner party at the Coles's house, 'along with the butter, the celery, the beetroot and all the dessert'. Mrs Austen had her own good recipes for such things as bread pudding, raised crust and shortcrust pastry, which were passed down in the family; she and her daughters would not themselves join in the cooking, but would have to know how to instruct the cook and her assistant cook-maid. When the socially inept Mr Collins first comes to Longbourn, he effusively admires the dinner Mrs Bennet has provided, and he 'begged to know to which of his fair cousins, the excellence of its cookery was owing. But there he was set right by Mrs Bennet, who assured him with some asperity that they were very well able to keep a good cook, and that her daughters had nothing to do in the kitchen.' In the autumn of 1798, while Mrs Austen was ill and confined to bed following her return from

The Swineherd, *oil on panel, by James Ward*, *1810*.

49

a trip to Kent, Jane wrote to Cassandra: 'I carry about the keys of the Wine & Closet, & twice since I began this letter, have had orders to give in the Kitchen: Our dinner was very good yesterday, & the Chicken boiled perfectly tender; therefore I shall not be obliged to dismiss Nanny on that account.' Mrs Austen did not recover for several weeks, and Jane wrote again to Cassandra:

> My mother desires me to tell you that I am a very good house-keeper, which I have no reluctance in doing, because I really think it my peculiar excellence, and for this reason – I always take care to provide such things as please my own appetite, which I consider as the chief merit in housekeeping. I have had some ragout veal, and I mean to have some haricot mutton tomorrow. . . . I am very fond of experimental housekeeping, such as having an ox-cheek now and then; I shall have one next week, and I mean to have some little dumplings put into it . . .

By early December Mrs Austen was much better, but Jane was still in charge of the housekeeping: 'Mr Lyford was here yesterday; he came while we were at dinner, and partook of our elegant entertainment. I was not ashamed at asking him to sit down to table, for we had some pease-soup, a sparerib, and a pudding.'

'. . . a love of the theatre is so general . . .'

As early as 1782, the seventeen-year-old James Austen had led his brothers and sisters in mounting their own amateur dramatic performances during the Christmas and summer holidays, when their Cooper cousins – and on one occasion Eliza de Feuillide too – could join in to swell the cast list. In December 1787 Kentish cousin Phylly Walter was invited to come to Steventon for the purpose, but refused, on the grounds of not wishing to perform in public, despite Eliza assuring her that the audience would be only 'a selected party of friends'. At first these performances were held in the rectory dining room, but later on the barn just across the lane was commandeered and fitted up 'quite like a theatre', including the construction and painting of a 'set of theatrical scenes', which later lay in the barn for years afterwards until finally sold off when Jane and her parents left Steventon in 1801. *Matilda*, a blank-verse costume drama supposedly set at the time of the Norman Conquest, was the first production, and James added in his own verses for prologue and epilogue. However, this may have been a bad choice, perhaps too difficult for the young actors or too dull to be universally popular with the family and their guests, since thereafter James and his troupe stuck to tried and tested comedies and farces, such as Sheridan's *The Rivals*, Mrs Centlivre's *The Wonder – a Woman keeps a secret!*, and Bickerstaffe's *The Sultan*. In this last, a witty English girl, Roxalana, persuades the Turkish Sultan to disband his harem and make her his one and only Empress, and possibly a recollection of Roxalana's teasing charm came to

Title-page of The Wonder; *first produced 1714; this edition of the text late eighteenth century.*

Jane's mind when she started creating Elizabeth Bennet and composing *First Impressions* (the original of *Pride and Prejudice*) eight years later.

Amateur theatricals were very popular at the end of the eighteenth century, and in Hampshire the Duchess of Bolton herself, at Hackwood Park, in 1787 invited her family and friends to perform the tragedy *Jane Shore*, the heroine of the title being one of the mistresses of Edward IV. Madam Lefroy was asked to take the part of 'Alicia' but, like Phylly Walter in real life, and like Fanny Price in fictional life years later, felt that, as a parson's wife, the play would be unsuitable for her, and so did not want to participate. She excused herself to the Duchess in a polite verse:

> Can I, a wife, a mother, tread the stage?
> Burn with false fire, and glow with mimic rage?
> Quit of domestic peace the calm retreat?
> As mad Alicia teach my heart to beat?

There is nothing to suggest that the young Austens quarrelled over the choice of play in the way the Bertrams did at Mansfield Park – who 'wanted a piece containing very few characters in the whole, but every character first-rate, and three principal women' – but it is unmistakably the experience of watching and performing on several occasions with the Steventon troupe during her teenage years that enabled Jane later on to make the production of *Lovers Vows* the turning point of the calamities that follow in *Mansfield Park*. Some literary critics believe that Jane herself must have disapproved of amateur theatricals, but in this case they fail to distinguish between real life and fiction. It is evident that all the Austens enjoyed both reading and acting plays at home and attending professional performances whenever they could; the difference in *Mansfield Park* is that the young Bertrams know their father would disapprove of such a pastime as amateur theatricals but go ahead with their plans nevertheless in his absence, coupled with the fact that Tom tactlessly chooses a risqué and unsuitable play which mirrors all too clearly the emotional stresses amongst his siblings, and so leads directly to the breakdown of Maria's marriage to Mr Rushworth and Edmund's subsequent disenchantment with Mary Crawford.

'In training for a heroine'

It may have been the extreme imbalance of boys in the household and in the wider Steventon neighbourhood that led the Austens to send Jane and Cassandra away in the summer of 1785 to Mrs Latournelle's Ladies' Boarding

Abbey Gate at Reading, *engraving, late eighteenth-century. The Abbey House was the building with tall windows, behind high brick walls, to the left of the old gateway.*

School in Reading. It occupied a large house that abutted upon the ancient Abbey Gateway, once the entrance to the now ruined medieval abbey, and so was sometimes referred to as the Abbey House School. In front of the school was the open space known as the Forbury, originally the outer courtyard of the abbey and now a rough playground for all the townsfolk, giving a very fine view across the River Thames into Oxfordshire on the opposite bank. At the Abbey House School Jane and Cassandra could 'scramble themselves into a little education', put aside their tomboyish games and make friends with other girls of their own age, since there were no such companions for them anywhere near the rectory. Life in a busy urban setting and in the company of some forty other girls and several teachers must have been a great change for the sisters, but that they were happy there is borne out by Jane's remembering in later years the school catchphrase: 'I could die of laughter at it . . .' and amusing herself by putting it into the mouth of noisy giggling Lydia Bennet.

The sisters were not leaving country life entirely behind them, however, for Reading was the county town of Berkshire, and as such the hub of commerce and trade. A visitor a few years later described the road from Basingstoke to Reading as 'most beautiful, very woody and lined with neat villages', and the town itself as being full of 'handsome houses and well-filled shops', and having an 'air of gaiety, bustle, wealth and gentility'. The Market Place was only a stone's throw away from Mrs Latournelle's establishment in the Abbey House, and every Monday there was a cattle market, chiefly for those animals driven up from further west of Reading and on their way to Smithfield in London, there to become more of the famed Roast Beef of Old England, and every Saturday a corn market. All the agricultural population of the district came to the Market Place for business or pleasure on these days, from the landed gentry down through all the cattle-dealers, brewers, millers, tradesmen and their apprentices, to the noisy boys, sturdy beggars and general riff-raff of the town. Quarrelsome old women selling fruit and vegetables sat against the wall of St Lawrence's church, which formed the top of the triangular Market Place; crockery-ware stalls were on the west side, and the respectable farmers' wives and daughters sat with their baskets of eggs, butter and poultry on the east side. There were also a few stalls set out here selling straw hats and caps and ribbons, to tempt these countrywomen, as well as boys offering rabbits or pigeons or caged birds, and small girls asking a few pence for little bunches of spring or summer flowers. Throughout the autumn months, huge four-horse waggons laden with grain would travel slowly into Reading from the surrounding countryside during the Friday night to be ready for the start of business at six in the morning on Saturday; a sample sack of wheat would be carried into the Market Place, and once a sale was agreed the waggon would then take the load on to the buyer's granary. The carters driving these waggons would take pride in making their horses look as smart as possible, with mane and tail neatly plaited and tied up with braids of various colours, and racks of small latten bells [an alloy of copper and zinc], tuned harmoniously, were fixed on the top of each animal's harness. The team of horses could therefore be heard in advance as the waggon approached down narrow country lanes, warning other road users to stand back out of the way. On market days the air was full with noises of every sort – the tinkling bells of these huge waggons, hooves of horses and donkeys clattering and wheels rumbling over cobble-stones, the shouts of passengers in some smaller cart as it was overturned or pushed aside by the irresistible momentum of these heavyweight teams, the lowing of cattle, the cackling of turkeys, geese, ducks and chickens, perhaps a crash of crockery knocked down from a stall by a cartload of turnips, and all the din of buyers and sellers talking together – not ceasing till well into the afternoon when the empty waggons and carts returned home.

It seems probable that it was during her time at the Abbey House School that Jane started reading the wildly incredible and romantic popular novels of the period that she subsequently parodied in *Northanger Abbey*. The school régime was very casual; after daily prayers and some formal lessons in the mornings, the girls could spend the afternoon hours as they pleased. There was a large garden behind the house, where the younger girls played and the older ones sauntered under the tall trees; and as one former pupil recollected many years later, there were also rambling yards and haylofts in the domestic quarters where it was perfectly possible for girls to hide away and read novels in peace, having perhaps borrowed them from Carnan & Smart's circulating library in the Market Place.

Going to Market, *drawing by Thomas Rowlandson (1756–1827)*.

But Jane and Cassandra's schooldays came to an abrupt end in December 1786, since Mr Austen's farm could not provide him with the funds to pay Mrs Latournelle's fees. The winter of 1785–6 had been very severe, with deep snowdrifts and cattle dying for lack of feed, and it was then followed by late frosts in May and blights in June that spoilt the fruit crops. Hay, straw and turnips were scarce and very dear, and many of the animals that had survived had lost too much weight to be properly fattened for market in the summer; and these difficulties were compounded by a plentiful harvest which reduced the average price of wheat by more than a quarter compared with the previous year. From now on the sisters lived at home, learning from their parents and brothers, as in due course do some of Jane's characters. Mrs Dashwood plans that while Elinor and Marianne are away in London, she will herself teach her youngest daughter: 'Margaret and I . . . shall go on so quietly and happily together with our books and our music! You will find Margaret so improved when you come back again!' Edmund Bertram earns Fanny Price's undying devotion by his kindness in her lonely childhood: 'Miss Lee taught her French, and heard her read the daily portion of History; but he recommended her taste, and corrected her judgement; he made reading useful by talking to her of what she read, and heightened its attraction by judicious praise.' It was remembered in the family that it was James Austen, the eldest of the brothers, who was in this respect a model for Edmund, directing Jane's reading and forming her taste.

In addition to instruction from her immediate family, at this stage of her life Jane had the benefit of encouragement in her studies from the Austens' neighbour, Madam Lefroy of Ashe, who was said to have 'an exquisite taste for poetry, and could almost repeat the chief English poets by heart, especially Milton, Pope, Collins, Gray, and the poetical passages of Shakespeare; and she composed easy verses herself with great facility . . .' Jane in turn is said to have regarded Madam Lefroy as 'a perfect model of gracefulness and goodness'; hence it is not surprising that when she composed *Susan* (the original title of *Northanger Abbey*) a few years later, the heroine Susan/Catherine learns appropriate extracts of Pope, Gray and Shakespeare, all of which volumes Jane would have found in her father's library. The Steventon schoolroom contained a copy of the 1771 edition of Oliver Goldsmith's *The*

History of England, from the Earliest Times to the Death of George II, and we know that Jane certainly read this in her early teens, since she could not resist scribbling flippant comments in the margins of the four volumes. Goldsmith's work remained in print for many years, and Jane probably imagined it was from these books that the Bertram sisters and Fanny Price read aloud the 'daily portion of History' to Miss Lee in the Mansfield Park schoolroom, just as she herself must have done sitting in the big room upstairs in Steventon rectory – it was remembered many years later in the family that Jane 'was considered to read aloud remarkably well'. The Austens also had a copy of Vicesimus Knox's *Elegant Extracts: or useful and entertaining Passages in Prose Selected for the Improvement of Scholars,* and here again Jane added her own sharp-tongued opinions to the extracts relating to her favourite historical character Mary Queen of Scots and Mary's opponent Queen Elizabeth Tudor. It was no doubt this popular anthology that Jane later envisaged as being one of the books owned by the aspiring young Robert Martin at Abbey Mill Farm.

It was probably also about now, when the young Jane was in a scribbling and irreverent mood, that she laid hands upon the official Marriage Register of St Nicholas's church, and left her unmistakable mark within it. In the past parish registers had been blank books – sometimes even loose leaves of paper – in which parsons and their parish clerks entered baptisms, marriages and burials haphazardly and often inaccurately; hence at the end of the eighteenth century the Church of England brought in pre-prepared volumes in order to regularize the recording of these important events in the lives of parishioners. The pages were laid out with numbered printed entries with spaces left to insert the individual names and dates, and the Marriage Register had an exemplar page at the beginning showing how to fill in the entries for both the calling of banns and the actual marriage service. These blanks were evidently too tempting to a future novelist; and Jane happily decided that the Banns of Marriage had been called between the romantically named gentleman *Henry Frederic Howard Fitzwilliam* of *London* and *Jane Austen* of *Steventon*; then that his equally romantic rival *Edmund Arthur William Mortimer* of *Liverpool* and *Jane Austen* of *Steventon* were Married in this Church; and finally that This Marriage was Solemnized between Us, the down-to-earth *Jack Smith & Jane Smith late Austen*, in the Presence of *Jack Smith, Jane Smith.*

THE

REGISTER-BOOK *of a Parish*

of Steventon For the Regiftering of all *in the County of South Hamp.*

BANNS and MARRIAGES,

Publifhed or folemnized

In the Parifh - Church of the Parifh of

Steventon in the County of South Hampton

Provided by the Church-Wardens of the faid Parifh, in
purfuance of the Statute of the Twenty-feventh Year of
his prefent Majefty King *G E O R G E* the Second,
Intituled, *An Act for the better preventing of Clan-
deftine Marriages*, which Act commenced from the
Twenty-fifth Day of *March* in the Year of our Lord
One Thoufand Seven Hundred and Fifty-four.

L O N D O N:

Printed for and fold by J. COLES, Stationer, in *Fleet-Street*.

MDCCLIV.

*Pages from the Steventon
Marriage Register, showing
Jane Austen's entries.*

The Form of an Entry of Publication of Banns.

The Banns of Marriage between *A. B.* of *London*
and *C. D.* of *Steventon* were duly publifhed in this
Church for the {firft / fecond / third} Time, on Sunday the
Day of in the Year One Thoufand Seven
Hundred and

J. J. Rector} Vicar } Curate}

The Form of an Entry of a Marriage.

A. B. of and *C. D.* of
were married in this Church by {Banns / Licenfe*} this
Day of in the Year One Thoufand Seven
Hundred and by me

J. J. Rector} Vicar } Curate}

This Marriage was folemnized between us *A. B. C. B.* late *C. D.*
in the Prefence of *E. F. G. H. Jack Smith, James Smith*

* Infert thefe Words, viz. *with Confent of* {Parents / Guardians} where both, or either
of the Parties to be married *by Licenfe*, are under Age.

LEFT *Cassandra's portrait of Jane Austen, c.1810;* RIGHT *Cassandra's drawing of Jane's back view, 1804.*

Lady Catherine de Bourgh would have been horrified to learn that no governess was engaged for Jane and Cassandra upon their return home, but Mr Austen did manage to pay for a few drawing lessons for his children, and Henry became sufficiently skilled to be able to instruct others in later years. Cassandra had no real talent, and was content to spend time in copying and tinting popular engravings, as does Elinor Dashwood – 'her drawings were affixed to the walls of their sitting-room' at Barton Cottage – but nevertheless it is to Cassandra that we owe the only two authentic representations of Jane – the half-length portrait (probably drawn about 1810) which is now in the National Portrait Gallery in London, and the back view (dated 1804), where Jane is wearing a blue dress and sitting down out of doors, which remains in family ownership. Jane was more interested in music, and when she was in her teens her father bought her a cheap pianoforte and arranged for her to have lessons from a visiting music-master, Mr Chard, who was the assistant organist at Winchester Cathedral. Unlike Catherine Morland – 'The day which dismissed the music-master was one of the happiest of Catherine's life' – although Jane never practised as much as Mr Chard would have liked, she enjoyed learning and collected into several music books her favourite pieces, both vocal and instrumental. In later years, when living in Chawton, she would sometimes sing to her own accompaniment in the evenings, and play dance music for the benefit of visiting nephews and nieces.

The Juvenilia

However, before she was sufficiently competent to offer her music as part of family entertainment, and apparently as soon as she had left school and was permanently at home again in the rectory, Jane embarked upon her career as a writer. Over the next seven years she composed numerous comic episodes, short stories and sometimes miniature plays or dramatic scenes, which she wrote down in three copy books, Volume the First, Volume the Second and Volume the Third. These early essays are now known collectively as her Juvenilia; they are dedicated to various members of the Austen family, and were evidently intended to be read aloud in the fireside circle. They are frequently parodies of the unnaturally elegant settings of the sentimental romances she had been reading, and hence are based firmly in the reality of the Hampshire country-side. In 'Frederic and Elfrida, a Novel' the characters propose to 'take a walk in a Grove of Poplars which led from the Parsonage to a verdant Lawn enamelled with a variety of variegated flowers & watered by a purling stream'; but then in 'Jack and Alice, a Novel' Lady Williams proposes 'a walk in a Citron Grove which led from her Ladyship's pigstye to Charles Adams's Horsepond'. 'Henry and Eliza, a Novel' opens immediately out in the fields in summer-time:

> As Sir George and Lady Harcourt were superintending the Labours of their Haymakers, rewarding the industry of some by smiles of approbation, & punishing the idleness of others, by a cudgel, they perceived lying closely concealed beneath the thick foliage of a Haycock, a beautifull little Girl not more than 3 months old. Touched with the enchanting Graces of her face &

delighted with the infantine tho' sprightly answers she returned to their many questions, they resolved to take her home &, having no Children of their own, to educate her with care & cost.

In 'Evelyn', young Mr Gower, rambling on horseback through Sussex, comes across the perfect elegant country villa:

As he approached the House, he was delighted with its situation. It was in the exact centre of a small circular paddock, which was enclosed by a regular paling, & bordered with a plantation of Lombardy poplars, & Spruce firs alternatively placed in three rows. A gravel walk ran through this beautiful Shrubbery, and as the remainder of the paddock was unencumbered with any other Timber, the surface of it perfectly even & smooth, and grazed by four white Cows which were disposed at equal distances from each other, the whole appearance of the place as Mr Gower entered the Paddock was uncommonly striking. A beautifully-rounded, gravel road without any turn or interruption led immediately to the house . . .

Laura and Sophia, the two heroines of 'Love and Freindship, a novel in a series of Letters', steal banknotes from their host and are turned out of his house in consequence: '. . . having walked about a mile and a half we sate down by the side of a clear limpid stream to refresh our exhausted limbs. The place was suited to meditation. A grove of full-grown Elms sheltered us from the East. – A Bed of full-grown Nettles from the West. – Before us ran the murmuring brook and behind us ran the turnpike road. We were in a mood for contemplation and in a Disposition to enjoy so beautifull a spot.' Laura and her lover Edward are so exquisitely high-minded and romantic that they are prepared to scorn 'the mean and indelicate employment of Eating and Drinking', but in this and in other of the Juvenilia pieces Jane gleefully provides her sentimental characters with such coarsely plebeian fare as fried cowheel and onion, tripe, pig's liver and crow [the mesentery, the membranes surrounding the internal organs of the beast], and the hashed-up remains of an old duck.

'A little quiet cheerfulness at home'

By some lucky chance a letter survives, written by Mrs Austen on 31 December 1786 to her husband's niece Phylly Walter, then living at Seal near Sevenoaks in Kent and tied at home by the demands of a possessive mother. Mr Austen's sister Mrs Hancock had moved to Paris some years previously, and her daughter Eliza had married the Comte de Feuillide and gone to live with him on his estate in the south of France, hence they were only infrequent visitors to Steventon. On the other side of the family, Mrs Austen's sister had died suddenly in 1783, leaving two teenage children, Edward and Jane Cooper, who turned to the Austens for family comforting. In her usual brisk and practical manner, Mrs Austen now gives a complete picture of life in the rectory in this deep midwinter, when other members of the family were able to visit while the pupils were away:

We are now happy in the company of our Sister Hancock, Madame de Feuillide & the little Boy; they came to us last Thursday Sennet [21 December] & will stay with us till the end of next Month. They all look & seem to be remarkably well, the little Boy grows very fat, he is very fair & very pretty; I don't think your Aunt at all alter'd in any respect, Madame is grown quite lively, when a child we used to think her too grave. We have borrowed a Piano-Forte, and she plays to us every day; on Tuesday we are to have a very snug little dance in our parlour, just our own children, nephew & nieces, (for the two little Coopers come tomorrow) quite a family party, I wish my <u>third niece</u> could be here also; but indeed, I begin to suspect your Mother never intends to gratify that wish. You might as well be in Jamaica keeping your Brother's House, for anything that we see of you or are like to see. Five of my Children are now at home, Henry, Frank, Charles & my two Girls, who have now quite left school; Frank returns to Portsmouth in a few days, he has but short holidays at Christmas. Edward is well & happy in Switzerland. James set out for La Guienne, on a visit to the Count de Feuillide, near Eight weeks ago, I hope he is got there by this time and am impatient for a Letter; he was wind-bound some weeks in the little Island of Jersey or he would have got to the end of his long Journey by the beginning of this Month. – Every one of our Fireside join in Love, & Duty as due and in wishing a happy '87 to our dear Friends at Seal.

Mrs Austen probably read out this letter before dispatching it, so that all those sitting round the Steventon fireside could truthfully add in their good wishes, as she said in her closing lines; and this may perhaps have inspired young Jane to compose 'Edgar and Emma, a tale', in which the activities of a huge family are described in tones just like those of her mother. Miss Emma Marlow is attached to Edgar, the eldest Willmot son, and hopes to see him when the family pay a call on the Marlows; the Willmot children

... were too numerous to be particularly described; it is sufficient to say that in general they were virtuously inclined & not given to any wicked ways. Their family being too large to accompany them in every visit, they took nine with them alternately. . . . Mr & Mrs Willmot with their three eldest Daughters first appeared, – Emma began to tremble. Robert, Richard, Ralph, & Rodolphus followed – Emma turned pale. Their two youngest Girls were lifted from the Coach – Emma sunk breathless on a Sopha. . . . 'Mrs Willmot, you do not stir from this House till you let me know how all the rest of your family do, particularly your eldest son.' . . . Mrs Willmot made the following eloquent oration: 'Our children are all extremely well but at present most of them from home. Amy is with my sister Clayton, Sam at Eton. David with his Uncle John. Jem & Will at Winchester. Kitty at Queen's Square. Ned with his Grandmother. Hetty & Patty in a Convent at Brussells. Edgar at college, Peter at Nurse, & all the rest (except the nine here) at home.' It was with difficulty that Emma could refrain from tears on hearing of the absence of Edgar; she remained however tolerably composed till the Willmots were gone when having no check to the overflowing

Outside the Ale House Door, *oil on canvas, by George Morland, 1792.*

of her greif, she gave free vent to them, & retiring to her own room, continued in tears the remainder of her Life.

'. . . a cottage tight & warm . . .'

Beyond the immediate Austen fireside circle lay the cottages where Mr Austen's parishioners lived, and from whose families the rectory servants were engaged. Apart from having been the foster-parents for the Austen babies, while Jane was growing up the Littleworths were still very much to the fore as members of her parents' household: John Littleworth was groom and coachman to Mr Austen and continued to work in this capacity for James Austen in later years, his wife Anne ('Nanny') was the cook; and the teenage Jane was godmother to their eldest daughter, born in 1789. Another Anne (also 'Nanny'), Mrs Hilliard, was the lady's-maid/housekeeper, and when she was ill for a few days in the autumn of 1798 Jane wrote to Cassandra: 'Our family affairs are rather deranged at present, for Nanny has kept her bed these three or four days, with a pain in her side and fever, and we are forced to have two charwomen, which is not very comfortable. She is considerably better now, but it must still be some time, I suppose, before she is able to do anything.' In the meantime, Nanny Littleworth had to be called upon to dress Jane's hair – a situation which Jane knew Cassandra would find amusing. There was also a widower William Littleworth, referred to as 'testy old Uncle Will'; and when he married again very late in life in 1796, this time Jane Austen could legitimately sign the marriage register as one of the witnesses. John Littleworth's sister Elizabeth ('Bet'), who had been the playmate and nursemaid for the fostered Austen babies in her childhood and was remembered as being rather small and delicate-looking, nevertheless as she grew up preferred to work in the fields or as an occasional gardener, like a man, rather than entering domestic service. She eventually became proudly self-sufficient, renting a few acres of land, owning a donkey and a cart, and finally a cow.

Out of doors, the most important of Mr Austen's agricultural workers was John Bond, his ploughman; James Austen remembered the pride John took in his well-kept team of plough horses and the thriving crops that his work produced, and John's sayings became part of Austen family usage. When Jane was on holiday

The Plough, *mezzotint by Valentine Green, 1801.*

in Bath in 1799 and bought herself a new cloak, she told Cassandra that: 'I like it very much, & can now exclaim with delight, like J. Bond at Hay-Harvest, "This is what I have been looking for these three years."' More than a decade later, when Jane's brother Edward Knight engaged a new governess for his children, Jane wrote: 'Miss Clewes seems the very Governess they have been looking for these ten years; longer coming than J. Bond's last Shock of Corn.' In 1798 he called at the rectory one autumn evening for instructions, and Jane told Cassandra: '[My father] & John Bond are now very happy together, for I have just heard the heavy step of the latter along the passage.' This interview meant a change in John's employment, for 'John Bond begins to find himself grow old, which John Bonds ought not to do, and unequal to much hard work; a man is therefore hired to supply his place as to labour, and John himself is to have the care of the sheep.' His interest in sheep was no less than in ploughing, and a tale of his shrewdness in his shepherding duties was passed down to later nineteenth-century family members:

> Mr Austen used to join Mr Digweed (his neighbour in Steventon Manor) in buying twenty or thirty sheep, and that all might be fair, it was their custom to open the pen, and the first half of the sheep

Labourers at Rest, *drawing by Thomas Rowlandson, 1790–5.*

which ran out were counted as belonging to the rector. Going down to the fold on one occasion after this process had been gone through, Mr Austen remarked one sheep among his lot larger and finer than the rest. 'Well, John,' he observed to Bond, who was with him, 'I think we have had the best of the luck with Mr Digweed today in getting that sheep.' 'Maybe not so much in the luck as you think, sir,' responded the faithful John. 'I see'd her the moment I come in, and set eyes on the sheep, so when we opened the pen I just giv'd her a "huck" with my stick, and out a' run.'

John's devotion to his employer's interests was probably in Jane's mind when she created William Larkins at Donwell Abbey, who is so pleased to think that Mr Knightley has been able to sell so many cooking apples – '... for William, you know, thinks more of his master's profit than any thing ...'

Apart from these valued and full-time employees, thought of by the Austens as friends in humble life, several other of the Steventon villagers are known to us: sometimes mentioned by name in passing in Jane's letters to Cassandra, and sometimes momentarily appearing under the tiny spotlights turned upon them in the brief memoir Jane's niece Anna Lefroy wrote many years later. There was Henrietta ('Henny') Lavender, 'who had been a beauty, the admired of my grandfather's elder pupils and late in life changed her fancy-sounding name for Dry – so neat, so clean and industrious, so discontented and dissatisfied – it was almost a treat to listen to her grumblings or a vexation, as the case might be.' The matriarchs of the village were known respectfully as 'Dame', and Jane mentions Dame Kew and Dame Staples – Anna added that Dame Staples had a 'pleasant face and tidy cottage', but had 'a sluttish nextdoor neighbour Betty Dawkins, with her sheepish, half-witted ragged husband, Phil.' There was a village schoolmistress, who wore a 'flattened bonnet approaching to a bonnegrace [a very old-fashioned shady hat worn by country-women], an elderly woman but still called young Dame Tilbury to distinguish her from an older dowager of that name.' A great friend of the Tilburys was the aged man nicknamed 'Old Shepherd' – his real name almost forgotten. He was 'always at leisure to assist by his presence in the cutting-up of our bacon pigs, guessing their weight, comparing past with present; and though I know not if I ever actually saw him doing anything, he was no doubt an important person in the parish.'

Dame Bushell was the Austens' washerwoman – this would be a part-time job, taking place perhaps once a month when large bundles of dirty linen had accumulated, and needed careful forward planning. Soap was an expensive item and required to be used in hot water, whereas other laundry methods could be done with cold. Additional alkaline detergent, 'lye', had to be home-made in advance, and one recipe instructed a young housewife to prepare this as follows:

> Take a butter-tub, or one of that size, and, with a gimblet, bore holes in it about half-way; put in your tub some clean straw, and over that about a peck of wood ashes; fill it with cold water, and set it into another vessel to receive the water as it runs out of the holes of the tub; if it is too strong a lye, add to it some warm water; wash your linen in it, slightly soaping the cloaths before

you wash them; two pounds of soap will go as far as six pounds, and make the cloaths whiter and cleaner, when you by experience have got the right way; if it is too strong for the hands, make it weaker with water.

The usual washday routine would be for the lye to 'run' from Friday until Monday; then washing started in the small hours of Monday and continued until about midday Tuesday; some ironing could be started on Tuesday and continued throughout Wednesday; and it was expected that by

Woman Churning Butter, *from W.H. Pyne's* British Costumes, *1805.*

Thursday everything would be clean and put away. Mansion-houses could afford to have special rooms set aside for laundry and special laundry-maids to work therein; but for the average home the necessity of washing-day completely upset the normal household routine, and all other occupations had to be put aside for the time being. When Dame Bushell retired in 1798 a replacement had to be found, and Jane wrote doubtfully: 'John Steevens' wife undertakes our Purification; She does not look as if anything she touched would ever be clean, but who knows?'

As well as Mrs Nanny Hilliard the lady's-maid/housekeeper and Mrs Nanny Littleworth the cook, there was usually a third maidservant at the rectory, who was expected to understudy for both these posts and help with the dairy-work as well. In the autumn of 1798 this position was vacant – perhaps

The Return from Market, *oil on canvas, by Francis Wheatley, 1789.*

the girl had gone off to the October hiring-fair in Basingstoke to seek a more lucrative job – and Jane wrote to Cassandra: 'We do not seem likely to have any other maid servant at present, but Dame Staples will supply the place of one.' By early December, however, Jane was able to write again to Cassandra: 'We are very much disposed to like our new maid; she knows nothing of a dairy, to be sure, which, in our family, is rather against her, but she is to be taught it all. In short, we have felt the inconvenience of being without a maid so long, that we are determined to like her, and she will find it a hard matter to displease us. As yet, she seems to cook very well, is uncommonly stout [that is, strong or sturdy], and says she can work well at her needle.'

In addition to these domestic servants, all the inhabitants of Steventon were known to Mr Austen and his family, and as Jane and Cassandra grew up they took part in visiting the cottagers, especially those most in need. Little Anna remembered how her grandfather used to refer to his daughters as 'the girls', and would sometimes ask his wife: 'Where are the Girls?' – 'Are the Girls gone out?' While Cassandra was away in the autumn of 1798, staying with brother Edward Knight at Godmersham in Kent, Jane told her: 'I called yesterday on Betty Lovell, who enquired particularly after you, and said she seemed to miss you very much, because you used to call in upon her very often. This was an oblique reproach at me, which I am sorry to have merited and from which I will profit.' It was the custom for landowners to give useful Christmas presents to their tenants, and Edward Knight provided his father with funds to distribute in this way amongst the Steventon cottagers; Mr Austen in turn delegated this task to his wife and daughters, to lay out the money in warm clothing. In 1798 Jane gave a pair of worsted stockings to each of Mary Hutchins, Dame Kew, Mary Steevens and Dame Staples, as well as a shift to Hannah Staples and a shawl to Betty Dawkins; and two years later Jane and her mother bought 'ten pair of worsted stockings, & a shift – The shift is for Betty Dawkins, as we find she wants it more than a rug. – She is one of the most grateful of all whom Edward's charity has reached, or at least she expresses herself more warmly than the rest, for she sends him a "sight of thanks".'

The clothes worn by these village wives were of necessity plain and simple and as warm as possible, hence the desirability of gifts of worsted stockings and shawls in the middle of winter. The basic garments for working women were a shift, an ankle-length petticoat, a pair of leather stays, a gown or overdress, and a colourful neckerchief or shawl, all covered by a cloak of fustian [a coarse strong twilled cotton] or frieze [a rough heavy woollen fabric], often red in colour, which must have shown up as bright spots in dark winter days. Buckled leather shoes worn with stockings, these latter held up by knitted garters tied above the knee; a check apron for indoors covered by a larger coarser one for outdoor work; and a small linen or cotton cap indoors, with a straw hat added on top for outdoors, completed their costume. The shift was made of linen, woven in either Ireland or Holland; it was something like a long shirt or underdress, worn next to the skin, and could also serve as a nightdress. Over this went a warm petticoat of linsey-woolsey [a coarse fabric of mixed wool and linen], and a pair of leather stays to give warmth and support to the waist and back. The overdress was a low-necked gown of common stuff [a cheap woollen fabric], revealing the edges of the shift at neck-line and sleeve ends; and a large kerchief or shawl filled in the bare neck, with its point hanging down the back and its ends tucked into the gown. The front of the gown was often tucked up at the waist to reveal the shorter petticoat, and to facilitate walking over muddy ground.

Unlike many European countries, England has never had a traditional peasant costume, and as it was the custom for the gentry to bequeath their clothes to their domestic servants, fashion between social ranks remained fluid – sometimes to the confusion of foreign visitors, indeed, who complained that at first sight it was impossible to tell the serving-maid from her mistress. The clothes which Jane and Cassandra wore during their Steventon days therefore differed in quality rather than style from those of the cottagers, hence Jane's purchase of Irish linen from the Overton scotchman in the autumn of 1798 to make shifts for herself and her sister. A few weeks later, she was planning to downgrade her old 'coarse spot' muslin dress and 'turn it into a petticoat very soon'; and when Elizabeth Bennet walks to Netherfield Park, 'crossing field after field at a quick pace, jumping over stiles and springing over puddles with impatient activity', finally arriving 'with weary ancles, dirty stockings, and a face glowing with the warmth of exercise', Bingley's sisters are not slow to sneer behind her back: 'I hope you saw her petticoat, six inches deep in mud, I am absolutely certain; and the gown which had been let down to hide it, not doing its office.'

When conditions were muddy underfoot, women would tie pattens on over their shoes – these were wooden soles mounted upon a large iron ring, which would therefore raise the wearer and her shoes above mud and water, and being of wood also helped to keep the feet warm. They were awkward in use, because the foot could not flex, and so the wearer had to stamp stiffly up and down instead of walking normally; but countrywomen could become accustomed to them – one old woman, indeed, living not far from Steventon, boasted that she had walked over twenty miles in one day, on pattens. Niece Anna wrote in later life: 'I recollect the frequent visits of my two Aunts, & how they walked in wintry weather through the sloppy lane between Steventon & Deane in pattens, usually worn at that time even by Gentlewomen' – and in *Persuasion*, when Anne Elliot enters Bath on a wet November afternoon, amongst the other city noises she hears 'the ceaseless clink of pattens' on the flagstoned pavements. Anna also remembered her aunts' bonnets: 'because though precisely alike in colour, shape & materials, I made it a pleasure to guess, & I believe always guessed right, which bonnet & which Aunt belonged to each other.' It seems to have been the fashion in the late 1790s for sisters to dress alike; when Jane Austen introduces her readers – and Catherine Morland – to the Thorpe daughters in Bath, she does so by saying that Isabella 'had great personal beauty, and the younger ones, by pretending to be as handsome as their sister, imitating her air, and dressing in the same style, did very well.'

ABOVE *Caricature of woman wearing pattens;*
BELOW *A pair of pattens.*

The male farm workers usually wore a shirt, waistcoat and neckerchief, and cord breeches with heavy woollen stockings, these latter protected by leather or fustian gaiters. Just as Jane and Cassandra did not scorn to use pattens like the village wives, so Mr Knightley wears thick leather gaiters when walking from Donwell Abbey to call on Mrs Weston. Over these garments went a wide smock-frock or slop, made of coarse linen or cotton gathered into thick folds or pleats held in place by ornamental stitching; this was warm and fairly waterproof, and was viewed as the distinctive garb of the farm labourer. The working smock might be brown, green or fawn, occasionally blue or grey, and the man would have another finer smock, in white linen, for church wear on Sundays or any other special event. He would naturally need strong footwear, and when Jane heard John Bond's 'heavy step' along the passage, this would be because he was wearing thick leather boots or shoes, perhaps double-soled for additional waterproofing. A hat was also considered essential, straw for summer and felt for winter; during the eighteenth century this was often a tricorne, or something else large and shady, but as fashions changed in

A Windy Day *(detail)*, *oil on canvas, by George Morland, undated (1790s)*.

men's-wear as in ladies', so the gentlemanly top-hat gradually appeared on the heads of villagers as well. The more senior of the villagers, or those in domestic service rather than working in the fields, might wear a wig, as does Wilcox the Mansfield Park coachman. Mr John Lyford, the Basingstoke doctor, was remembered by Jane's nephew James-Edward Austen-Leigh as being a fine tall old gentleman who always wore a remarkable flaxen wig; and every two years, as it began to show signs of wear, he would pass it on to an old man at Steventon, 'as tall and fine-looking as himself, producing thereby a ludicrous resemblance between the peasant and the doctor.'

CHAPTER 3
A YEAR IN THE COUNTRYSIDE

D URING THE SECOND HALF OF THE EIGHTEENTH CENTURY the
English weather, fickle and changeable at best, was more than usually
unpredictable and extreme; agricultural records show that there were
frequently excessively cold winters, very wet late springs, summers that were
either very cold and wet or else excessively dry, followed by yet more weeks of
rain in early summer and autumn – all of which could prove devastating to the
rural community in one way or another. Stormy wet weather would beat down
the arable crops, and ruin the newly cut hay; frost and infestation of turnip fly
would destroy this root crop, now mainstay winter fodder for livestock; summer
droughts meant animals died for lack of water and grass; cold spells in midsummer would cause many newly shorn sheep to die; there could be mildew in
wheat, blight on fruit and vegetable crops; and wet weather could lead to out-
breaks of the painful and contagious foot-rot in sheep flocks; while cattle which
had struggled through the year in poor condition would probably not survive
the coming winter. Poor harvests meant the price of wheat rose, and the price of
bread, the staple food, rose correspondingly – the farmers profited but the poor
were brought to famine level, and food riots sometimes occurred under such
circumstances. If a harvest was good the situation was reversed – a fall in the
price of wheat and bread benefited the poor but could mean ruin for the farmers.

Mr Austen and his family lived in Deane and Steventon from 1764 till early
1801, and as well as enduring all the vicissitudes of bad weather in his capacity as a farmer, he had to encourage his parishioners to endure them as well,
in his capacity as their rector. It was customary in the countryside to bless a
plough in early January, on what was known as Plough Monday, which was

Sunday Morning, a Cottage Family going to Church, *stipple and etching with aquatint, by William Bigg, 1795.*

considered to be the start of the English agricultural year since it was the first working day after the twelve days of Christmas and New Year. This ceremony was not officially noted in the Book of Common Prayer, but in days when work was scarce in winter, the observance looked forward hopefully to the time of sowing and the promise of a harvest to come, and it therefore seems likely that Mr Austen would have continued the tradition. The teenage Jane, certainly, noted very solemnly in the family copy of Goldsmith's *The History of England, from the Earliest Times to the Death of George II*: 'Every ancient custom ought to be sacred unless prejudicial to Happiness.'

A day which was noted officially by the Church of England this month was 30 January, when prayers were said to commemorate the execution of King

Charles I in 1649; and since Jane wrote a parody of Goldsmith in her own *The History of England from the reign of Henry the 4th to the death of Charles the 1st, by a partial, prejudiced, and ignorant Historian* in order to praise the Stuart family, she must have been delighted to hear her father read these prayers in church.

If the weather in January was favourable, it might be possible for the farmer to do a little early ploughing to sow spring wheat, otherwise the tasks in this month for him and his labourers were those of maintenance and preparation for the coming year: feeding and tending the surviving cattle which had been brought into sheltered farmyards and enclosures and perhaps fattening a few very early lambs and calves for marketing in the summer, repairing implements and tools, clearing ditches and drains, spreading manure, pruning fruit trees and planting orchards, felling timber and grubbing up the roots and stumps to burn as firewood. In 1799 Jane reported to Cassandra that a pig had recently been killed at Cheesedown and the meat cut up to be salted and sent as a gift to their brother Edward, now living in Kent, also that: 'We have had one dead lamb.' Some of the landowners and other local gentry would by now be in London for the fashionable social season, escaping the long cold nights and short cold days of life in the country by gathering together for parties and dances – Queen Charlotte's official birthday was celebrated on 18 January – and Mrs Jennings in *Sense and Sensibility* decides to return from Devonshire to her house in Upper Berkeley Street, near Portman Square, taking the Dashwood sisters with her. Others, like Sir John Middleton and Willoughby, would remain on their estates to enjoy foxhunting and other field sports until such time as frost and snow made these impossible. Mrs Jennings knows that 'Sir John will not like leaving Barton next week; 'tis a sad thing for sportsmen to lose a day's pleasure'; while Marianne Dashwood, longing for Willoughby to come to London, '. . . saw every night in the brightness of the fire, and every morning in the appearance of the atmosphere, the certain symptoms of approaching frost'. At Mansfield Park, Fanny Price has to sit in her little East Room study wrapped in a shawl and shivering while there is snow on the ground outside because, unknown to Sir Thomas Bertram, spiteful Aunt Norris has forbidden the housemaids to lay a fire there for her niece's benefit – an order which Sir Thomas promptly overrules as soon as he becomes aware of it.

Mr Austen was rarely away from his parishes for more than a couple of weeks at a time, and could not in any case have afforded to rent a house in London for several months. The family therefore stayed at home over the winter, entertaining their relatives and amusing themselves with their amateur dramatic productions, and exchanging dinner party visits with their nearest neighbours. As Jane and Cassandra grew up, they attended private dances organized by these neighbouring families and also the local assembly balls, held once a month from September or October to March or April in Basingstoke town hall, on the Thursday nearest the full moon, so that – assuming the night was not overcast – the participants would have the maximum possible light when driving home afterwards. In Jane's first surviving letter, that of 9–10 January 1796, she teases Cassandra:

> You scold me so much in the nice long letter which I have this moment received from you, that I am almost afraid to tell you how my Irish friend [Tom Lefroy] and I behaved. . . . I can expose myself, however, only once more, because he leaves the country soon after next Friday, on which day we are to have a dance at Ashe after all. He is a very gentlemanlike, good-looking, pleasant young man, I assure you. But as to our having ever met, except at the three last balls, I cannot say much; for he is so excessively laughed at about me at Ashe, that he is ashamed of coming to Steventon, and ran away when we called on Mrs Lefroy a few days ago.

In 1799 she went to Lady Dorchester's ball at Kempshot Park: 'It was a pleasant Ball, & still more good than pleasant, for there were nearly 60 people, & sometimes we had 17 couples.' On another occasion, in 1801, after some 'dreadfully mild and unhealthy weather', Jane was dining at Deane with James and his second wife Mary Lloyd, and while she was there 'a sudden fall of snow rendered the roads impassable, and made my journey home in the little carriage much more easy and agreeable than my journey down'.

On 2 February there was the Feast of Candlemas, when lights and candles were blessed; lengthening of the days became apparent, and towards the end of the month it would be possible to dine without candles, an event which good housewives might note in their pocketbooks, since candles, especially good quality wax ones, were expensive items in the domestic budget. Dining by natural light at this time of the year was in fact not so unlikely as it sounds, since at this period dinner, especially in the country, was taken very much earlier in the day, quite often in mid-afternoon – in 1798, when Cassandra was away staying at Godmersham, Jane wrote to her: 'We dine now at half after Three, & have done dinner I suppose before you begin . . .' Out of doors, in mid-February the wives and children of the labourers could add to the family income by planting beans – bean-setting, as it was called – a task which lasted for about a month. Beans had to be hand-set one by one – no machine had yet been invented for the task – so women and boys would meet at the granary door to be given their daily allowance of seed beans, which could be four gallons for a woman, two gallons for a strong teenager, and one gallon for a smaller child. The troop then set off for the arable lands, and spent the day in this simple but back-breaking task, drilling holes in the earth with a little stick – a dibber – and dropping a bean into each. They were paid according to the quantity planted, and sometimes the women would be accused of 'clumping' – that is, dropping more than one bean into a hole in order to finish all the sooner. Those fields that had been ploughed the previous autumn and left open for frost to shatter the clods, could now be sown with wheat and barley. A seed-drill had been invented in Berkshire early in the eighteenth century by Jethro Tull, a hands-on gentleman farmer like Mr Knightley; this was the first attempt to sow seed by machine rather than by hand, and there had been later improvements to the drill as the century progressed, but sowing was still much more frequently done by hand, like the bean-setting: the labourer had a bag of seed corn at his waist, and would throw out handfuls left and right as he walked slowly and carefully up and down the furrows, and it was said that an experienced sower could cover a ten-acre field very evenly using twenty bushels of corn. Mr Austen's congregation could well appreciate the Biblical parable of those seeds which fell by the wayside and were eaten by birds, or those which fell upon stony places or amongst thorns, and at last rejoice in the thought of the success of those which fell into good ground and brought forth a fine harvest.

More lambs would be dropped in this month and early wildflowers would start to appear, and if the weather was mild these intimations of spring meant the month could be delightful. Country dwellers who had been kept at home by winter weather could now think again of travelling beyond their own parishes. It is at the end of January or very early in February that the Allens and Catherine Morland go to Bath, and a few days later she drives out with John Thorpe in his gig, with 'all the enjoyment of air and exercise of the most invigorating kind, in a fine mild day of February . . .'; but after another two days rain returns in the morning and spoils the plans for a country walk with Henry Tilney and his sister. Fanny and William Price travel from Mansfield Park to Portsmouth 'as expeditiously as could rationally be hoped in the dirty month of February', staying overnight at Newbury and arriving in Portsmouth 'while there was yet daylight for Fanny to look around her, and wonder at the new buildings'. In February 1801, when Jane herself visited Baughurst, a village several miles beyond Basingstoke and hitherto unknown to her, she told Cassandra: 'The place is not so pretty as I expected, but perhaps the Season may be against the beauty of Country.' In contrast, in the February when Frank Churchill comes to visit his father for the first time since childhood, and Emma is looking forward to becoming acquainted with this handsome young man who is bringing a breath of fresh air into her confined Highbury life, Jane gives us a quick glimpse into the symbolism at work in Emma's sub-conscious mind, as she looks at the hedges and thinks 'the elder at least must soon be coming out'; and there follows a spell of 'fine, dry, settled weather' which enables Mrs Weston, Emma and Frank to walk about together 'for an hour or two – first round the shrubberies of Hartfield, and afterwards in Highbury'.

The farming year started to become really busy in March, when the possibility of dryer weather meant that the plough-teams were out, jangling and trampling along the lanes on their way to the fields, much ploughing was done and most of the sowing was undertaken; hedges were cut and laid, on the principle that a hedge trimmed in March had all the year to grow into the proper shape; and shepherds were fully occupied with the main lambing season, watching the flocks and hand-feeding the lambs if necessary. The hay meadows had to be prepared, and boys walked up and down with baskets to pick up all the stones which might injure the scythes when the hay was cut later in the year,

ABOVE Ellis's Drill, *from William Ellis, The Farmer's Instructor, 1750.*

BELOW Ploughman at Work, *from John Boys's* General View of the Agriculture of Kent, *1796.*

81

after which cartloads of manure were spread over the field and the boys would harrow it in; they were followed by a little troop of women who would tear up any weed or root which they could see. The wild flowers were appearing in force – celandines, violets, daffodils, primroses – and coltsfoot, mallows, yarrow, tansy, camomile and others could all be used to brew herbal teas or were pulped into medicinal salves and syrups. The tender shoots of young nettles were considered by the villagers to be a great purifier of the blood, and so were gathered and cooked like spinach, as well as being brewed into nettle beer. Ale and beer proper were also brewed, and March beer was noted for its excellence. Lady Day, 25 March, was one of the quarter days, when farms often changed hands – and the day when both domestic servants and farm labourers could make a year's agreement with their employers that they would not change their situation during the following year. If notice were not given it was assumed that the employee was content and would remain till the end of the coming year.

For those of Jane's heroines who were already out and about on their adventures, March seems to have been rather wet, cold and windy. As Catherine Morland drives up to Northanger Abbey with Henry Tilney in his curricle, 'a sudden scud of rain driving full in her face . . . fixed all her thoughts on the welfare of her new straw bonnet . . .' and she has no time to look at the outside of the Abbey itself before hurrying into the house. 'The night was stormy; the wind had been rising at intervals the whole afternoon; and by the time the party broke up, it blew and rained violently. . . . The wind roared down the chimney, the rain beat in torrents against the windows . . .' The next morning, however, is dry, and General Tilney takes her out of doors to show her the house and grounds. 'She was struck however, beyond her expectation, by the grandeur of the Abbey, as she saw it for the first time from the lawn. The whole building enclosed a large court; and two sides of the quadrangle, rich in Gothic ornaments, stood forward for admiration. The remainder was shut off by knolls of old trees, or luxuriant plantations, and the steep woody hills rising behind to give it shelter, were beautiful even in the leafless month of March.' When Sir William and Maria Lucas take Elizabeth Bennet with them to visit the newly married Charlotte Lucas at Hunsford parsonage in Kent, the weather is fine but cold, despite which Mr Collins gives them a long-winded tour of his garden.

Here, leading the way through every walk and cross-walk, and
scarcely allowing them an interval to utter the praises he asked
for, every view was pointed out with a minuteness which left
beauty entirely behind. He could number the fields in every
direction, and could tell how many trees there were in the most
distant clump . . . From his garden, Mr Collins would have led
them round his two meadows, but the ladies not having shoes
to encounter the remains of a white frost, turned back . . .

The Dashwood sisters fare better during their stay in London, when there
is 'so fine, so beautiful a Sunday as to draw many to Kensington Gardens,
though it was only the second week in March'; and Fanny Price has the best
March day of all, when she is walking with her family on the ramparts at
Portsmouth after attending Sunday morning service at the Garrison Chapel:

The day was uncommonly lovely. It was really March; but it was
April in its mild air, brisk soft wind, and bright sun, occasionally
clouded for a minute; and every thing looked so beautiful under
the influence of such a sky, the effects of the shadows pursuing
each other, on the ships at Spithead and the island beyond, with
the ever-varying hues of the sea now at high water, dancing in
its glee and dashing against the ramparts with so fine a sound . . .

But later on, when Fanny is still in Portsmouth and longing to return to
Mansfield, she misses seeing spring in the countryside, '. . . from the earliest
flowers, in the warmest divisions of her aunt's garden, to the opening of
leaves of her uncle's plantations, and the glory of his woods'.

In Jane's own life, the winter of 1794–5 was again very severe, with frost
and snow starting in December and ending in floods as the ice melted in
mid-March. Their neighbour Mrs Bramston wrote to her Gloucestershire
cousin Mrs Hicks Beach about its effects at Steventon:

As you live on the top of a hill, I will not ask you how you like
floating on the Waters, & as we live on the Side of a one, I

cannot tell you from Experience, but our neighbours say they rather like the Ground floor than the upper apartments, Mr Austens family did not descend for two days, Mr James Austen lost 2 fat pigs, one poor farmer had but 60 Ewes & above 20 were drown'd, Corn carried out of the Barns, & numberless Accidents did the sudden thaw create . . .

When the ground floor of the rectory had dried out, Mr Austen had to spend £11 early in April buying new carpets from John Ring's firm in Basingstoke. April 1795 continued to be very wet and cold with food in short supply, and a mob at Portsea near Portsmouth attacked the butchers' and bakers' shops and compelled them to sell meat and bread at low prices.

During March and April 1798 there was insurrection in Ireland which brought in its wake the threat of landings there by a French army, and this in turn led to the English Government's preparations against invasion along the vulnerable Channel coast. 'In Hampshire every person from 15 to 60 years of age is summoned to arms, and the Mayor, Aldermen and Burgesses of Portsmouth have unanimously offered their services in defence of his Majesty . . .' and the Government sent out a questionnaire under the Defence of the Realm Act to check on the state of preparedness of the Hampshire countryside. Mr Austen sent in the required returns, which give a snapshot of the parish of Steventon just at the turn of the century: there were thirty-nine able-bodied men and ten infirm incapable men; no one was serving in the volunteer militia; no foreigners; no Quakers; and seventy-eight non-combatants who would need help to be evacuated. Live and dead stock amounted to 5 cows, 1,100 sheep and goats, 64 pigs, 4 riding horses and 34 draft horses; 12 waggons, 5 carts; 20 ovens which could be used to bake regular supplies of bread; 380 quarters of wheat, 250 quarters of oats, 200 quarters of barley, 220 loads of hay, 10 loads of straw, 50 quarters of vetches, 1 threshing machine. Thirty men were prepared to fight on foot and five on horseback, but they had no military weapons, only their agricultural tools – axes, spades, shovels, billhooks and saws; the remaining four men would act as guides or servants. Luckily, as in 1940, the danger passed off, and after another similar scare in 1804, Nelson's victory at Trafalgar in 1805 meant it was no longer possible for Napoleon to contemplate a cross-Channel invasion of England.

In April the hay meadows, once cleared and harrowed, were closed off to allow the grass to grow; some sowing of corn still continued but should finish by the end of the month, as also should all ditching, hedging and draining. Ideally there should be warm rain for the corn to start growing, but all too often there were dry frosts instead. Sheep and lambs were now grazing in the fields, but there was always the danger that they could overeat upon lucerne and clover and bloat themselves into violent indigestion, which caused suffocation and was rapidly fatal; also both sheep and cows could develop 'the staggers', a deficiency disease due to a lack of magnesium in new grass – as this is a mineral which aids muscle control – and which was another quick killer. John Bond may have dosed his flock with a home-made recipe such as one preserved in an Austen family household book: 'Cinnabar of antimony two drams, mash half a dram gum asafoetida, half an ounce valerian root in powder half an ounce, winters bark in powder half an ounce, made into a ball with honey', which was then pushed down the animal's throat.

The sowing of peas, clover, lucerne, vetches, sainfoin and lesser crops such as woad, madder, flax, hemp, mustard, rhubarb and other medicinal plants would be in full swing, and the end of the month was the time to plant turnips, potatoes, mangolds and swedes – this last vegetable being introduced to England just at the end of the eighteenth century, and known then as rutabaga or 'Swedish turnips'. Women and children were employed on hoeing out weeds from wheat fields, and later on in hacking up the root crops and slicing them into cattle feed. As always, Mrs Austen's poultry yard was full of newly hatched chicks – she kept turkeys, ducks, chickens and guinea fowl – and farming manuals pointed out that these demanded much of the good housewife's cares.

Marianne Dashwood, sunk in grief after Willoughby's cruel public jilting of her in January, followed by his rapid marriage to

The Turkey, *wood engraving by Thomas Bewick.*

the rich Miss Grey in February, now cannot bear to remain in London. She 'sighed for the air, the liberty, the quiet of the country', and when Charlotte Palmer and her husband decide to return to their home in Somerset, she and Elinor leave London with them very early in April. As soon as they arrive at Cleveland, Marianne steals away through the

> . . . winding shrubberies, now just beginning to be in beauty, to gain a distant eminence; where, from its Grecian temple, her eye, wandering over a wide tract of country to the south-east, could fondly rest on the farthest ridge of hills in the horizon, and fancy that from their summits Combe Magna [Willoughby's estate] might be seen. . . . She returned just in time to join the others as they quitted the house, on an excursion through its more immediate premises; and the rest of the morning was easily whiled away, in lounging round the kitchen garden, examining the bloom upon its walls, and listening to the gardener's lamentations upon blights; – in dawdling through the greenhouse, where the loss of her favourite plants, unwarily exposed, and nipped by the lingering frost, raised the laughter of Charlotte, – and in visiting her poultry yard, where, in the disappointed hopes of her dairy-maid, by hens forsaking their nests, or being stolen by a fox, or in the rapid decease of a promising young brood, she found fresh sources of merriment.

But after two rainy days, when Marianne persists in walking out at twilight, 'not merely on the dry gravel of the shrubbery, but all over the grounds, and especially in the most distant parts of them, where there was something more of wildness than in the rest, where the trees were the oldest, and the grass was the longest and wettest', she develops a violent cold which turns to pleurisy or pneumonia, and nearly proves fatal.

Other heroines have much happier Aprils: Catherine Morland goes to see Henry Tilney in his parsonage at Woodston, 'a new-built substantial stone house, with its semi-circular sweep and green gates'; and although 'the General seemed to think an apology necessary for the flatness of the country' – Jane had imagined both Northanger and Woodston as being situated on the flood-plain of the River Severn in Gloucestershire, somewhere near Slimbridge – Catherine 'preferred it to any place she had ever been at, and looked with great admiration at every neat house above the rank of a cottage, and at all the little chandlers' shops which they passed'. By the end of the story we know that in about a year's time Woodston parsonage will indeed be her home, and she will be sitting in the 'prettily-shaped' drawing-room, with its windows reaching to the ground and a view from them over green meadows, including a 'sweet little cottage' amongst the apple trees, or strolling in the shrubbery which Henry has just planted, though at present 'there was not a shrub in it higher than the green bench in the corner'. In Kent, since 'all field sports were over', Darcy and Colonel Fitzwilliam stay on at Rosings with their aunt Lady Catherine de Bourgh, and call at Mr Collins's parsonage almost every day to see Elizabeth Bennet – calls which climax in Darcy's first tactless proposal to her. Lizzy notices that the 'five weeks which she had now passed in Kent, had made a great difference in the country, and every day was adding to the verdure of the early trees' – and it is while she is 'tempted, by the pleasantness of the morning, to stop at the gates and look into the park', that Darcy presents her with his long letter of explanation.

May Day, 1 May, was a traditional holiday in the countryside, when doors were decorated with fresh green sprays picked from shrubs and young branches, perhaps tassels of green larch, and in some villages a maypole was set up and decorated likewise, with dancing to follow. May was a fairly slack month for the farmer since all the crops had been sown; some were now sprouting and required to be weeded by the women and children of the village; and the children would also have the pleasant task of gathering cowslips to be made into wine. Apple trees were coming into bloom, but sudden frosts could kill the blossom and spoil the future crop; and although rain would be needed to benefit both corn and hay, this month too, like March, could be wet, cold and windy. When Jane went to Bath in May 1799 with her brother Edward and his family, she wrote home to Cassandra: '. . . it has rained almost all the way, & our first view of Bath has been just as gloomy as it was last November twelvemonth'.

The cattle were now grazing on the abundance of fresh grass and the cows were in full milk, hence the milkmaid would carry her stool and buckets out to the herd and milk them in the fields, returning with full buckets hung from a yoke across her shoulders. The farmer's wife became busy with all the cares and processes of dairy work, skimming and churning the milk and producing rich cream, sweet butter – butter made in May was said to be the best – curds, syllabubs, custards and various kinds of cheese. Making cheese alone required several different processes – pressing the curd, shaping into individual weights and storing and turning them for months until sufficiently mature. Even with only three cows in the rectory field, there would be no lack of employment for Mrs Austen and the dairymaid; also her poultry broods still demanded careful attention to protect them from marauding hawks and foxes that raided hen coops and roosts; and the rectory garden needed to be sown and weeded. Another traditional event this month that would have delighted Jane was Royal Oak Day, 29 May, when special prayers and thanksgivings were said in church to commemorate the birthday of Charles II and also his return to England and the restoration of the Stuart monarchy in May 1660 after the dreary years of Cromwell's Puritan republic.

After the long lead-in to *Mansfield Park*, beginning with Fanny Price's arrival there to join the Bertram family as a frightened little ten-year-old, Jane Austen starts the main action in the spring some six or seven years later, by which time Maria and Julia Bertram were 'fully established among the belles of the neighbourhood' and Maria has just become engaged to Mr Rushworth; Fanny is companion to her indolent Aunt Bertram and the object of spiteful Aunt Norris's harassment and bullying. The sisters each had their own horse, and so they 'took their cheerful rides in the fine mornings of April and May; and Fanny either sat at home the whole day with one aunt, or walked beyond her strength at the instigation of the other . . .' a situation which leads kind Edmund to provide a horse for her to ride as well. The story unfolds over the following year, and in February Fanny is sent away to Portsmouth; when she returns, it is May again, and 'her eye fell every where on lawns and plantations of the freshest green; and the trees, though not fully clothed, were in that delightful state, when farther beauty is known to be at hand . . .'

Easter usually falls in April and forty days after Easter, just before Ascension Day in May, were the days of Rogation-tide in the church's calendar, when the parson would invoke a blessing on the fields and livestock: he and his congregation would walk round the boundary of the parish [this was known as 'beating the bounds'], stopping off at some well-known landmarks to read an appropriate extract from the Gospels or preach a short sermon. At any time of the year there might be the necessity of prayers to avert an agricultural crisis, whether in times of drought: 'Send us, we beseech thee, in this our necessity, such moderate rain and showers, that we may receive the fruits of the earth to our comfort, and to thy honour . . .'; or in too wet a season: 'We humbly beseech thee, that although we for our iniquities have worthily deserved a plague of rain and waters, yet upon our true repentance thou wilt send us such weather, as that

A Shady Corner, *oil on canvas, by William Shayer senior, 1840.*

The Shearers, *oil and tempera on panel, by Samuel Palmer, 1833–4.*

we may receive the fruits of the earth in due season . . .'; and from any kind of crop failure: 'Behold, we beseech thee, the afflictions of thy people; and grant that the scarcity and dearth, which we do now most justly suffer for our iniquity, may through thy goodness be mercifully turned into cheapness and plenty . . .'

June was traditionally the month for washing the sheep and then shearing them; as there was no stream running through Steventon, Mr Austen and the Digweeds presumably drove their flocks through the man-made ponds in the village, one just off the main street and the other on the Warren land. Mr Austen seems to have kept his flock more for mutton than fleece, and Jane has no personal comment to make in her letters regarding his sales of wool. However, the naïve Harriet Smith, when telling Emma about her recent holiday with the Martin family at Abbey Mill Farm, says proudly that Robert Martin '. . . had a very fine flock; and while she was with them, he had been bid more for his wool than any body in the country'.

As soon as sheep-shearing was over, haymaking started and usually continued into July, depending upon weather conditions. In the long summer days the troops of haymakers would start work before dawn so that a rest could be taken beneath the shade of trees in the heat of midday, then work again until the stars came out in the evening sky. The first into the meadow were the actual mowers, the men working together in a rhythm one behind the other each in his own swathe, wielding their sharp scythes with regular strokes, and the long grass falling before them with a gentle hissing noise into smooth waves. After them came the tedders, tossing the grass into the air with pronged forks and spreading it out in order to start the drying process. Next it would be drawn together with rakes into small rows – 'wind-raked' – and on the following day turned over and raked into larger rows or 'beds'. At night these would be divided into 'half-cocks'; the next day all the hay was thrown out again and turned over, and finally got up into 'full cock', which was then nearly ready to carry. The raking and turning of the hay had to continue for at least three days or until it was as dry as possible, since if damp hay were built into a haystack this would lead to spontaneous combustion inside the stack. The huge empty waggons waited at the edge of the meadow, and, as haymaking was one of the natural festivities of the farming year, the patient old horses were decked with flowers and honey-suckle, and the carters fixed branches of ash leaves over the horses' heads to keep the tormenting flies at bay. Once loaded, they would set off for the farmyard, harness-bells tinkling, and while the haystack was being built would be back down again for the next load.

The younger children could play in the haycocks and ride on the waggons while their parents and elder brothers worked, and Jane would have known from a very early age the importance of the hay-harvest in the life of the community; she was probably no more than thirteen when she wrote one of her Juvenilia items, 'Henry and Eliza, a Novel', which starts with a haymaking scene. In later years, she mentioned haymaking in *Mansfield Park*: Henry and Mary Crawford come to stay at Mansfield Parsonage in July, and Mary is trying to get her harp sent after her from London, but finds it is stuck at Northampton and there is no transport available for the last leg of its journey. She tells Edmund Bertram, with amused annoyance: 'To want a horse and cart in the country seemed impossible, so I told my maid to speak for one directly; . . . I thought it would be only ask and have, and was rather grieved that I could not give the advantage to all. Guess my surprise, when I found that I had been asking the most unreasonable, most impossible thing in the world, had offended all the farmers, all the labourers, all the hay in the parish.' Edmund points out to her that they are presently in the middle of a very late hay harvest: 'You could not be expected to have thought on the subject before, but when you *do* think of it, you must see the importance of getting in the grass. The hire of a cart at any time, might not be so easy as you suppose; our farmers are not in the habit of letting them out; but in

harvest, it must be quite out of their power to spare a horse.' Mary starts to betray her basically mercenary nature when she replies: 'I shall understand all your ways in time; but coming down with the true London maxim, that every thing is to be got with money, I was a little embarrassed at first by the sturdy independence of your country customs.'

In her last, unfinished, novel, the fragment now known as *Sanditon*, Jane again started with a haymaking scene. Mr and Mrs Parker have been overturned in their carriage while driving up a very rough lane at Willingden in Sussex, and Mr Parker has badly sprained his ankle. Mrs Parker stood,

The Country round Dixton Manor, *oil on canvas, English School, c.1725. Dixton is near Cheltenham in Gloucestershire and Jane would have seen this sort of countryside when going to visit her Leigh relations at Stoneleigh Abbey.*

Haymaking at Dixton Manor, *oil on canvas, English School,* c.*1725. This panorama shows all the stages of haymaking: the curve of the mowers working in lines, the rows of cut grass being raked up into haycocks by women, the haywains waiting to be loaded, and finally the haymakers leaving the field (bottom right) in a merry morris-dance.*

terrified & anxious, neither able to do or suggest anything – & receiving her first real comfort from the sight of several persons now coming to their assistance. The accident had been discerned from a Hayfield adjoining the House they had passed – & the persons who approached, were a well-looking Hale, Gentlemanlike Man, of middle age, the Proprietor of the Place, who happened to be among his Haymakers at the time, & three or four of the ablest of them summoned to attend their Master – to say nothing of all the rest of the field, Men, Women & Children – not

very far off – Mr Heywood, such was the name of the said
Proprietor, advanced with a very civil salutation . . . very cor-
dially pressing them to make use of his House . . . 'And here
come my Girls to speak for themselves & their Mother, (two or
three genteel looking young Women followed by as many Maid
servants, were now seen issuing from the House) – I began to
wonder the Bustle should not have reached them. A thing of this
kind soon makes a Stir in a lonely place like ours.'

Of all Jane's works, *Emma* contains the most emphasis on the weather and
its effect upon the life of an agriculturally based community, from the umbrellas
lent by Farmer Mitchell of Broadway-lane when it began to mizzle, through Mr
Elton's embarrassing proposal to Emma in the cold coach trip at snowy Christmas,
and so on to the two midsummer parties which provide the final complications of

the plot. The first party is that organized by Mr Knightley at his home: 'Donwell was famous for its strawberry-beds . . . and Mrs Elton, in all her apparatus of happiness, her large bonnet and her basket, was very ready to lead the way in gathering, accepting, or talking – strawberries, and only strawberries, could now be thought or spoken of. . . . hautboys very scarce – Chili preferred – white wood finest flavour of all . . .' While Mrs Elton is monopolizing the conversation, Emma herself enjoys walking round the grounds of the Abbey in the sunshine:

> . . . its ample gardens stretching down to meadows washed by a stream . . . its abundance of timber in rows and avenues, which neither fashion or extravagance had rooted up . . . the delicious shade of a broad short avenue of limes, which stretching beyond the garden at an equal distance from the river, seemed the finish of the pleasure grounds. It led to nothing; nothing but a view at

View of Box Hill from Norbury Park, Surrey, *drawing by Thomas Sandby* c. *1775.*

the end over a low stone wall with high pillars . . . a charming walk, and the view which closed it extremely pretty.

Emma sees that Mr Knightley and Harriet are walking about together distinct from the rest: 'She joined them at the wall, and found them more engaged in talking than in looking around. He was giving Harriet information as to modes of agriculture, &c . . .' She herself pauses to look at the view:

The considerable slope, at nearly the foot of which the Abbey stood, gradually acquired a steeper form beyond its grounds; and at half a mile distant was a bank of considerable abruptness and grandeur, well clothed with wood; and at the bottom of this bank, favourably placed and sheltered rose the Abbey-Mill Farm, with meadows in front, and the river making a close and handsome curve around it . . . with all its appendages of prosperity and beauty, its rich pastures, spreading flocks, orchard in blossom, and light column of smoke ascending.

When *Emma* was published at the very end of 1815, the Austen family remembered that Jane's brother Edward teased her about this scene, asking: 'Jane, I wish you would tell me where you get those apple trees of yours that come into bloom in July.' However, one modern meteorologist considers that this is not an error on Jane's part, but a clue to the date of composition of this chapter. Jane had started writing *Emma* on 21 January 1814 and May and June of that year had been remarkably cold with only a brief warm spell in the middle of June, hence blossoming could have been delayed; and Jane stayed with her Cooke cousins at Great Bookham in Surrey from 24 June until 7 July 1814. Great Bookham is only a few miles from Leatherhead, and in later years the Austen family recorded that Jane had based Highbury upon this latter small town; perhaps it was during this visit that she saw some Leatherhead apple trees in very late blossom – fitting in with her vision of the thriving Donwell Abbey estate in midsummer: 'It was a sweet view – sweet to the eye and the mind. English verdure, English culture, English comfort, seen under a sun bright, without being oppressive.'

Mr Weston's picnic party to Box Hill, a genuine and well-known beauty spot rising to more than 600 feet and so providing fine views of the Surrey countryside for miles around, takes place the next day after the trip to Donwell Abbey. 'They had a very fine day for Box Hill . . . Seven miles were travelled in expectation of enjoyment, and every body had a burst of admiration on first arriving; but in the general amount of the day there was deficiency. There was a languor, a want of spirits, a want of union, which could not be got over. They separated too much into parties.' The Eltons in particular choose to be offended and stand aloof. Frank Churchill flirts violently with Emma in order to punish Jane Fairfax for quarrelling with him the day before; Emma does not as yet know that Frank and Jane are secretly engaged, but senses the tension in the atmosphere and although chattering away brightly is nevertheless unhappy within herself – 'such another scheme, composed of so many ill-assorted people, she hoped never to be betrayed into again' – and in exasperation is rude to Miss Bates, for which she is then roundly scolded by Mr Knightley, thus completing the unhappiness of the day. 'Emma felt the tears running down her cheeks almost all the way home, without being at any trouble to check them, extraordinary as they were.'

'Rare Old Port, Strawberries & Cream, Ladies!', *oil on board, artist and location unknown, date late eighteenth century. The scene is a visitors' day at a farm or small house in the country; smaller than Donwell Abbey and earlier in date than Mr Knightley's picnic, but with the same interest in the strawberry beds and orchards.*

There is further unhappiness in store for Emma, when she believes for a time that Mr Knightley has decided to marry Harriet Smith. Harriet instances some apparent proofs of his intentions:

> The first, was his walking with her apart from the others, in the lime walk at Donwell, where they had been walking some time before Emma came, and he had taken pains (as she was convinced) to draw her from the rest to himself . . . and seemed to be almost asking her, whether her affections were engaged. – But as soon as she (Miss Woodhouse) appeared likely to join them, he changed the subject, and began talking about farming. . . . Till now that she was threatened with its loss, Emma had never known how much of her happiness depended on being *first* with Mr Knightley, first in interest and affection.

The weather is correspondingly wretched:

> The evening of this day was very long, and melancholy, at Hartfield. The weather added what it could of gloom. A cold

stormy rain set in, and nothing of July appeared but in the trees and shrubs, which the wind was despoiling, and the length of the day, which only made such cruel sights the longer visible. The weather affected Mr Woodhouse, and he could only be kept tolerably comfortable by almost ceaseless attention on his daughter's side, and by exertions which had never cost her half as much before. . . . The weather continued much the same all the following morning; and the same loneliness, and the same melancholy, seemed to reign at Hartfield – but in the afternoon it cleared; the wind changed into a softer quarter; the clouds were carried off; the sun appeared; it was summer again. With all the eagerness which such a transition gives, Emma resolved to be out of doors as soon as possible. Never had the exquisite sight, smell, sensation of nature, tranquil, warm, and brilliant after a storm, been more attractive to her . . . she lost no time in hurrying into the shrubbery.

This is where Mr Knightley presently finds her, and all misunderstandings are resolved.

After Jane's birth at the start of the freezing winter of 1775–6, the strangest summer of her young life was that of 1783, as the Revd Gilbert White wrote afterwards in his *Natural History of Selborne*:

The summer of the year 1783 was an amazing and portentous one, and full of horrible phenomena; for, besides the alarming meteors and tremendous thunderstorms that affrighted and distressed the different counties of this kingdom, the peculiar haze, or smokey fog, that prevailed for many weeks in this island, and in every part of Europe, and even beyond its limits, was a most extraordinary appearance, unlike anything known within the memory of man. By my journal I find that I had noticed this strange occurrence from June 23rd to July 20th inclusive, during which period the wind varied to every quarter without making any alteration in the air. The sun, at noon, looked as blank as a clouded moon, and shed a rust-coloured ferruginous light on the ground, and floors of rooms; but was particularly lurid and blood-coloured at rising and setting. All the time the heat was so intense that butchers' meat could hardly be eaten on the day after it was killed, and the flies swarmed so in the lanes and hedges that they rendered the horses half frantic and riding irksome. The country people began to look with a superstitious awe, at the red, louring aspect of the sun; and indeed there was reason for the most enlightened person to be apprehensive; for, all the while, Calabria and part of the isle of Sicily, were torn and convulsed with earthquakes; and about that juncture a volcano sprung out of the sea on the coast of Norway.

Gilbert White could not have known at the time, but these strange conditions were due to the eruption of the Laki volcanic fissure in Iceland, the deadliest volcanic eruption in history. For several months during 1783–4 the fissure not only poured out lava on the ground but also blew clouds of poisonous hydrofluoric acid and sulphur dioxide compounds into the atmosphere, thus contaminating subsequent rainfall. Over half of Iceland's livestock died as a result, as did a quarter of the island's human population; there were crop failures in Europe, and famines as far away as India and Japan.

The farmers and their labourers would still be busy haymaking, carting and stacking during July, but for those not personally involved in agriculture the long light days and the promise of a spell of more settled warm weather would lead to plans for holiday tours. Mr and Mrs Gardiner invite Elizabeth Bennet to join them in a trip to Derbyshire and set off in mid-July, and this timing enables Elizabeth to see Darcy's Pemberley estate at its best:

> The park was very large, and contained great variety of ground. They entered it in one of its lowest points, and drove for some time through a beautiful wood, stretching over a wide extent. . . . On reaching the house, they were shewn through the hall into the saloon, whose northern aspect rendered it delightful for summer. Its windows opening to the ground, admitted a most refreshing view of the high woody hills behind the house, and of the

beautiful oaks and Spanish chestnuts which were scattered over the intermediate lawn.

It is probably also during July that Robert Ferrars and Lucy Steele get married and travel to Dawlish in Devon for a seaside honeymoon. In real life Jane and Cassandra travelled to Gloucestershire to stay with their Leigh relations at Adlestrop in July 1794; and in July 1817 a Race Week was held at Winchester, with its accompanying balls and theatrical performances in the evening to amuse the gentry who had gathered to enter their horses and watch the sport.

August saw the climax of the agricultural year, the month for the harvesting of the crops upon which the life of the community depended, and which had taken a whole year's labour to bring to maturity. Corn – wheat, barley, oats and rye – had to be allowed to grow and ripen for as long as possible, but cutting had to begin before there was any danger of the grain falling out of the ears. The corn harvest started early in August as soon as haymaking had finished, and lasted for the month; everything about it was urgent – there was a greater variety of tasks involved than in the normal rural routine and they all had to be performed simultaneously, since no crop was safe until it had been stored. The standing corn was cut at its foot by dragging a toothed sickle through it, or by slashing with a sharp long-bladed reaping-hook; the cut stalks were then bundled into sheaves, which were loosely stacked together in stooks to dry out; once cutting had begun the crop in the field was in constant danger from a change in the weather which could ruin its quality, hence the sheaves were carted to the barn as soon as possible to be stored until winter, when they were threshed. The farm waggons would travel all day and far into the twilight between the field and the farmyard, passing and re-passing along the lanes, and the big cart-horses returning with an empty waggon were urged to gallop like two-year-olds. Harvesting involved the whole village – the skilled carters driving the waggons, the labourers loading them, and the women and children helping to stook the sheaves and afterwards gleaning across the field for a few fallen wheat-stalks to gain their own little supplies of flour for the forthcoming year. Even those who were not farm workers would join in – the carpenters, wheelwrights, masons and all other tradesmen would lay down their tools to help get the precious corn in. When the last

Wheat, *oil on canvas, by John Linnell, 1860.*

load was piled high on the waggon, perhaps even by moonlight, and it set off swaying and lurching dangerously along the narrow lanes on its final trip to the farmyard, the weary but proud workers followed behind, shouting and singing to let the neighbourhood know: 'Harvest home, harvest home, merry merry merry harvest home!' or 'We have ploughed, we have sowed, we have reaped, we have mowed, ne'er a load overthrowed – Harvest Home!'

Such a cheerful Harvest Home was the ideal outcome of the year's work, but all too often adverse weather conditions prevailed; 1795 and 1796 were years of great scarcity, when wheat harvests failed throughout Europe, and the gentry were urged by newspapers to use less flour and bread, and plant potatoes instead: 'It is recommended to noblemen and gentlemen, who have large parks, to break up a part of them to be planted with potatoes, those grounds generally lying dry, will be very proper for the purpose and fit for immediate planting with that root.' Yet another bad year was 1799, when from 22 June to 17 November there were only eight days without rain; harvest in many districts did not begin till September and much of the corn was never got in. The following year saw the price of wheat rise to 113s.10d a quarter

/ JANE AUSTEN'S COUNTRY LIFE

[about £5.70 in modern currency], which was double the average price of the last ten years, and food riots occurred again. *The Times* of 22 February 1800 repeated its advice to landowners to use spare land to grow more potatoes.

The apple harvest started in late August and continued until mid-October, and all the village families would again set to work in the orchards filling large baskets; the early dessert varieties would not keep well and so needed to be sold straight away, other varieties would be pressed into cider, and those which ripened later, usually cooking apples, could safely be stored in the farm-houses' cool apple lofts to be used during the coming winter. Pears and damsons were also ripe now, and blackberries, cobnuts, sweet chestnuts, filberts and walnuts were all to be gathered in the hedgerows as the calendar moved into September. Robert Martin went three miles out of his way one day, in order to bring Harriet some walnuts, because she had said how fond she was of them. Beechmast was starting to fall in the woodlands, so the villagers' pigs could be set free to roam and grow fat upon it during the next three months. Rabbiting – using ferrets to flush rabbits out of their burrows and catch them in nets – provided extra meat until the following March; and 'green' geese [that is, young ones] were turned out into the now empty cornfields to pick up the scattered loose grain and fatten themselves into 'stubble' geese. At Mansfield Park, Dr Grant – described by his sister-in-law Mary Crawford as an 'indolent, selfish bon vivant, who must have his palate consulted in every thing, who will not stir a finger for the convenience of any one, and who, moreover, if the cook makes a blunder, is out of humour with his excellent wife' – has been in a bad temper all day because of 'a disappointment about a

The Last Load Home at Harvest. *Early-nineteenth-century engraving.*

green goose, which he could not get the better of. My poor sister was forced to stay and bear it.' Once the harvest had been gathered in and the stubble-geese driven off to fairs and markets, ploughing would start for new sowings of wheat and barley; and the cycle of cultivation and growth would begin again, with preparation for the coming winter: in September 1796 the Digweed family were planning to carry out some repairs at the Manor Farm, and Edward Knight's steward was due to call and look over the work. Michaelmas, 29 September, was another quarter day and an important date in agriculture; farm tenancies often ran from Michaelmas and farmers would seek to hire new men if any were needed. By now the various crops probably had been harvested and stored safely in the barns, hence the farmer was better able to judge how much profit he might have made during the past year, and see if he could fulfil the proverb: 'If you eat goose on Michaelmas Day you will never want for money all the year round' – a proverb Jane refers to in her letter of 11–12 October 1813.

No fewer than four of Jane's novels start their main action in September: *Sense and Sensibility*, *Pride and Prejudice*, *Emma* and *Persuasion*. This is not accidental, but tacitly acknowledges that the slight pause after the hectic and anxious time of harvesting gave the opportunity for both farmers and gentry to plan for agricultural and social life respectively. Horse races could be held on cleared fields before ploughing had to start again, and with races went race-balls and arrangements for both private and assembly balls over the forthcoming winter months. Partridge-shooting started on 1 September (until a new Game Act in 1796 moved the date forward to the 14th of the month); it was an important date for gentlemen, and Jane mocked this devotion to the sport in one of her Juvenilia items, 'Sir William Mountague', written perhaps as early as 1788.

> Lady Percival was young, accomplished & lovely. Sir William adored her & she consented to become his Wife. Vehemently pressed by Sir William to name the Day in which he might conduct her to the Altar, she at length fixed on the following Monday, which was the first of September. Sir William was a Shot & could not support the idea of losing such a Day, even for such a Cause. He begged her to delay the Wedding a short time. Lady Percival was enraged & returned to London the next

Morning. Sir William was sorry to lose her, but as he knew that he should have been much more grieved by the Loss of the 1st of September, his Sorrow was not without a mixture of Happiness, & his Affliction was considerably lessened by his Joy.

At the end of August Tom Bertram returns home from his holiday in Weymouth to start partridge shooting on his father's estate as soon as possible; and 'the season and duties which brought Mr Bertram back to Mansfield, took Mr Crawford into Norfolk. Everingham could not do without him in the beginning of September. He went for a fortnight; a fortnight of such dullness to the Miss Bertrams, as ought to have put them both on their guard . . .' and when Henry Crawford returns to Mansfield and the party is joined by Tom's new friend acquired in Weymouth, the feather-headed young John Yates, the next phase of the plot starts, with the calamitous choice of the play *Lovers Vows* that acts as the catalyst to break up the Bertram family circle.

Mrs Dashwood and her daughters move from Sussex to Devonshire very early in September.

The whole country about them abounded in beautiful walks. The high downs which invited them from almost every window of the cottage to seek the exquisite enjoyment of air on their summits, were an happy alternative when the dirt of the valleys beneath shut up their superior beauties; and towards one of these hills did Marianne and Margaret one memorable morning direct their steps, attracted by the partial sunshine of a showery sky, and unable longer to bear the confinement which the settled rain of the two preceding days had occasioned. . . . They gaily ascended the downs, rejoicing . . . at every glimpse of blue sky; . . . and when they caught in their faces the animating gales of an high south-westerly wind . . . they pursued their way against the wind, resisting it with laughing delight for about twenty minutes longer, when suddenly the clouds united over their heads, and a driving rain set full in their face.

Sir John Nelthorpe, 6th Baronet, out shooting with his dogs in Barton Field, Lincolnshire, *oil on panel by George Stubbs, 1776.*

It is as they run back down the hill to Barton Cottage that Marianne falls and sprains her ankle and is picked up by Willoughby, out for some shooting with his gun and two pointers.

Pride and Prejudice starts in early September, as Mrs Bennet tells her husband: '. . . Mrs Long says that Netherfield is taken by a young man of large fortune from the north of England; that he came down on Monday in a chaise and four to see the place, and was so much delighted with it that he agreed with Mr Morris immediately; that he is to take possession before Michaelmas, and some of his servants are to be in the house by the end of next week.' The first Meryton assembly ball of the season is held in late September or early October, and the action of the plot runs round for almost exactly a year, with

Jane and Bingley becoming engaged at the end of the September following, and Darcy and Elizabeth after them in early October. Before these engagements, Lydia Bennet, now Mrs Wickham after her elopement and forced marriage in London during August, returns briefly to Longbourn and noisily demonstrates her devotion to her new husband: 'He was her dear Wickham on every occasion; no one was to be put in competition with him. He did every thing best in the world; and she was sure he would kill more birds on the first of September, than any body else in the country.'

The Elliots too leave their Somerset estate in early September, since their new tenants Admiral Croft and his wife were to take possession of Kellynch Hall at Michaelmas. Anne Elliot was 'dreading the possible heats of September in all the white glare of Bath, and grieving to forego all the influence so sweet and so sad of the autumnal months in the country' – but in the event it happens that she stays on till later in the year, dividing her time between her sister Mary's home at Uppercross Cottage and Lady Russell's Kellynch Lodge. After moving in '. . . the Admiral and Mrs Croft were generally out of doors together, interesting themselves in their new possessions, their grass, and their sheep, and dawdling about in a way not endurable to a third person, or driving out in a gig, lately added to their establishment.' Like Anne Elliot, Jane herself seems to have preferred cool weather, and in September 1796 grumbled to Cassandra: 'What dreadful Hot weather we have! – It keeps one in a continual state of Inelegance.'

Emma starts late in September, on the day of Miss Taylor's marriage to Mr Weston; Frank Churchill's letter of congratulation to his father is dated 28 September, written from Weymouth where he is presently on holiday – and, as we later learn, entering into a secret engagement with Jane Fairfax. The action, like that of *Pride and Prejudice*, runs round the year, with Harriet Smith and Robert Martin being married before the end of the following September, Emma and Mr Knightley in October, and Jane Fairfax and Frank Churchill in November, once the three months' official 'deep' mourning for old Mrs Churchill had been completed.

Pheasant shooting starts on 1 October, and depending on the weather fox-hunting will also begin this month, or during November at the latest. There will still be blue skies and sunshine, though strong winds blowing through the woods bring down the red and yellow leaves and the acorns and beechmast off the trees, which fatten up the herds of roving pigs turned out to forage before they are slaughtered. Any hay carried so late in the year, and any cider made from old or leftover apples, will not be of good quality. The corn harvest is finished and the fields are being ploughed again to receive a new sowing of autumn wheat, while timber felling will start at the end of the month.

Lady Susan begins some time in the autumn, when the newly widowed adventuress tells her friend Mrs Johnson that she intends to inflict her company upon her Vernon in-laws in 'that insupportable spot, a Country Village, for I am really going to Churchill. – Forgive me my dear friend, it is my last resource. Were there another place in England open to me, I would prefer it' – and flirts with Reginald de Courcy, the brother of her hostess, who anxiously writes to their mother: 'You must not expect Reginald back again for some time. He desires me to tell you that the present open weather induces him to accept Mr Vernon's invitation to prolong his stay in Sussex that they may have some hunting together. He means to send for his Horses immediately, & it is impossible to say when you may see him in Kent.'

The Watsons definitely starts in October, and the unfinished text takes us on for about a month thereafter. 'The first winter assembly in the Town of D. [presumably Jane intended that this would be Dorking] in Surry was to be held on Tuesday Octr. ye 13th . . .' and the eldest Watson daughter, Elizabeth, cheerfully undertakes to drive her younger sister Emma in 'all her finery in the old chair to D. on the important morning', splashing along the dirty lane. 'The next turning will bring us to the Turnpike. You may see the Church Tower over the hedge, & the White Hart is close by it.' The gauche young Lord Osborne later tries to interest Emma Watson in attending a meet of his foxhounds: 'My Hounds will be hunting this Country next week – I believe they will throw off at Stanton Wood on Wednesday at 9 o'clock. – I mention this, in hopes of your being drawn out to see what's going on. – If the morning's tolerable, pray do us the honour of giving us your good wishes in person.'

In Devonshire, the Dashwood sisters have to stay at home for several days while Marianne nurses her sprained ankle, and Willoughby constantly visits them at Barton Cottage.

When Marianne was recovered, the schemes of amusement at home and abroad, which Sir John had been previously forming, were put in execution. The private balls at the Park then began; and parties on the water were made and accomplished as often as a showery October would allow. . . . A party was formed this evening for going on the following day to see a very fine place about twelve miles from Barton . . . the grounds were declared to be highly beautiful, and Sir John, who was particularly warm in their praise, might be allowed to be a tolerable judge, for he had formed parties to visit them, at least, twice every summer for the last ten years. They contained a noble piece of water; a sail on which was

'Meeting the Hounds returning home', *drawing by Diana Sperling, 1817.*

to form a great part of the morning's amusement; cold provisions were to be taken, open carriages only to be employed, and every thing conducted in the usual style of a complete party of pleasure. To some few of the company, it appeared rather a bold undertaking, considering the time of year, and that it had rained every day for the last fortnight . . . Their intended excursion to Whitwell turned out very differently from what Elinor had expected. She was prepared to be wet through, fatigued, and frightened; but the event was still more unfortunate, for they did not go at all.

This was because Colonel Brandon, whose presence is necessary to introduce them to the Whitwell household, has to leave suddenly for London. Instead of driving to Whitwell, therefore, Willoughby takes Marianne up in his curricle and rushes her off to see Allenham Court, the house he will inherit from his elderly cousin Mrs Smith; and Marianne, thinking she will soon be married to him, later tells Elinor with delight:

'There is one remarkably pretty sitting room up stairs; of a nice comfortable size for constant use, and with modern furniture it would be delightful. It is a corner room, and has windows on two sides. On one side you look across the bowling-green, behind the house, to a beautiful hanging wood, and on the other you have a view of the church and village, and, beyond them, of those fine bold hills that we have so often admired. I did not see it to advantage, for nothing could be more forlorn than the furniture – but if it were newly fitted up – a couple of hundred pounds, Willoughby says, would make it one of the pleasantest summer rooms in England.'

At Mansfield Park, Sir Thomas Bertram horrifies his children by returning from the West Indies unexpectedly early, in October instead of November as he had previously intended; and Tom gabbles frantically about pheasant shooting in order to delay for as long as possible the subject of their amateur dramatics and the production of *Lovers Vows*, since he knows his father will disapprove:

A Party Angling, *oil on canvas, by George Morland, 1789.*

We have had such incessant rains almost since October began, that we have been nearly confined to the house for days together; I have hardly taken out a gun since the 3d. Tolerable sport the first three days, but there has been no attempting any thing since. The first day I went over Mansfield Wood, and Edmund took the copses beyond Easton, and we brought home six brace between us, and might each have killed six times as many; but we respect your pheasants, sir, I assure you, as much as you could desire. I do not think you will find your woods by any means worse stocked than they were. *I* never saw Mansfield Wood so full of pheasants in my life as this year. I hope you will take a day's sport there yourself, sir, soon.

The Anglers' Repast, *oil on canvas, by George Morland, 1789.*

In Jane's own life, she and her parents stayed at Godmersham in Kent
for about two months in the late summer of 1798, returning to Steventon at
the end of October. As she told Cassandra: 'We had one heavy shower on
leaving Sittingbourne, but afterwards the clouds cleared away, and we had
a very bright <u>chrystal</u> afternoon.' However, when they arrived home, they
found that 'there has been a great deal of rain here for this last fortnight,
much more than in Kent . . . Steventon lane has its full share of it, & I do
not know when I shall be able to get to Deane. . . . there are some Grapes
left, but I believe not many; – they must be gathered as soon as possible, or
this Rain will entirely rot them.' By contrast, in 1800 late October provided
'delightful weather', and Jane and her parents took advantage of it by walking out to see James and Mary Lloyd at Deane, the Bramstons at Oakley
Hall, and to Deane again to call on the Harwoods. 'The weather does not
know how to be otherwise than fine.' Less satisfactory news for Cassandra

to hear was that Mr Austen's farming activities had left him only £300 clear profit for the past year.

Although October can be very fine and even warm, November is usually dank and grey, with mists filling the valleys and sometimes not lifting all day. However, it was a busy month for farmers, with the checking of flocks and herds and the slaughtering of surplus cattle unlikely to survive the coming winter. The pigs kept by the individual cottagers were always killed around Martinmas, 15 November; some of the fresh meat was eaten at once, and flitches of bacon and hams were salted down and stored on racks in the kitchen or smoked in the open chimney for use during the winter, with the remnants of the animal turned into brawn and sausages and other meat products. In her letter of 17–18 November 1798 Jane tells Cassandra that: 'We are to kill a pig soon.' Privies had to be cleared out and the contents used to manure the fields, since all next year's wheat should have been sown by now. The task of threshing the August harvest started this month, and continued over the winter. It was a long and dusty job, and hated by all. The sheaves were pitchforked down on to the hard-surfaced threshing-floor in the centre of the barn, and then a group of labourers would rhythmically belabour the heap with flails – stout wooden cudgels hinged together with leather loops – which knocked the grain out of the dry chaff of the ears. The wide doors of the barn were kept open, and the wind blowing through winnowed the threshed heap by wafting the chaff away, so that the valuable grain could be shovelled up and taken to be stored in the granary; the monotonous thumping of the flails could be heard all over the farmstead and surrounding village. By 1813 the Digweed family at Steventon Manor Farm had spent the huge sum of £250 upon constructing a threshing mill for wheat – 'the horse-walk of which is 30 feet, and the horizontal wheel 14 feet in diameter' – as an agricultural journalist reported admiringly. It was powered by four horses and needed two men and four boys to operate it, but the Digweeds calculated that it was still cheaper and produced better quality grain than hand-threshing did, and so would presently pay for itself.

In late November 1798 autumn was lingering in Hampshire, and Jane wrote to Cassandra in Kent: 'What fine weather this is! Not very becoming perhaps early in the morning, but very pleasant out of doors at noon, and

Slaughterman, *from W.H. Pyne's* British Costumes, *1805.*

very wholesome – at least everybody fancies so, and imagination is every-thing. To Edward, however, I really think dry weather of importance. I have not taken to fires yet.' In the villages the only fuel used was wood since coal was expensive and in short supply, and even then it was desirable to delay starting domestic fires for as long as possible in the autumn in case stocks of firewood ran out before winter was over. In 1800, only a few days after Jane had told Cassandra of the very fine weather which Steventon had been enjoy-ing at the end of October, everything changed in early November:

We have had a dreadful storm of wind in the fore-part of this day, which has done a great deal of mischief among our trees. – I was sitting alone in the dining room, when an odd kind of crash startled me – in a moment afterwards it was repeated; I then went to the window, which I reached just in time to see the last of our two highly valued Elms descend into the Sweep!!!!! The other, which had fallen I suppose in the first crash, & which was the nearest to the pond, taking a more easterly direction sunk amongst our screen of Chestnuts & firs, knocking down one spruce fir, beating off the head of another, & stripping the two corner chestnuts of several branches, in its fall.

Barn at Park House Farm, Donyatt, with threshing in progress, *drawing by W.W. Wheatley, 1850.*

– This is not all – . One large Elm out of two on the left hand side, as you enter what I call the Elm walk, was likewise blown down, the Maypole bearing the weathercock was broke in two, & what I regret more than all the rest, is that all the three Elms which grew in Hall's meadow & gave such ornament to it, are gone. – Two were blown down, & the other so much injured that it cannot stand.

A few days after this, Jane went to stay with her friend Martha Lloyd at Ibthorpe, a little village close to the county boundary with Berkshire, and wrote from there:

> . . . – it is too dirty even for such desperate Walkers as Martha & I to get out of doors, & we are therefore confined to each other's society from morning till night, with very little variety of Books or Gowns. Three of the Miss Debaries called here the morning after my arrival, but I have not yet been able to return their civility; – You know it is not an uncommon circumstance in this parish to have the road from Ibthrop to the Parsonage much dirtier & more impracticable for walking than the road from the Parsonage to Ibthrop.

November is a significant month for several of Jane Austen's heroines. Mr Bingley holds his promised ball at Netherfield Park, and remembers the date precisely, as he later says to Elizabeth: '"It is above eight months. We have not met since the 26th of November, when we were all dancing together at Netherfield." Elizabeth was pleased to find his memory so exact; and he afterwards took occasion to ask her, when unattended to by any of the rest, whether *all* her sisters were at Longbourn' – which she hopes means he is thinking of Jane in particular.

At Mansfield Park, Fanny had been sent into the village on some errand by her aunt Norris, and was overtaken by a heavy shower close to the Parsonage, from one of the windows of which she could be seen endeavouring to find shelter under the branches and lingering leaves of an oak just beyond their premises. Mary Crawford in her turn had been reduced by the gloom, dirt and loneliness of a November day to a very desponding state of mind, sighing over the ruin of all her plan of exercise for that morning; hence 'the sound of a little bustle at the front door, and the sight of Miss Price dripping with wet in the vestibule, was delightful. The value of an event on a wet day in the country, was most forcibly brought before her.' This leads to a 'sort of intimacy which took place between them', with Fanny calling at the Parsonage every two or three days, although she does not really enjoy these meetings as she and Mary have no ideas in common.

She went however, and they sauntered about together many an half hour in Mrs Grant's shrubbery, the weather being unusually mild for the time of year, and venturing sometimes even to sit down on one of the benches now comparatively unsheltered, remaining there perhaps till in the midst of some tender ejaculation of Fanny's on the sweets of so protracted an autumn, they were forced by the sudden swell of a cold gust shaking down the last few yellow leaves about them, to jump up and walk for warmth.

Anne Elliot is the heroine for whom November is the most important month in her story. While she is staying at Uppercross Cottage with her sister Mary and family, Charles Musgrove and Captain Wentworth go out shooting together one very fine day, but return early because an untrained young dog had spoilt their sport. Anne and Mary, with the two young Musgrove girls, Louisa and Henrietta, were just setting off on a walk, and so are joined by the gentlemen, and the sextet ramble along the narrow paths across the fields. Anne tries to keep close to Charles and Mary while Captain Wentworth walks with Louisa and Henrietta, and occupies her mind with 'the view of the last smiles of the year upon the tawny leaves and withered hedges, and from repeating to herself some few of the thousand poetical descriptions extant of autumn, that season of peculiar and inexhaustible influence on the mind of taste and ten-derness, that season which has drawn from every poet, worthy of being read, some attempt at description, or some lines of feeling'; but cannot help over-hearing Wentworth and Louisa talking together. Henrietta takes the group on to the path leading to Winthrop, and 'after another half mile of gradual ascent through large enclosures, where the ploughs at work, and the fresh-made path spoke the farmer, counteracting the sweets of poetical despondence, and mean-ing to have spring again, they gained the summit of the most considerable hill, which parted Uppercross and Winthrop, and soon commanded a full view of the latter . . .' Anne sits down 'on a dry sunny bank under the hedgerow' on the other side of which, in the rough channel down the centre, Wentworth and Louisa are walking in search of hazel-nuts; and overhears him telling her to be firm-minded – 'let those who would be happy be firm'.

This advice has unfortunate repercussions, for when the same party visits Lyme a few days later, Louisa insists upon showing her firmness and strength of character by jumping down the steep steps on the Cobb, which results in her near-fatal accident. However, the visit also results in Wentworth's attention being drawn again to Anne: 'She was looking remarkably well; her very regular, very pretty features, having the bloom and freshness of youth restored by the fine wind which had been blowing on her complexion, and by the animation of eye which it had also produced' – and his old love for her starts to revive, especially when he realizes that her cousin Mr William Elliot, whom they meet at Lyme, admires her. But once back at Uppercross, the weather has changed, and Anne sits sad and alone waiting for Lady Russell's carriage to arrive, 'on a dark November day, a small thick rain almost blotting out the very few objects ever to be discerned from the windows . . .'

Autumn Sowing of Grain, *watercolour and graphite, by J.M.W. Turner, c.1794.*

Another traditional custom which provided encouragement as winter weather really started, was the arrival of the popularly named Stir Up Sunday at the end of November – the fifth Sunday before Christmas, and the last before Advent – so called because the Collect for the Day in the Book of Common Prayer begins: 'Stir up we beseech thee, O Lord, the wills of thy faithful people.' This reminded housewives to start making their Christmas and Twelfth Night cakes, and also cheered up boys at boarding school with the thought that Christmas holidays were approaching. December is likely to bring in the worst of the winter weather in the run up to Christmas, which would make these weeks exceptionally dull for ladies in particular if they were confined indoors by rain and snow, with little to do and little hope of visitors to bring variety to the domestic scene. James Austen wrote in his verses of the '. . . moonless nights / And hollow roads filled up with snow . . .' which prevented neighbours joining each other for dinner parties. James hated cold weather and admitted he dreaded having to ride out on December Sundays to take his church services and could hardly keep warm even in bed; and Mrs Austen did not like the cold either. Edward Knight, on the contrary, enjoyed it – 'he is all alive & chearful', as Jane said; and in 1798, when Cassandra was staying at Godmersham, Jane wrote: 'I find great comfort in my stuff gown . . .' adding that: 'I enjoyed the hard black Frosts of last week very much, & one day while they lasted walked to Deane by myself.' A few days later, however, she wrote: 'I was to have dined at Deane to day, but the weather is so cold that I am not sorry to be kept at home by the appearance of Snow . . .' but the next morning was able to reassure her sister: 'The Snow came to nothing yesterday, so I did go to Deane, & returned home at 9 o'clock at night in the little carriage – & without being very cold.'

Unless and until frost set in really hard or snow lay too long on the ground, gentlemen could still go out foxhunting in December, as Edmund and Henry Crawford do; but when Henry's horse loses a shoe at some distance from Mansfield he is obliged to give up and make the best of his way back. As he tells the family group playing cards at the Park that evening, in his ramblings he passed an old farm house with yew trees around it, and then found himself 'upon turning the corner of a steepish downy field, in the midst of a retired little village between gently rising hills; a small stream before me to be forded, a church standing on a sort of knoll to my right – which church was strikingly large and handsome for the place, and not a gentleman or half a gentleman's house to be seen excepting one – to be presumed the Parsonage, within a stone's throw of the said knoll and church . . . I told a man mending a hedge that it was Thornton Lacey, and he agreed to it.' Thornton Lacey is the parish of which Edmund will become rector once he has been ordained, and in the ensuing conversation he makes it clear that he intends to leave Mansfield Park and live full-time in this retired little village in the depth of

A Village Snow Scene, *watercolour and gouache by Robert Hills. 1819.*

the country. This is unwelcome news to Mary Crawford, who 'startled from the agreeable fancies she had been previously indulging on the strength of her brother's description, [is] no longer able, in the picture she had been forming of a future Thornton, to shut out the church, sink the clergyman, and see only the respectable, elegant, modernized, and occasional residence of a man of independent fortune . . .'

In *Sense and Sensibility* Jane Austen refers to Christmas, tongue in cheek, as 'that festival which requires a more than ordinary share of private balls and large dinners to proclaim its importance'. The idea of bringing a live fir-tree into the house, to decorate it and make it the central point in the room for the exchanging of presents, had not yet arisen, and would not become a necessary part of Christmas festivities until the middle of the nineteenth century, when Prince Albert introduced the English royal family to this custom from his childhood in Germany. The Yule Log would certainly be brought in, to provide a huge blaze in the living-room, and also any form of evergreens – holly, ivy, mistletoe, rosemary, bay and laurel – were pinned up to decorate rooms. Preparations for Christmas would start early in December, as Jane describes in *Persuasion*, when Anne Elliot and Lady Russell visit the Musgrove family:

> The Musgroves came back to receive their happy boys and girls from school, bringing with them Mrs Harville's little children, to improve the noise of Uppercross, and lessen that of Lyme. . . . Lady Russell and Anne paid their compliments to them once, when Anne could not but feel that Uppercross was already quite alive again. Though neither Henrietta, nor Louisa, nor Charles Hayter, nor Captain Wentworth were there, the room presented as strong a contrast as could be wished, to the last state she had seen it in. Immediately surrounding Mrs Musgrove were the little Harvilles, whom she was sedulously guarding from the tyranny of the two children from the Cottage, expressly arrived to amuse them. On one side was a table, occupied by some chattering girls, cutting up silk and gold paper; and on the other were tressels and trays,

bending under the weight of brawn and cold pies, where riotous boys were holding high revel; the whole completed by a
roaring Christmas fire, which seemed determined to be heard,
in spite of all the noise of the others. Charles and Mary also
came in, of course, during their visit; and Mr Musgrove made
a point of paying his respects to Lady Russell, and sat down
close to her for ten minutes, talking with a very raised voice,
but, from the clamour of the children on his knees, generally in
vain. It was a fine family-piece. . . . 'I hope I shall remember, in
future,' said Lady Russell, as soon as they were reseated in the
carriage, 'not to call at Uppercross in the Christmas holidays.'

The 'silk and gold paper' is presumably being used to make artificial decorations in addition to the natural greenery, and the 'tressels and trays bending
under the weight of brawn and cold pies' suggests that at least some of the
time food will be served as a cold buffet rather than as a sit-down dinner.
The idea of the Christmas Pudding as we now know it, a solid steamed con-
coction full of dried fruits and eaten only at Christmas and New Year, also
dates to the middle of the nineteenth century, and was largely popularised by
Charles Dickens in his novels. In the mid-eighteenth century Hannah Glasse
in her *The Art of Cookery made Plain and Easy* gave a recipe for something
which we would probably recognize if we saw it on our dessert plates – 'A
Boiled Plumb-Pudding: Take a Pound of Suet cut in little Pieces, not too fine,
a Pound of Currants, and a Pound of Raisins stoned, eight Eggs, half the
Whites, the Crumb of a Penny-loaf grated fine, half a Nutmeg grated, and a
Tea Spoonful of beaten Ginger, a little Salt, a Pound of Flour, a Pint of Milk;
beat the Eggs first, then half the Milk, beat them together, and by degrees stir
in the Flour and Bread together, then the Suet, Spice and Fruit, and as much
Milk as will mix it all well together and very thick; boil it five Hours' – but she
does not relate this in any way to Christmas. Instead, she has another recipe,
called specifically 'Plum-Porridge for Christmas', similar to the above but
with more breadcrumbs and no flour and including a lot of sugar as well as
pints of sherry and claret, and which seems to result in, as the title suggests, a
very thick sweet alcoholic porridge-type confection.

The closest we get to Christmas itself is in *Emma*, when Mr John Knightley
and his family come from London to stay at Hartfield for the holidays.
Harriet has fallen ill with a bad sore throat, and on 24 December, the day of
Mr Weston's dinner party, Emma has been to visit her that morning at Mrs
Goddard's house; on her way home she is 'overtaken by Mr John Knightley
returning from the daily visit to Donwell, with his two eldest boys, whose
healthy, glowing faces shewed all the benefit of a country run, and seemed to
ensure a quick dispatch of the roast mutton and rice pudding they were has-
tening home for'. It is on the return from Mr Weston's party that the slightly
drunken Mr Elton proposes to Emma, and a scene embarrassing and annoy-
ing to both of them ensues. The next morning Emma is relieved to find that
she will not immediately have to meet Mr Elton again; the 'weather was most
favourable for her; though Christmas-day, she could not go to church. . . .
The ground covered with snow, and the atmosphere in that unsettled state
between frost and thaw, which is of all others the most unfriendly for exercise, every morning beginning to rain or snow, and every evening setting in
to freeze, she was for many days a most honourable prisoner.'

In December all the farmer's operations would now be concentrated
around the farmstead: attending and feeding sheep in their sheltered pastures, young cattle and colts in their sheds, and all the other livestock – the
cows, pigs and poultry. There would be abundant employment in cutting hay
from last summer's stacks and chopping straw; hacking up, bringing home
and slicing turnips for their feed, and seeing that they were well cleaned
and bedded; fattening some for market, choosing some for breeding, and
killing others for meat. Threshing of corn continued, with the grain being
sacked and carried to market; implements such as flails and sieves, nets and
traps, needed to be made or repaired. If there were spells of clear frosty
weather manure could be carried out to the fields; and there was always the
maintenance work of hedging and ditching around the property. At night
foxes could be heard barking in the woodland, stealthy poachers might be
on their rounds checking their pheasant-traps, and shepherds would be out
in their huts in the fields watching for midnight lambings. In the farmhouse
itself the family might call in a local fiddler or two, with a boy to bang a
jangling tambourine, push aside the furniture and dance up and down the

Farmer Giles's Establishment, Christmas Day 1800, *coloured engraving, published London 1830.*

big brick-floored kitchen, with their music and songs floating out of the casement windows and up the chimneys to let any stray passers-by know that the New Year was being welcomed in style; they might perhaps finish off with a lantern-lit trip to the apple orchard to encourage the spirits of the trees with a song:

> Stand fast root, bear well top,
> Pray God send us a good howling crop;
> Every twig, apples big;
> Every bough, apples enow;
> Hats full, caps full
> Full quarter sacks full!

. . . before work began again after Twelfth Night in January.

125

CHAPTER 4
THE HARDSHIPS AND PLEASURES OF RURAL LIFE

Illnesses, accidents, calamities and deaths

WHEN THE JOHN KNIGHTLEY FAMILY COME to spend Christmas at Highbury with Mr Woodhouse and Emma, and discuss together Mr Weston's recent marriage to Miss Taylor, Isabella Knightley cries out in praise of him: '. . . ever since his particular kindness last September twelvemonth in writing that note, at twelve o'clock at night, on purpose to assure me that there was no scarlet fever at Cobham, I have been convinced there could not be a more feeling heart nor a better man in existence. – If any body can deserve him, it must be Miss Taylor.' To us nowadays this may sound as if Isabella is being as hypochondriacal as her father, since Cobham is several miles away from Leatherhead – the basis for Jane's creation of Highbury – but with so many vaccines available today we have forgotten just how easy it was, two centuries ago, for epidemics to arise and spread, and how fatal they could be, especially for children. Scarlet fever could kill or perhaps leave a survivor profoundly deaf for life, and if the John Knightleys had stopped to change horses and eat a meal at a Cobham inn, infection from some local outbreak would be a definite risk. Jenner's discovery in the late eighteenth century that vaccination with cowpox prevented infection with smallpox meant that that disfiguring and frequently fatal illness was gradually abating, but James Austen's second wife, Mary Lloyd, had fallen victim to a smallpox epidemic in the 1770s when she was a toddler and her face remained scarred for the rest of her life, while her elder brother, aged six, had died of it. Tuberculosis ('consumption', or 'a decline') was rife and incurable – it had killed Colonel Brandon's first love, the unhappy Eliza Williams; Tom Bertram's neglected fall and subsequent fever makes his family 'apprehensive for his lungs'; Jane Fairfax's young mother had sunk 'under consumption and grief' soon after her soldier husband's death abroad on active service, and Mrs and Miss Bates are terrified that Jane too may be harbouring the seeds of the disease. Diphtheria ('putrid sore throat') was another potential killer, hence Mr Elton's officious and would-be-lover-like concern when Emma tells him that she has been to visit Harriet who is in bed with a bad sore throat: 'A sore throat! – I hope not infectious. I hope not of a putrid infectious sort. . . . Indeed you should take care of yourself as well as of your friend. Let me entreat you to run no risks.' Typhoid ('putrid fever') and cholera could all be fatal; these last three were water-borne infections – though this was as yet unrealized – caused by cesspits or graveyards soaking through into nearby wells; and when the Austens were looking for a house to rent in Bath in the summer of 1801, they rejected Green Park Buildings because of '. . . the observation of the damps still remaining in the offices of an house which has been only vacated a week, with reports of discontented families & putrid fevers . . .' The two terraces, Green Park Buildings East and West, were low-lying and close to the River Avon, and so received all the drainage from the city on the hills behind them.

The Revd Gilbert White of Selborne, writing in 1778, not long after Jane's birth at Steventon, was pleased to think how much healthier the average farm-workers in Hampshire were now, compared with the earlier part of the eighteenth century. This he rightly put down to better diet and an increase in cleanliness: meat and fish were more often eaten fresh instead of salted, and the consumption of vegetables was vastly increased; there was

> . . . plenty of good wheaten bread . . . instead of that miserable sort which used in old days to be made of barley or beans. . . . Every decent labourer also has his garden, which is half his support, as well as his delight; and common farmers provide plenty of beans, peas, and greens for their hinds to eat with

their bacon. . . . The use of linen changes, shirts or shifts, in the room of sordid and filthy woollen, long worn next the skin, is a matter of neatness comparatively modern; but must prove a great means of preventing cutaneous ails.

Steventon and Deane certainly seem to have been generally healthy villages, since during the eighteenth century the parish registers show no signs of any unusual number of burials occurring at one time, which would indicate a local epidemic. But still the cleanliness of Deane left something to be desired, since in June 1799, when Jane was staying in Bath, she wrote to Cassandra: 'I am heartily glad that You have escaped any share in the Impurities of Deane . . . What have you going on in Hampshire besides the Itch from which you want to keep us?' 'The Itch', as it was popularly called, was scabies: a contagious skin infection caused by the tiny, barely visible parasitic mite *Sarcoptes scabiei*, which burrows between folds of the host's skin and sets up an intense allergic itching, and the harbouring of such mites is the result of bodies remaining unwashed in dirty clothing. If Mrs Austen had a copy of *The Compleat Housewife* ready to hand, she might have taken one of the recipes given by Eliza Smith and mixed up the following ointment for use by the sufferers from scabies: 'Take elecampane-roots, or dock-roots dried, and beaten to powder, and a little beaten ginger, both searced [sifted] very fine; mix it up with fresh butter, and anoint with it in the joints.' Another

Harvest-bug *(much enlarged), from* The Naturalist's Miscellany *by George Shaw, 1789–1813.*

similar skin affliction was seasonal, occurring in the hot months of summer, when the microscopic bright scarlet larvae of the mite *Trombicula autumnalis* – nicknamed by the country people 'harvest bugs' – like the scabies mite could get under the skin where the allergic reaction raised tumours which itched intolerably, but it was realized that this could to some extent be prevented by keeping the hands covered and wearing gloves when harvesting.

Eliza Smith's recipes cast a gloomy light upon the illnesses that were rife in the eighteenth century, and whether her 'cures' did any good seems very doubtful. By far the largest number are for chest complaints – coughs, colds, consumption, asthma, pleurisy, haemorrhages – followed by those in the stomach and bowels: colic, constipation, diarrhoea, piles, worms in children, jaundice, dropsy, gravel and stones in the kidneys; then agues [regularly recurring malarial fevers] and all other unexplained fevers, and the internal pains of rheumatism, toothache and gout – any pain anywhere in the body could be diagnosed as 'flying gout' – and the external ailments of burns and scalds, cancers and ulcers, bruises, cuts, sores and sprains, bites from mad dogs, rashes, pimples, boils and the reddened pits and puckering scars caused by smallpox. At that period freckles were also viewed as a skin blemish, to be bleached away if at all possible – Lydia Bennet refers to Wickham's latest flirt, Mary King, as being 'such a nasty little freckled thing' – and Elizabeth Elliot tells Anne that she is quite sure their father could never fall in love with the widowed Mrs Clay: 'Freckles do not disgust me so very much as they do him:

The Sick-Bed, wood engraving, by Thomas Bewick.

I have known a face not materially disfigured by a few, but he abominates them. You must have heard him notice Mrs Clay's freckles.' What Elizabeth does not know, however, is that Sir Walter has been recommending Mrs Clay to use the harsh caustic Gowland's Lotion as a face-wash, and believes that 'it has carried away her freckles' – though 'it did not appear to Anne that the freckles were at all lessened'.

Mrs Norris, officious as ever, enjoys every opportunity to inflict treatments upon the Mansfield Park servants – the poor old coachman Wilcox is hardly able to sit on the box on account of the rheumatism for which she has been doctoring him for months – and during the Bertram family's fateful visit to Sotherton Court she had convinced the gardener there that his grandson's illness was an ague and promised him a charm for it. It may sound somewhat odd that the widow of an Anglican cleric should talk of 'charms', but perhaps this was no more than something such as preparing a bag containing grated horseradish to be worn around the neck of the sufferer to ward off the next attack of fever. If there were no lady of the manor or parson's wife interested in reading medical books and from them offering help and advice to their tenants and parishioners, then the cottagers themselves might turn to a 'wise woman' or 'cunning man' for cures: at Bramley, not far from Steventon, Olive Sweetzer was the unofficial midwife of the parish, noted for her skill in nursing women in childbirth; and when anyone had the misfortune to run a thorn into hand or finger they went to her to have it 'whispered away'. Her custom was to wet her longest finger on her tongue, rub the place over with it, and whisper, but what she whispered the patient must not know, or the charm would have no effect. Mrs Sam Tubb of Sherfield Farm was noted for her ointment, curing all kinds of sores, and old Mrs Pink was famous for her distilled essences of peppermint and other herbs, while Thomas Allwright could cure St Vitus' Dance. This was the popular name for what was later medically classified as Sydenham's chorea, a nervous affliction which may follow on from infection with rheumatic fever; but sufferers recover spontaneously in time, hence this could account for Thomas Allwright's 'cures'.

A farming community is always liable to suffer from accidents caused by animals, and country newspapers filled up their columns by repeating gruesome tales of calamities that had happened in other parts of the United

Kingdom. In 1804 the *Ipswich Journal* reprinted the account of the death of Mr Sam Tully of Huntington, near Hereford, 'an eminent farmer and breeder of cattle – . . . The death of this truly worthy man was occasioned by a violent attack made upon him the preceding Tuesday by a favourite bull belonging to his own stock, which turned upon him and forced him to the ground with such violence with his head, as to break several of his ribs, and occasioned so much other injury, that he survived the accident only two days.' The *Maidstone Journal* reported in October 1787 a story from Yorkshire: 'A woman having left her child (about half a year old) in the cradle, with a little boy to rock it till she came back; when, soon after she was gone, he left it alone and a pig belonging to the family went in, tore the child out of the cradle and ravenously devoured it.' An almost identical tale was reported, again in 1804, by the *Ipswich Journal*: 'On Tuesday sennight, a shocking circumstance occurred at Cottingham, near Hull. A woman having left a child a few months old, in the cradle, while she went out upon some occasion, and negligently omitted to shut the door, on her return found the child lying on the floor, and both its hands nearly eaten off by a sow which had got into the house.' When Elizabeth Bennet cries out at the noise and confusion caused in Mr Collins's parsonage because Miss de Bourgh and her companion have stopped their low phaeton at the front gate, likening it mockingly to the noise caused when pigs get into the garden, she is only half-joking – pigs are large and dangerous animals when fully grown, and will not only rootle up a garden and its vegetables but also eat anything else they come across as they do so, young babies included.

Winter weather would bring its own particular kinds of calamity: at Salisbury in January 1784 a lone traveller was found frozen to death on the downs about five miles outside the city,

Pigs getting into a garden, *wood engraving, by Thomas Bewick.*

while the boy who brought the mail from Devizes to Heytesbury was nearly dead when he arrived there – 'he was lifted from the horse almost motionless, and it was some hours before he totally recovered'. The Morland family at Fullerton, nine miles from Salisbury, would have experienced this sort of weather and Mr Morland would have had to bury any such unknown person when the body was eventually discovered. The following month the *London Chronicle* reported an accident in Surrey which could have occurred to Robert Martin or his father at Donwell's Abbey Mill Farm: 'On Saturday last a miller went on the mill wheel, at Byfleet, near Guildford, to clear the cogs of the ice, which with some pains he accomplished. The millers in the inside, finding the machinery free, set the mill a-going, without considering the situation of the poor man, who, at that time, stood on the shafts; but being unable to extricate himself, he was broke to pieces by the going round of the mill wheel.'

Over the years Steventon seems to have had a number of accidents caused by horses, and these are mentioned by Jane in her letters and also appear in the burial register when the result was unhappily fatal. Thomas Gilbert, Hugh Digweed's servant, was kicked to death by a horse in 1789; and in December 1798 Jane wrote: 'James Digweed has had a very ugly cut – how could it happen? – It happened by a young horse which he had lately purchased & which he was trying to back into its stable; the Animal kicked him down with his forefeet, & kicked a great hole in his head; he scrambled away as soon as he could, but was stunned for a time, & suffered a good deal of pain afterwards. – Yesterday he got up the Horse again, & for fear of something worse, was forced to throw himself off.' Two years later: 'Mr Heathcote met with a genteel little accident the other day in hunting; he got off to lead his horse over a hedge or a house or a something, & his horse in his haste trod upon his leg, or rather ancle I believe, & it is not certain whether the small bone is not broke.' In March 1801 one of Jane's last actions before leaving Steventon for good, was to enter in the burial register the record of that of Nathaniel Martell junior, a boy who was 'killed by a Waggon going over him'. Large waggons, with several horses harnessed to them, could easily become dangerously out of control – like a modern juggernaut on a motorway if the brakes failed – and the *Ipswich Journal*

A Mill in Bonsall Dale, *Derbyshire, by John Glover (1767–1849)*.

reported that one young farm worker had been convicted 'for riding on
the shafts of his master's waggon with six horses; he was driving very rapidly, without any person by the side of the horses to guide them.' Another
accident occurred in East Anglia in 1804: 'As the son of Mr Wiseman was
riding the shaft-horse in an empty harvest waggon, the animal fell down,
which frightening the other two horses, they ran away with the waggon,
dragging the young man and the horse till the rein he held broke, when the
wheel went over his body and he received very severe injuries, but hopes

'Harry tumbling off his Colt: June 1816', *drawing by Diana Sperling.*

are entertained of his recovery.' Perhaps something similar had happened to young Nathaniel Martell.

After Mr Austen had retired, James moved into the rectory as his father's curate, and further accidental deaths are noted in the register in later years: John Staples, aged fifteen, probably a son or grandson of the Dame Staples of the 'pleasant face and tidy cottage' who had been one of the rectory servants, was killed by falling from a tree; Michael Taylor, in his twenties, killed by a fall from a horse; and Frances Stevens, a young woman in her twenties, 'found dead'. On one windy March night in 1808 a fire broke out close to the rectory, burning down a cottage and adjacent barn containing £80-worth of corn belonging to the Digweeds; and poor old Betty Lovell, who lived in the cottage and had so much appreciated visits from Jane and Cassandra, was badly injured and died three days later. This barn was probably that in which the young Austens had performed their Christmas theatricals in past years, and the flattened mound where it had stood was still visible at the end of the nineteenth century. At Ashe, one of the Lefroy sons, Anthony, died at the age of sixteen as a result of a riding accident two years previously; and worst of all, in 1804 Jane's great friend Madam Lefroy was herself killed in a riding accident on 16 December, Jane's birthday. Years later James's daughter Caroline remembered:

> She was riding a very quiet horse, attended by a servant, as usual. My father saw her in Overton, and she observed the animal she rode was so stupid and lazy, she could scarcely make him canter. My father rode homeward, she staying to do some errands in Overton; next morning the news of her death reached Steventon. After getting to the top of Overton Hill, the horse seemed to be running away – it was not known whether anything had fright-ened him – the servant, unwisely, rode up to catch the bridle rein – missed his hold and the animal darted off faster. He could not give any clear account, but it was supposed that Mrs Lefroy in her terror, threw herself off, and fell heavily on the hard ground. She never spoke afterwards, and she died in a few hours.

It is not therefore surprising that Mrs Austen, ten years later, was worrying about the potential danger of her grand-daughter Anna riding a 'high-spirited mare'.

Mr Austen and his family seem to have enjoyed excellent health when living in Steventon and their strong constitutions – with the sad exception of Jane herself – took them on into old ages ripe even by modern standards and still more so when compared with contemporary lifespans. Mr Austen retired to Bath in 1801 at the age of seventy, and died there four years later, possibly from a stroke; and although Mrs Austen often complained of various ailments in her later life, this may not have been entirely due to hypochon-dria: she had had eight live births and possibly one miscarriage within the first fourteen years of her marriage, all of course without anaesthesia or any pre- or post-natal care; and by the age of forty-nine in 1788 had 'lost several fore-teeth which makes her look old', as her niece Phylly Walter commented. Family memories confirm that she suffered much from rheumatism in her last years, but nevertheless lived on to be eighty-seven. Looking to the future: of Jane's siblings, James was the unluckiest, breaking his arm and twice breaking a leg before dying aged fifty-four of what seems to have been bowel or stomach cancer. Her second brother, George junior, although having some mental impairment, was evidently quite fit physically, since under the careful fostering of the respectable Cullum/Culham cottager family at Monk Sherborne he lived to be seventy-two and died there of 'dropsy' – that is, heart failure. Edward Knight died peacefully in his sleep one evening at Godmersham, aged eighty-five; Henry was seventy-nine when he died of gastritis at Tunbridge Wells; Cassandra was seventy-two when she died of a stroke; Rear-Admiral Charles was still on active service aboard the steam-sloop HMS *Pluto* on the Irrawaddy River in Burma, when he died of cholera aged seventy-three. Admiral of the Fleet Francis was the last survivor of the family; in later life he became crippled with rheumatism like his mother, but reached the great age of ninety-one. Jane, as we know, was only forty-one when she died in 1817, possibly of Addison's disease, which is of tubercular origin – and leaving behind her those tantalizing first twelve chapters of her seventh novel, now known to us as *Sanditon*.

It may perhaps have been this very healthy background to Jane's life that resulted in the almost complete absence of death and disease in her novels – none of the tear-jerking deathbed scenes so beloved of later nineteenth-century authors. Such deaths as are mentioned have happened off-stage before the action begins: General Tilney's wife, Emma Woodhouse's mother, Anne Elliot's mother, Fanny Price's sister little Mary – and none of these has any great influence upon the plot. The only two of any significance are those of Mr Henry Dashwood, which means that his wife and daughters have to leave their home at Norland in Sussex and move to Devon; and of Mrs Churchill of Enscombe in Yorkshire, which means that Frank Churchill is at last free to marry the penniless Jane Fairfax. It is not that Jane Austen was unaware of the precariousness of human life – over the years her letters record the illnesses and deaths of numerous acquaintances, friends and family connections – but she preferred to think of stories in sunshine rather than in shadow.

Crime and punishment:
highwaymen, poachers, gipsies, thieves

As well as dangers from animals and from the weather, rural communities were also at risk from human activities, and against these there was almost as little protection as against the former, since no police forces as such existed. The Justices of the Peace for the county would appoint some respectable villager to be the local unpaid constable for his parish, and it was up to him to catch criminals and take them before magistrates for incarceration in county gaols until such time as they were brought to trial; but the successful apprehension of criminals was in fact largely dependent on informers who were enticed by the prospect of monetary reward. Landowners and farmers might join together in setting up some sort of anti-crime group, such as the Overton Association for the Prevention of Thefts and Felonies and for Prosecuting Offenders, which would have been well-known to the Austens – but all the Association could do was offer rewards, with the cost of these and legal fees being spread amongst their subscribers.

Highwaymen were a well-known class of robbers, who lurked in woodland near main roads, especially those leading to London or other wealthy provincial cities such as Bath, so that they could intercept solitary coaches and then gallop off into hiding before anyone else came on the scene. In the London area their favourite haunts were Finchley Common on the north side, Blackheath on the south-east, Hounslow Heath and Maidenhead Thicket on the west. Further out to the south-west Bagshot Heath in Surrey was also dangerous, since the little town of Bagshot was an important staging post on one of the main coach-roads out of London, and at one time had no less than fourteen inns to cater for travellers. In the summer of 1770 Mr Austen's sister Mrs Philadelphia Hancock and her little daughter visited Steventon rectory; Philadelphia was of an impetuous and thoughtless nature, and when going back to her home in London put herself considerably at risk, as Mrs Austen reported, with some exasperation in her tone, to her other sister-in-law Mrs Walter:

Sister Hancock staid with us only a few days, she had more Courage than you had and set out in a Post Chaise with only her little Bessy, for she brought neither Clarinda or Peter [servants] with her, but believe she sincerely repented, before she got to her journey's end, for in the middle of Bagshot Heath the Postilion discover'd She had dropped the Trunk from off the Chaise. She immediately sent him back with the Horses to find it, intending to sit in the Chaise till he return'd, but was soon out of patience and began to be pretty much frighted, so began her Walk to the Golden Farmer [one of the Bagshot coaching inns] about two miles off, where she arrived half dead with fatigue, it being in the middle of a very hot day. When she was a little recover'd she recollected she had left all the rest of her things (amongst which were a large parcel of India Letters, which she had received the night

Dick Turpin surprised by the sight of a gibbet, *engraving, 1836.*

before, and some of them she had not read) in the Chaise
with the Door wide open, She sent a man directly after them
and got them all safe and after some considerable time the
Driver came with the Trunk, and without any more misfortune got to Bolton Street about Nine oclock . . .

Years later, little Bessy Hancock, now grown up, re-named more elegantly
as 'Eliza' and married to the Comte de Feuillide, visited Blenheim in August
1788, and wrote to Mrs Walter's daughter Phylly: 'We returned to Town on
Sunday and of all the dreadful storms of Thunder Lightning & Rain I ever
remember, I think that we experienced on that aimiable place called Hounslow
Heath was the worst, however I believe it saved us from being robbed as we
afterwards heard that two Highwaymen were at that very moment in waiting
for their Prey & nothing but the violent storm prevented their stopping us.'
    In the summer of 1793 this form of lawlessness came most uncomfortably
close to Steventon rectory, when there was such an outbreak of highway
robberies in the neighbourhood of Overton that the local county newspaper, the *Reading Mercury*, which circulated in South Berkshire and North
Hampshire, published a long article on the subject in its issue of 19 August:
'. . . many robberies have of late been committed in and about the neighbourhood of Overton, in the County of Southampton, by a person, supposed to
be a stranger . . .' and gave details of three. At about ten o'clock at night
on 6 June the carriage of the Austens' friend Mrs Bramston was stopped at
Hyde Hill, near Overton, and the two ladies inside were robbed of eleven or
twelve guineas. On 5 July, again at about ten o'clock, '. . . a servant of the
Revd Mr Lefroy was attacked by the same person in Kingsdown Lane, the
road leading to Kingsclere and Newbury, and who, on making some resist-
ance, was much beaten with a bludgeon.' On 12 July Mrs Trevor of London,
with two other ladies, 'travelling in their own carriage, were stopped in the
vicinity of Popham lane, by a man in a smock frock, with a handkerchief
or crape over his face, and armed with pistols, who robbed them of nine
guineas, their gold watches, and ear rings from their ears, value together
about £100. The villain came out of Popham wood, and tied his horse to a
gate, whilst he committed the robbery.' Most interestingly, Mrs Bramston's

139

own account of this attack survives, as she wrote to tell her Gloucestershire kinswoman Mrs Hicks Beach about it on 6 July 1793: '. . . I have been very much frightend Lately, by being Stopd returning from drinking tea with Mrs Lefroy, by a footpad, who put his pistol Close to me & said he would blow out my brains if I did not give him my Money I lost 8 Guineas which I did not like at all, beside its having made my head Ache ever since & I now Start at my own Shadow but am getting better . . .'

The *Reading Mercury* continued its report: '. . . the person supposed to have committed these robberies has been seen hovering about the neighbour-hood of Overton for several weeks past, and is supposed to have sheltered himself principally in the adjacent woods. He is a stout lusty man about 35 years of age, from five feet eight to ten inches high, darkish hair, not tied, pale sodden complexion, roundish face, with high cheek bones, flattish in front, and long nose, not very aquiline; he has generally been seen in a dark coloured coat, a cross barred flowered linen or cotton waistcoat, dark ribbed corduroy breeches, light blue ribbed stockings, half boots and a round high crowned hat. Has generally had with him another coat of a darkish colour, like a great coat; and a bundle in a diamond-spotted handkerchief, supposed to contain a round frock; he has a singularity in his walk, as if he had been lamed, and speaks quick; he neither talks nor appears like a countryman, but rather like a man who has been in some business, or in a gentleman's service.' Mr Greene, attorney-at-law in Basingstoke, advertised a reward of £40 for any infor-mation leading to his arrest; this never happened but seems to have had the effect of making him move on from the Overton district, as no further cases occurred at that time. However, he may have returned to his favourite area in later years, because on 27 January 1800 the *Hampshire Chronicle* reported, as part of the news from Winchester: 'Last Sunday evening as Charles Parkhurst, Esq, of Brambridge, and some of his servants, were coming from London, the servants were stopped by a highwayman, between Basingstoke and Popham-lane, who thrust a pistol through the window of the chaise, and slightly wounded one of them (a female) in the face. Fortunately, Mr and Mrs Parkhurst were in the first carriage, by which means they escaped.'

In 1793 all the Austen sons had left home, and Mr Austen himself was past sixty, hence the knowledge that such a criminal was at large, with fresh cases being reported every month, must have caused consternation and alarm in Steventon rectory, and very probably curtailed the journeyings of Mrs Austen and her daughters for some time. The road to Bath seems to have been considered especially dangerous, for when Jane travelled there in May 1799 she wrote to Cassandra: 'Our Journey yesterday went off exceedingly well; nothing occurred to alarm or delay us' – and again in May 1801: 'Our Journey here was perfectly free from accident or Event . . .' This emphasis on safe journeying to Bath reappears in *Northanger Abbey*, when Catherine Morland goes there with Mr and Mrs Allen and Jane Austen mocks the clichés of the romantic Gothic novel: '. . . the parting took place, and the journey began. It was performed with suitable quietness and uneventful safety. Neither robbers nor tempests befriended them, nor one lucky overturn to introduce them to the hero. Nothing more alarming occurred than a fear on Mrs Allen's side, of having once left her clogs behind her at an inn, and that fortunately proved to be groundless.'

Poachers and mantraps

Mantraps had been invented about 1770, and some landowners chose to employ these devices throughout their estates to protect their deer, wild game-birds, and fruit crops from village poachers. The trap consisted of an iron plate balanced upon springs, which was concealed under grass or dead leaves in the centre of the woodland path; when the poacher stepped on the plate, and the springs sank under his weight, this released iron bars on each side, which sprang up and gripped him by the leg, at shin- or thigh-height, lacerating and perhaps even breaking it. Locking devices meant he could not release himself, even with the assistance of friends, but had to await the arrival of the gamekeeper doing his rounds the next morning. The use of these traps was not made illegal till 1827. Spring-guns were another kind of booby-trap: a shot-gun would be fixed unobtrusively to a tree or a post, and a trip-wire across the path would pull the trigger and discharge the shot in the poacher's direction – the gun could be angled to fire at legs or body.

The *Morning Chronicle* of 27 September 1784, carried the following cautionary but sympathetic tale: 'A few days since a young woman, servant to Mr Woodnorth, at Chatham in Kent, walked in her sleep into the garden, where she was caught by the leg in a man-trap. The trap being old, and the spring having but little power, the wound she received is but slight; but the terror occasioned by the accident, threw her into violent convulsions, from which her life is still judged to be in great danger.' Across the Border, the Scots were more ferocious: a handbill issued in Edinburgh on 17 September 1788, gave public warning that the garden at St Bernard's, between Stockbridge and the Water of Leith, was defended by steel traps of the largest sort, with spring-guns and an armed watchman under cover, as well.

Much closer to Steventon, on 16 March 1789 the *Reading Mercury* carried the following advertisement: 'Whereas some person or persons did on Monday night last break into the garden of the Revd William St John, at Dogmersfield, and maliciously pull up and destroy all the Melon and Cucumber plants, with large fruit thereon; He does hereby offer a reward of £10 to any person who will give such information as to convict the offender or offenders thereof. Spring guns, thigh snappers, and body squeezers, are and will continue to be set in various parts of the said garden and all other premises in the occupation of the said William St John.'

The St John family were well known to the Austens and are mentioned in Jane's letters; and it may well have been this advertisement, which must have been read and discussed in Steventon rectory, that gave Jane the idea for her short story 'Jack and Alice', which appears in Volume the First of

The 'humane' man-trap had no teeth on the jaws.
Illustration from William Bullock & Co. catalogue.

her Juvenilia and was probably written late in 1789. Two of the characters, Lady Williams and Alice Johnson, are out walking together and quarrelling as they go, when they see:

A lovely young Woman lying apparently in great pain beneath a Citron tree, [which] was an object too interesting not to attract their notice. Forgetting their own dispute they both with simpathizing tenderness advanced towards her & accosted her in these terms: 'You seem fair Nymph to be labouring under some misfortune which we shall be happy to releive if you will inform us what it is. Will you favour us with your Life & adventures?' – 'Willingly Ladies, if you will be so kind as to be seated.' They took their places & she thus began. . . . [It turns out that the lovely young woman, Lucy, is a stalker, pursuing the incredibly handsome Charles Adams]: 'On enquiring for his House I was directed thro' this Wood, to the one you there see. With a heart elated by the expected happiness of beholding him I entered it & had proceeded thus far in my progress thro it, when I found myself suddenly seized by the leg & on examining the cause of it, found that I was caught in one of the steel traps so common in gentlemen's grounds . . . I screamed as you may easily imagine till the woods resounded again & till one of the inhuman Wretch's servants came to my assistance & released me from my dreadfull prison, but not before one of my legs was entirely broken.' . . . Lady Williams now interposed & observed that the young Lady's leg ought to be set without farther delay. After examining the fracture therefore, she immediately began & performed the operation with great skill which was the more wonderfull on account of her having never performed such a one before. Lucy, then arose from the ground & finding that she could walk with the greatest ease, accompanied them to Lady Williams's House at her Ladyship's particular request. . . .

Gipsies

More so than highwaymen, gipsies were hated and feared in the country-side, since they operated in gangs and pilfered from homes and gardens as well as threatening and robbing travellers; newspapers frequently carried articles about their depredations, and authors and journalists commented in identical terms upon the crimes they committed. In 1775 the Revd Gilbert White of Selborne wrote to his friend Daines Barrington: 'We have two gangs or hordes of gypsies which infest the south and west of England, and come round in their circuit two or three times in the year. . . . while other beggars lodge in barns, stables, and cow-houses, these sturdy savages seem to pride themselves in braving the severities of winter, and in living in the open air the whole year round.' At this date gipsies did not live in what we now think of as the traditional caravan, but camped in primitive tents in any likely secluded place; and James Austen in his poetry mentions the black circles on grassy wasteland caused by their fires as they moved on from day to day. In the Reading district, as Jane and Cassandra might have seen in their schooldays . . .

> a party of gipsies had pitched their tent and tethered their donkeys in Kibes-lane, and fowls were disappearing from the hen-roost, and linen vanishing from the clothes-line, as is usual where an encampment of that picturesque but slippery order of vagabonds takes place. The party in question consisted as usual of tall, lean, suspicious-looking men, an aged sibyl or two of fortune-telling aspect, two or three younger women with infants at their backs, and children of all ages and sizes from fifteen downwards.

The radical political journalist William Cobbett came upon a similar group in Hampshire in 1815, and reported angrily upon such populous gangs and the robberies which they constantly committed, drawing a pen-picture on this occasion of the 'blackguard ruffians of men and the

Country Lane with Gypsies, *oil on canvas, by Thomas Sidney Cooper (1803–1902).*

nasty ferocious looking women with pipes in their jaws', and 'the poor asses that went bending along beneath their burdens laid on them by their merciless masters' while an 'extraordinarily ill looking fellow, with two half starved dogs, performed the office of rearguard'.

Apart from pilfering whatever they could lay hands on, gipsies also claimed to be able to foretell the future, and expected to be paid for telling the fortunes of those gullible enough to believe them. This also of course gave great scope for robbery, and in October 1784 *Jackson's Oxford Journal* carried the following warning news item: 'Last Friday in the afternoon one of those vagrants stiled gypsies, in a field between Kentish Town and Copenhagen House [on the outskirts of north London], calling to a young man and asking him if he would have his fortune told, and the latter foolishly agreeing to it, she took him behind a hedge, where was another woman, with a man, who robbed the youth of all the money he had, stripped him to his very shirt, and it was with some difficulty he prevailed on them not to take even the shirt also.' Every now and then some local authority would try to enforce the law, and in August 1797 *The Times* reported a police raid on a gipsy encampment south of London: 'On Sunday morning, about five o clock, ten police officers came to Norwood in three hackney coaches, threw down all the gypsey tents, and exposed about thirty men, women and children [and] carried them to prison, to be dealt with according to the Vagrant Act.' They had been 'telling fortunes for foolish young girls and even well experienced dames'.

It is this well-understood danger from gipsies which makes Harriet Smith and her friend Miss Bickerton so frightened when they go for a walk along

> . . . the Richmond road, which, though apparently public enough for safety had led them into alarm. About half a mile beyond Highbury, making a sudden turn, and deeply shaded by elms on each side, it became for a considerable stretch very retired; and when the young ladies had advanced some way into it, they had suddenly perceived at a small distance before them, on a broader patch of greensward by the side, a party of gipsies. A child on the watch, came towards them to beg . . . Harriet was soon assailed by half a dozen children, headed by a stout woman and a great boy, all clamorous, and impertinent in look, though not absolutely in word. More and more frightened, she immediately promised them money, and taking out her purse, gave them a shilling, and begged them not to want more, or to use her ill . . . she was followed, or rather surrounded by the whole gang, demanding more . . .

She is only saved by the appearance of Frank Churchill, who frightens them off.

Thieves and robbers

Pilfering and robbery by gipsies, and destruction of property, were the most usual types of crimes committed in rural areas, and Jane's family and neighbours suffered upon various occasions. In 1759, when her uncle James Leigh Perrot was enclosing the estate he owned at North Leigh near Oxford, *Jackson's Oxford Journal* reported that '. . . certain ill-disposed Persons did . . . destroy the Fences, and new-planted Quick-Hedges, upon Norleigh-Heath, in the County of Oxford, belonging to James Leigh Perrot esq.' Some years later the Leigh Perrots moved to Scarlets in Wargrave parish in Berkshire, and in 1772 their hen house was broken open and a number of fowls stolen, for which a reward of ten guineas was offered. Also in 1772 the *Reading Mercury* published a formal warning: 'Whereas great damage has been done for many years past, to the hedges, lands, and coppices at Popham in the County of Southampton by several idle and dis-orderly people, by gathering of mushrooms and nuts, this is to give notice, that whoever is found trespassing thereon for the future will be prosecuted to the utmost severity of the law . . .' In 1786 'two fat hogs were stolen from out of the hog-stye of Hugh Digweed, of Steventon, and drove away in the night of Friday the 15th of December' – for which Mr Digweed offered a reward of ten guineas, with an added inducement for encouraging offenders to betray each other: 'And if any one of the offenders will make a discovery of his or her accomplices, so that they may be brought to justice, he shall be intitled to the same reward and a free pardon.' A few years later another farm which Hugh Digweed owned elsewhere in Hampshire was the subject of an arson attack, and the entire property – houses, barns and crops – was destroyed by a fire started in a hayrick.

In 1788 the Revd George Lefroy at Ashe had three horses stolen; Thomas Marshall of Deane lost a 'handsome ram lamb, the off horn a little broken' in 1797; and a large quantity of potatoes, three ducks and one fowl were taken from John Lovett's property at Overton in 1798. In *Persuasion* Mr Shepherd the sharp lawyer – perhaps not appreciating there could be such a thing as a Christian spirit of forgiveness – remembers that when

Captain Wentworth's brother, Revd Edward Wentworth, was the curate of
Monkford, he refused to prosecute a farm labourer who had broken into his
orchard – 'wall torn down – apples stolen – caught in the fact; and afterwards, contrary to my judgement, submitted to an amicable compromise.
Very odd indeed!' Jane Austen used such domestic crimes to provide the
final happy ending for Emma and Mr Knightley, whose marriage is delayed
due to Mr Woodhouse's selfish fears of being left alone at Hartfield thereafter and consequent refusal to give his consent. Although the gipsies who
had frightened Harriet 'did not wait for the operations of justice [but] took
themselves off in a hurry', it would seem that they presently returned to
their old haunts, because some weeks later '. . . Mrs Weston's poultry-house
was robbed one night of all her turkies – evidently by the ingenuity of
man. Other poultry-yards in the neighbourhood also suffered. – Pilfering
was *housebreaking* to Mr Woodhouse's fears . . .' and on the understanding
that Mr Knightley would move into Hartfield after the marriage instead of
taking Emma away to Donwell Abbey, he finally did consent.

Murders

Murders too happened from time to time, especially those of lone travellers
who were known or believed to have money with them. Farmers returning
late from market might be expected to have sold their stock successfully,
and in July 1784 a typical case was reported by the *Public Advertiser*: 'They
write from Town Malling in Kent, that Farmer Jackson, going from thence
about Nine o'Clock on Wednesday Night the 21st Instant was set upon
about a Mile from that Place by several Men and Women, who pulled him
off his horse, and robbed him of Twelve Guineas and some Silver. The
Women were for murdering him, that he might tell no Tales; but one of
the Men said, it was Crime enough to rob him. They then turned his Horse
loose and made off.' Sailors unwisely showing off their prize-money were

A Gibbet, *drawing by Thomas Rowlandson (1756–1827)*.

149

also likely targets, and such a murder occurred just over the Hampshire border, near Farnham in Surrey: in September 1786 a sailor was walking from London to Portsmouth to join a ship, when he met three men at Esher; he paid for food, drink and lodging for the group, and was last seen alive with them at the Red Lion inn at Thursley; his body was later found on the slope of the Devil's Punchbowl at Hindhead, near the Portsmouth road. The men were caught and executed, and their bodies were hung in chains on Gibbet Hill, the highest point of the Portsmouth Road, 900 feet above sea-level. Perhaps Jane had been reading some similar tale in the papers in January 1799, for when she wrote to Cassandra: 'You express so little anxiety about my being murdered under Ash Park Copse by Mrs Hulbert's servant, that I have a great mind not to tell you whether I was or not . . .' it sounds as if this was a very wry joke.

Markets, fairs and festivities

The harshness of rural life and the never-ending drudgery of the agricultural year, often exacerbated by great poverty, was cheered by church and seasonal festivals and visits to local markets and fairs, with now and then – particularly during these wartime years – some special occasion that called for countrywide civic rejoicing. After the Twelve Days of Christmas the first holiday proper would be in the early spring: Mothering or Mid-Lent Sunday, the fourth Sunday in Lent, when young men and maidservants who were working and living away from home would be allowed the day off to return to their native villages and give some little present to their mothers – for those who could afford it, to bake a simnel cake for them. The seasonal festivals were usually arranged by the villagers themselves under the leadership of the local inn-keeper, and sometimes the landowners or lords of the manor would throw parties for their tenants and workforce to celebrate sheep-shearing, haymaking and harvesting. May Day celebrations were very popular – in 1791 the *Morning Post* of 2 May reported: 'Yesterday being the 1st of May, according to annual and superstitious custom, a number of persons went into the fields and bathed their faces with dew on the grass, under

Maypole on Monument Green, *oil on wooden board, date and artist unknown.*

the idea that it would render them beautiful.' In its issue of 8 May 1815, the *Hampshire Courier* reported lengthily on the May Day festivities at Cheriton near Alresford the previous week. A maypole about 70ft high had been erected, which had 'a very grand and pleasing appearance'. Near this was constructed a 'commodious bower' of green boughs and ornamented with garlands and wreaths of flowers, where about fifty couples danced till night-fall. The dancing was repeated the next day, and 'many highly respected farmers were observed among the assembly'. There are no references to May Day celebrations as such in Jane's surviving letters, but in that of 8–9 November 1800 she tells Cassandra that the maypole at Steventon had been broken by a storm – had the Austens perhaps given May Day parties for their children and pupils in earlier years? Niece Anna, born in 1793 and writing down in old age her memories of her childhood life at Steventon, calls it only 'a tall white pole surmounted by a weathercock' standing at the end of the rectory garden near the Elm Walk shrubbery, with no suggestion that it was or had been a maypole proper. Was Jane perhaps joking in referring to it as a 'maypole'? It does not seem that there were ever May Day celebrations involving the whole parish, perhaps because there was never an inn or a village green to provide a focal point. Indeed, the Knight family appear to have insisted upon sobriety for their tenants – in 1754 the widowed Jane Brown was granted a lease of her cottage at Hatch Gate on the outskirts of the village provided she did not make it a beerhouse or sell liquor there. If the villagers did not brew at home, they would have to walk to either the Deane Gate Inn or the Wheatsheaf at Popham Lane for their alcoholic refreshment. In later years, after Jane and her parents had left Steventon, her sister-in-law Mary Lloyd noted in her pocket-book on several occasions going to Oakley Hall to drink tea with Mr Bramston and see the Mayings, as well as going to North Waltham to see the dancing – but there is no mention of any such festivities at Steventon.

Another Hampshire-born authoress, Mary Russell Mitford (1787–1855), has left graphic descriptions of May Day celebrations in the villages not far to the north of Steventon. Mary was the grand-daughter of the Austens' old neighbour, the Revd Dr Richard Russell, rector of Ashe until his death in 1783, when he was succeeded by the Revd George Lefroy. Jane and Mary never met, since the Mitfords had moved away from Ashe before Mary was born; and in later years Mary became far more famous in her lifetime than ever Jane did in hers, when she wrote the essays on rural life that were subsequently published under the title *Our Village*. She explained that: 'A country Maying is a meeting of the lads and lasses of two or three parishes, who assemble in certain erections of green boughs called May-houses, to dance.' These Mayings were held on village greens, such as the one at Bramley which she attended:

> . . . a little turfy spot, where three roads meet, close shut in by hedgerows, with a pretty white cottage and its long slip of garden at one angle. . . . In the midst grows a superb horse-chestnut, in the full glory of its flowery pyramids, and from the trunk of the chestnut the May-houses commence. They are covered alleys built of green boughs, decorated with garlands and great bunches of flowers, the gayest that

The Village Festival, *oil on canvas, by William Shayer senior, 1843. The scene was composed from sketches made at Alverstoke in Hampshire.*

blow – lilacs, guelder-roses, peonies, tulips, stocks – hanging down like chandeliers among the dancers; for of dancers, gay dark-eyed young girls in straw bonnets and white gowns, and their lovers in their Sunday attire, the May-houses are full.

Outside,

. . . were children laughing, eating, trying to cheat, and being cheated, round an ancient and practised vendor of oranges and gingerbread; and on the other side of the tree lay a merry

153

Back-swording, *wood engraving by Richard Doyle, 1859.*

group of old men, in coats almost as old as themselves, and young ones in no coats at all . . . There were a few decent matronly-looking women sitting in a cluster; and young mothers strolling about with infants in their arms; and ragged boys peeping through the boughs at the dancers . . .

This Maying at Bramley seems to have been a very modest affair, perhaps due to the fact that the roads in that part of Hampshire were notoriously bad and known to be almost impassable for wheeled traffic. In less isolated villages Mayings could be much larger and become a revel, a feast day or a festival, when many more people attended – the men in clean white smocks or velveteen or fustian coats, with rough plush waistcoats of many colours, the older women in their traditional long scarlet cloaks and the younger in modern stuff shawls. The dancers were joined by cheapjacks with their green covered carts and assorted wares, small traders with arrays of fairings and

A Smock Race at a Country Fair, *drawing by Thomas Rowlandson, 1811.*

eatables, quack doctors and tooth-drawers, performing animals, penny peep shows, and games of quoits and bowls and ninepins.

A ring or a stage would also be set up for wrestling matches and back-swording or cudgel-playing contests, this latter being a peculiarly ferocious sport whose sole object was simply to 'break' the opponent's head – that is, to hit the crown of the other man's head sufficiently hard to split the skin and make blood flow visibly for at least an inch anywhere above the eyebrow. The weapon was a stout ash stick with a large basket handle, and lots were drawn for opponents; the left elbow had to be kept up to head-height and the stick used only in the right hand in order to beat down the other man's guard and succeed in hitting his head. The *Reading Mercury* advertised in its issue of 29 June 1782 that the Berkshire village of Yattendon was to hold its Revel on 10 July: 'and for the encouragement of gentleman gamesters and others, there will be given an exceedingly good Gold-laced Hat of 27s. value, to be played for at Cudgels, the man that breaks most heads to have the prize. Two shillings will be given to each man that positively breaks a head, for the first ten heads that are broken the blood to run an inch, or to be deemed No Head.' A hat of 15s. value was to be wrestled for, and another 27s. value gold-laced hat to be bowled for. The next day there were still more cudgels and bowling matches, again for gold-laced hats of 27s. value, and a half-guinea prize for a donkey race. The women of the village were not neglected, since they could run races to win a fine Holland smock, and join in a jingling match for a very good petticoat. Jingling matches were a single-sex sport: about a dozen people, men or women, all blindfolded, would try to catch one man, not blinded, with a bell hung round his neck and his hands tied behind him. There might also be such appropriately agricultural games as sack races, climbing a greasy pole to grab a ham or leg of mutton fixed to the top, trying to catch a greasy pig or one with a well-soaped tail, or grinning through a horse-collar – that is, a prize for whoever could pull the ugliest grimace when framed by the heavy leather harness.

All towns had weekly markets, which were held in some convenient central road or square where country people could come together to sell their home-grown food to the townsfolk – poultry, eggs, dairy produce, honey, vegetables – but over time some of these gatherings began to sell cattle as well, thus becoming too big for any town's market place, and so had to be held in fields outside the town, where they were known as fairs. The fairs grew still larger when traders and stallholders moved in to cater for people wanting to stock up for a year ahead with such durable items as bacon, cheese, leather, cloth, hats, gloves and shoes, earthenware, tools and ironmongery; then booths and sideshows were set up to provide food, drink and entertainment for the fairgoers; for those not interested in purchasing livestock rural sports and games, such as the above, were added to the proceedings; and after the serious cattle-dealers and farmers had done their business and left, the day inevitably ended with noisy drunken dancing and brawling. A family visiting Yorkshire in 1805 passed through Thorne, which the young diarist of the party thought was '. . . an ugly village & was not embellished by a crowd of dirty noisy tipsy people who were assisting at a horse-fair, thro' which we drove to the Red Lion, a shabby Inn – The noise of Drums, Fiddles, dancing & drunken people was so great as rather to alarm us, & happy we were to get out of it with a sober Postboy.' In its issue of 3 June 1800, *The Times* reported a brawl at Farnham in Surrey, when the Irish recruits of the 25th and 27th Regiments, which were then quartered in the town, came to the fair armed with large bludgeons and knocked down everything they could reach, destroying the stalls. The fairgoers returned, armed with hop poles and other clubs, and beat the Irish back, killing some of them. The local militia had to be called in to quell the riot, and *The Times* commented approvingly: 'The great utility of volunteer corps was never more apparent than on this occasion, for had not the Farnham Volunteers instantly turned out, the whole town must have been in the greatest danger from a furious and provoked mob, and the Irish soldiers in quarters were at that very moment joining their comrades who were becoming desperate.' The inquest on the bodies of the Irish soldiers gave a verdict of justifiable homicide.

In Reading, the fairground was the Forbury, the rough open space outside the old Abbey Gateway, so that the boys at Dr Valpy's school on one side of the Forbury and the girls in the Abbey House school on the other, could see everything of the four big fairs which were held there during the year, and which usually lasted for several days. The first was at Candlemas, 1–2 February, which was mainly for the sale of horses; during May there was another livestock fair for horses and cows; on St James's Day, 25 July, it was for horses and seasonal fruit; and the biggest of the four was the Cheese Fair on St Matthew's day, 21 September. This was a hiring fair for domestic servants and farm labourers, as well as being one of the principal markets in the region for the sale of cheese, offering over a thousand tons of the different cheeses made in the dairy-lands of the south-western counties of England.

Mary Russell Mitford and her parents lived for many years at Grazeley and then at Three Mile Cross, villages to the south of Reading, and Mary knew the town well. She was able to describe the Cheese Fair in detail, as Jane and Cassandra would have seen it from their school-room windows:

Factors from the West and dealers from London arrived days before the actual fair-day; and waggon after waggon, laden with the round, hard, heavy merchandise, rumbled slowly into the Forbury, where the great space before the school house, the whole of the boys' play-ground, was fairly covered with stacks

A Country Fair, *by W.H. Pyne, from* British Costumes, *1805.*

of Cheddar and North Wilts. Fancy the singular effect of piles of cheeses several feet high, extending over a whole large cricket ground, and divided only by narrow paths littered with straw, amongst which wandered the busy chapmen, offering a taste of their wares to their cautious customers the country shopkeepers (who poured in from every village within twenty miles), and the thrifty housewives of the town, bewildered by the infinite number of samples . . . When lighted up at night, it was perhaps still more fantastic and attractive . . . [including as it did] the travelling wild beasts, whose roars and howlings at feeding-time used to mingle so grotesquely with the drums, trumpets and fiddles of the dramatic and equestrian exhibitions and the laugh and shout and song of the merry visitors.

Mary wrote again about the Cheese Fair, describing how the Mitfords' young groom Ben wandered round the different side-shows: laughing at Punch and Judy, staring at the wild beasts, admiring clever horsemanship, and preparing to enjoy the delights of a threepenny play where the actors in full costume were exhibiting themselves on a platform in front of the booth in order to attract an audience for the entertainment about to commence inside it – these included 'a black boy in a turban flourishing a tambourine, a gentleman in a helmet and spangles, a most Amazonian lady in a robe and diadem, and a personage, sex unknown, in a pair of silver wings, gold trousers, and a Brutus wig . . .' The black boy was in fact a gipsy with burnt cork rubbed on his face, and the tambourine had previously been stolen from Ben, who was able to lay claim to it and prove his ownership in front of the justices.

Apart from a very few private zoos, such as that at Exeter Exchange in the Strand in London, which Jane mentions in *Sense and Sensibility* as being where John and Fanny Dashwood take their little Harry to see the wild beasts, the only chance the average person had to see foreign animals would be when some travelling menagerie visited a fairground. A headline event occurred on the night of 20 October 1816 when a lioness escaped from such a menagerie encamped in the middle of Salisbury Plain and attacked one of the horses drawing the Quicksilver mail coach on its way to London; the lioness was recaptured and the horse survived, and the pair became an added attraction for the showman's business. *Bonner and Middleton's Bristol Journal* for 28 August 1784 published an advertisement for a more docile animal, on display at the fair at St James' Barton in central Bristol:

To the admirers of the wonderful Productions of Nature: To be seen alive in a Caravan in the Horse-Fair, during the time of the Fair, a most astonishing Creature called the

The Lioness attacking the horse of the Exeter Mail Coach, *engraving, 1816.*

Ethiopian Satyr, or real Wild Man of the Woods. – It may be justly asserted that this animal is of a different Species from any Creature ever seen in Europe, and seems to be the link between the rational and brute Creation. It was brought from the Desarts of Abyssinia in Ethiopia Superior, to Amsterdam in a Dutch ship, and purchased by the Proprietor for a large sum. This astonishing Creature, when he stands erect, is near five feet high . . . he sits in a chair in a very pleasing and majestic attitude, to receive and eat his food; he is very affable and obedient to the commands of his keeper . . .

From the rest of the lengthy description, a modern zoologist has suggested it was probably a drill (*Mandrillus leucophaeus*), a species of large forest baboon coming from the border area of Nigeria and Cameroon in West

Africa. These are about 3ft high when on all fours but would be about 5ft tall when standing on their hind legs.

The biggest and most ancient of the Hampshire fairs was that held annually at Weyhill, a village on open downland just to the west of Andover. It lasted for several days during the first half of October, and in the eighteenth century was one of the most important markets in southern England for all types of agricultural products, but specializing in sheep – in the 1790s it was said to sell 140,000 sheep each year. Two days were devoted to selling sheep only, followed by one day for a horse fair, another day for farmers to hire their servants, and then ending with sales of cheese and hops, these last having been brought in from Hampshire, Surrey and Kent. Standing places and pens for the animals were laid out, and tents were erected all over the hill; in fine weather everything would have a thin coating of chalky dust, but if the autumn was wet even the sheep would be sodden, the buyers' hat-brims full up and spilling every time they moved, and the auctioneer scooping rain from his face and wringing out his beard. October 1813 was just such a rainy season, and Jane commented to Cassandra: 'Poor Basingstoke Races! – there seem to have been two particularly wretched days on purpose for them; & Weyhill week does not begin much happier.' In later years some of the tents used by the hop sellers were superseded by permanent booths, simple constructions with cob walls and slate roofs, and window shutters that dropped down to form a counter. These booths still survive, now modernised, and are used for a rural craft centre and Weyhill's parish council offices.

Apart from the villagers' own amateur Mayings and the organized fairs and markets, it was usual for landowners and prosperous farmers to give parties to celebrate the important summer events of sheep-shearing, haymaking and harvesting. These always followed much the same pattern: long tables and benches were laid out, either inside a barn or just outside in its shade, and at about midday the labourers sat down to dine off roast meat and suet puddings, with the farmer carving at the principal table and his wife at another, while the daughters of the house and their friends circled the tables with vegetable dishes and beer jugs. In October 1775 William Marshall, a bad-tempered agricultural journalist who farmed for a time in Surrey until he quarrelled with his partners, wrote in his diary:

I have given the labourers, who were all very ready to help, a Sunday's dinner, and some ale in the evening; but sent them home sober to their wives and children. Farmer _____ made his men so intolerably drunk the other night, that one of them was suffocated by the liquor, leaving a widow and four children to be kept by the parish – such is the effect of harvest suppers!

Some of these parties could be very large indeed. In October 1784 the *Nottingham Journal* reported on the harvest home dinner given by Sir Richard Hill of Hawkstone. His employees went first of all to a church service, at which the 65th Psalm was sung, as this includes the verse: 'Thou crownest the year with thy goodness, and thy paths drop fatness.' After the service,

> ... no less than 200 workmen, reapers &c repaired to a regale, given them by Sir Richard and managed under the direction of his servants, consisting of five sheep, two of which were roasted whole, several pieces of beef pies, plumb puddings &c., when all was conducted with so much regularity, as happily to blend temperance and hospitality together, a union which it was so much to be wished was always observed upon such occasions. Though the number of guests was so great, yet they behaved with the utmost decorum, and returned early to their respective families, without the least appearance of clamour, riot, or excess.

As the newspaper report hinted, and as William Marshall stated, it was quite true that such dinners often ended with all the guests becoming dead drunk; and army recruiting parties would prowl the countryside at this time of year, looking for those young men who were so drunk as to sign up for military service without realizing what they were doing.

Although Jane herself makes no mention of any parties being given for the Steventon workforce, in 1813 one of James-Edward's school friends, twelve-year-old William Heathcote, visited Steventon rectory during the summer holidays, and on 19 July wrote a vivid letter to his cousin Margaret Blackstone, describing the

. . . merry-making at Steventon, which Mr. Digweed gave (on Saturday evening) to his haymakers, when all his hay was got in. There were donkey races, merely for the sport, old women in wheel-barrows blindfolded, for two blue ribbon bows, young women to run a race for a straw bonnet, girls for two pink ribbons, boys to run in sacks for harvest gloves not bugs, to roll down an hill for a plum pudding, to run a race for a hand-kerchief, & lastly to dip their heads into a bucket of water for some oranges. I got a donkey lent me to run (the one I used to ride), [James-]Edward Austen was my jockey, he was dressed in this manner, he had a black velvet cap, with a yellow button on the top, & a yellow band in front, & buff coat with black sleeves, we managed that in this manner, first he put on a black velvet spencer of Mrs. Austen's, & over that, a buff waistcoat, it looked very well I assure you. I think you would be quite amused to see the old women wheel their barrows, in one part of the field there was a rake, to which the prizes were hung, which was the goal, & another stick for the starting post, they did not run a race all at the same time, as perhaps you suppose, but one at a time & they (not seeing the goal) but [to] go on as long as they liked & stop whenever they thought they were near the end of their journey, so that some women, by letting one hand lower than the other might turn their barrows completely round thinking that they were as straight as any of them all the time, when all had all done they measured the distance of each woman's barrow from the goal, & that one which was nearest obtained the prize.

It would be nice to think that Jane too had visited her old home and seen these harvest sports, but on Saturday 17 July 1813 she and Cassandra and their mother were all dining at the Great House in Chawton, as her niece Fanny Knight noted in her diary.

Apart from the regular round of seasonal festivities, markets and fairs, the twenty years of hostilities with France – the French Revolutionary wars which were followed immediately by the Napoleonic Wars – called forth national rejoicings when notable victories occurred. On 1 June 1794 Admiral Lord Howe, in command of the Channel fleet, met the French fleet off Ushant, and captured or sank seven of their ships without losing any of his own. This battle is now known in English naval history as the Glorious First of June, and in its issue of 1 July 1794 the *Kentish Gazette* reported:

> On Wednesday 18th June the general inhabitants of Godmersham assembled in the village, to celebrate the important victory obtained by Lord Howe, and the Brave British Tars, over the French Fleet; and to testify their loyalty and attachment to their King and Country . . . they paraded two and two in front of the house of Thomas Knight, Esq, accompanied by a band of music, and singing 'God Save the King', 'Rule Britannia' &c in which they were joined by Mr Knight, Lord Willoughby de Broke, and several other respectable visitors. They adjourned afterwards to the park, where they were liberally entertained at the expense of Mr Knight. Many loyal and constitutional toasts were drank, and the whole was concluded with a brilliant display of fireworks and rural dances &c &c to the entire joy and satisfaction of every person in the neighbourhood.

There was a brief cessation of hostilities, a period known as the Peace of Amiens, for a few months during 1801–2, and when preliminary peace talks started in October 1801 householders created their own decorations to mark the occasion – 'illuminations' were all the rage, which were made by fixing a wooden triangle in each window pane, on which were stuck tallow candles. Another form of decoration was a black painted board with a few coloured oil lamps arranged in the form of a crown, with 'GR' [for George Rex] on either side, or spelling out the word PEACE. Flags would be hoisted and church bells rung; the mail coaches carried placards announcing PEACE WITH FRANCE in large capitals to spread the news along the main roads out of London, and the coachmen all wore a sprig of laurel in their hats, as an emblem of peace.

The King's birthday on 4 June, and the Queen's official birthday held on 18 January, were always celebrated with assembly balls; but the Golden Jubilee of the King's Coronation fell in 1809, and this called for special celebrations and parties throughout the land. In Hampshire, Mr and Mrs William John Chute at the Vyne in Sherborne St John gave a dinner for all the poor of the parish on 10 October, and their adopted daughter Caroline Wiggett recalled that tables were laid out on the avenue in front of the house, and two old villagers who had worked for fifty years were placed at top and bottom of the tables, with crowns on their heads which had been specially made by someone in the village. Old Bush, the butler at the Vyne, had also served the Chute family for fifty years, and he made some fireworks which were let off at the end of the evening. There was a special assembly ball at Basingstoke on 24 October, and the next day James Austen and the Digweed family gave a dinner for all the inhabitants of Steventon parish, which was held in the Digweeds' barn.

In January 1799 Jane had gone to one of the assembly balls in Basingstoke, which was poorly attended due to illness amongst the local families, and later she told Cassandra: 'Our ball was chiefly made up of Jervoises and Terrys, the former of whom were apt to be vulgar, the latter to be noisy' – but Jane danced with Colonel George Jervoise nevertheless. In this jubilee year of 1809 the Colonel, as an officer in the militia, probably felt some particularly patriotic display was required of him, and at Herriard Park he was farsighted enough to create a truly lasting memorial by planting a beech avenue more than one mile long following the parish boundary between Herriard and Lasham. This avenue grew and flourished and remained intact until 1941, when most of it was cut down in order to build Lasham airfield during the Second World War.

CHAPTER 5
CROPS, LIVESTOCK, AND PLEASURE-GROUNDS

ALL READERS OF *PRIDE AND PREJUDICE* instinctively feel that Jane Austen must have put much of her own character, her own likes and dislikes, into the creation of Elizabeth Bennet; hence it may strike some as slightly odd that her love and knowledge of the countryside should appear specifically in the creation of Fanny Price – most timid, meek and shy of all Austenian heroines, and the complete antithesis of witty talkative Lizzy. Certainly, when Sir William Lucas, accompanied by Lizzy and his daughter Maria, are travelling into Kent to see Charlotte Lucas, now married to Mr Collins, we are told that: 'Every object in the next day's journey was new and interesting to Elizabeth . . .' but it is Fanny's thoughts that are described in detail in *Mansfield Park*. When the Bertram family visit the Rushworths at Sotherton Court on a hot August day, Fanny is one of the party travelling in Henry Crawford's barouche; the others are Henry, who is driving his own carriage, with Julia Bertram sitting beside him on the box so that he can flirt with her under pretext of teaching her how to drive; Maria Bertram, who is already obviously preferring Henry's company to that of her stupid fiancé Mr Rushworth, and so is therefore bitterly jealous of her sister; Mary Crawford, who watches the situation between Maria and Julia with sardonic amusement, knowing as she does her brother's propensity for deliberate cold-hearted flirting; and imperceptive Aunt Norris, 'all delight and volubility', since she prides herself on having made the match between Maria and Mr Rushworth. Edmund is following the barouche, travelling separately on his own horse. Jane Austen then gives us this sudden insight into Fanny's character:

Their road was through a pleasant country; and Fanny, whose rides had never been extensive, was soon beyond her knowledge, and was very happy in observing all that was new, and admiring all that was pretty. She was not often invited to join in the conversation of the others, nor did she desire it. Her own thoughts and reflections were habitually her best companions; and in observing the appearance of the country, the bearings of the roads, the difference of soil, the state of the harvest, the cottages, the cattle, the children, she found entertainment that could only have been heightened by having Edmund to speak to of what she felt.

Steventon countryside

What then did Jane observe and admire, when walking or driving around Steventon in her childhood and, later on, travelling further afield in Hampshire to Winchester and Southampton or *en route* to Bath, London and Kent? The parish of Steventon is a long narrow strip of land, about three miles long by one mile wide, running approximately north–south and lying 450 feet above sea level, and amounting to just over 2,000 acres; the subsoil is chalk with flints and includes clay and gravel outcrops, which allows for both heathland, woodland, fields for cultivation and meadows for grazing. The high heathland above Steventon could look bleak and barren, without trees or lush grasses and tufted with thorn bushes, furze and juniper instead, but it provided very good rough grazing for sheep. The Digweeds at Manor Farm were probably now following what was then called the 'new Norfolk' four-course rotation of crops, as this idea had originated in East Anglia: each field would bear a different crop every year – cereals, roots or grass – so that the soil did not become exhausted. In 1800 there were serious food shortages, and in the following year the Government instructed country clergymen to report on the crops being cultivated in their parishes; Mr Austen's reply gives another snapshot of Steventon farming as it was in 1801: out of 2,155 acres, 267 acres were growing wheat, 250 barley, 250 oats, 60 turnips or rape, 28 rye, 12 peas, and only 1½ acres of potatoes; the remaining acreage was woods and pasture. Around the village, therefore, the fields would alternately show the blueish greens of bushy turnip tops and of the tall swaying wheat and oats, as well as the yellower green of barley; then the emerald green of hay meadows contrasted with the pinks and crimson of sainfoin and clover, followed in late summer by the golden brown of ripe cornfields; and finally the regular furrows ploughed across the bare brown soil of those fields which were to be left fallow. Timber too was viewed as a crop to be rotated, hence the established woodlands of deciduous trees, pollarded or coppiced according to their kind, the new plantations to replace mature trees, and quickset hedges thickening into hedgerows, would show a whole variety of tints of green in spring, yellow and russet in autumn; and when the deciduous trees were reduced to a tracery of bare branches in winter there would still be the dark evergreen firs.

Every Sunday Jane and her family would take the footpath between these fields up to Mr Austen's church, St Nicholas. It was a small and very plain building consisting only of a nave and a chancel, built by the Norman lords of the manor about the year 1200. There was no good building stone in Hampshire, hence the church had to be constructed out of the local flints, the walls then being rendered over and lime-washed inside and out. Some centuries later a bell-turret had been added at the west end, above the main west door, and this housed three small bells, ringing just powerfully enough to alert the cottagers in the village street below that service was due to begin; here too at the west end stood an evergreen yew tree, its great age making it a symbol of life everlasting and an emblem of the Resurrection.

There had also been a Norman manor house facing the church, likewise built of flints but with the addition of stone brought from Binstead in the Isle of Wight to provide more elegant door and window frames. However, in the sixteenth century the then owners of the estate, the Brocas family, had demolished most of this and re-used the stones and flints in building the first wing of what had been intended to become a very large mansion but which was never in fact completed. This one long ivy-covered wing was now the Manor Farm, where the Digweed family had lived as Mr Knight's tenants since 1758, and the remnants of the Norman house were used as stables and barns. It was noted by contemporary agricultural journalists travelling in this part of Hampshire that the farm houses were mostly of great antiquity, and that the building materials were very mixed, including flint, brick, cob and half-timbering, with thatch or tile roofs – a description which could equally well apply to Steventon rectory. The Manor Farm must have seemed very old-fashioned indeed to Jane, for the other houses in the neighbourhood which she knew best – Deane House, Oakley Hall, Ashe Park and Ashe Rectory – were all modern, since they were built or rebuilt in the 1780–90s, symmetrically planned and constructed in warm red brick throughout.

She might also have noted that although most of the cottages in her father's parishes were comfortable enough by the standards of the day – and obviously those occupied by the Littleworth family were suitable for the Austen babies to be fostered therein – some were little more than hovels. Her brother James talks in his poetry of damp, earthen-floored huts with thin rotting thatch, the bed-chamber without any fireplace and containing only a straw-stuffed mattress, a comfortless place for the sick and old. Such hovels may have been in Jane's mind when she wrote of Emma calling upon 'a poor sick family, who lived a little way out of Highbury . . . it was sickness and poverty together

Steventon Manor House, *wood-engraving by George Pearson, 1869, from an Austen family drawing.*

which she came to visit . . . all the outward wretchedness of the place and the still greater within . . .' There are cottages near Sotherton Court which Maria Bertram loftily condemns as 'a disgrace', but she makes no suggestion that Mr Rushworth intends to rebuild them in the future. In *Sanditon*, when Mr Parker is in Sussex and notices 'the neat-looking end of a Cottage, which was seen romantically situated amongst wood on a high Eminence at some little Distance', he hopes it may be occupied by a surgeon who can attend to his badly sprained ankle. This hope is dashed by the squire, Mr Heywood: 'But as to that Cottage, I can assure you Sir that it is in fact (in spite of its spruce air at this distance) as indifferent a double Tenement as any in the Parish, and that my Shepherd lives at one end, & three old women at the other.'

Sheep

As Jane walked on the footpath to and from the church and manor house, or took the muddier lane to Deane, or drove with her family in their chariot to Basingstoke, she would see and hear the animals grazing in the fields on each side; in fact by ancient custom Mr Austen was entitled to graze his sheep and cows in the actual churchyard of St Nicholas if he so chose. However, thanks to his subscription to *The Annals of Agriculture* he would have been able to discuss with his family all the latest information and theories about improvements in stockbreeding, a topic that was currently of interest to every landowner from the King himself downwards. Indeed, George III bore the nickname of 'Farmer George' thanks to his practical interest in agriculture – he was well-known, and jeered at by some, for his custom of frequently making personal unplanned visits to the tenants of his farms around Windsor, as well as contributing several letters to the *Annals*, under the pseudonym of 'Ralph Robinson', regarding his experimental farm at Petersham in Surrey. The merino sheep in Spain were noted for their excellent wool and in 1792 the King purchased

'Affability', *engraving by James Gillray, 1795: George III and Queen Charlotte pay an unexpected visit to a startled farmer.*

Pub.d Feb.y 10, 1795, by H.Humphrey, N.o 37. New Bond Street

AFFABILITY.

J.G.y des.

" *Well, Friend, where a'you going. Hay?__ whats your Name, hay?__ where d'ye Live, hay?__ hay?* "

forty to create a flock at Kew Palace; and from these a group was sent out to Australia in 1804, where it laid the foundation of all fine wool production in that country.

The man who led the way in stockbreeding in the mid-eighteenth century and whose name is still prominent in agricultural history was Robert Bakewell (1725–95), who farmed at Dishley in Leicestershire and was one of Europe's first great livestock improvers; he owned large flocks of the indiscriminately mixed local sheep and by careful selection created a distinctive breed which became known as Leicester Longwools. They were tall beasts, with a heavy bulky fleece which enabled them to withstand severe winter conditions, and also produced large meaty carcases; they were quiet to handle, fattened quickly and well even upon poor pasture-land, and had small bones and heads, with long straight backs and swelling rumps, thus yielding the most meat from the least food. Robert Bakewell hired out his best young rams to other breeders so that they could in turn improve their own stock – it was stated in 1788 that one Bakewell ram had earned its owner £400 for the season.

We know that Mr Austen certainly kept Leicesters, for Jane mentions them in one of her letters to Cassandra during November and December 1798: 'I am likewise to tell you that one of his [my father's] Leicestershire sheep, sold to the butcher last week, weighed 27 lb. & ¼ per quarter. . . .You must tell Edward that my father gives 25s. a piece to Seward for his last lot of sheep . . . Mr Lyford gratified us very much yesterday by his praises of my father's mutton, which they all think the finest that was ever ate.' Since Jane specifies Leicesters in this letter, it may be that Mr Austen also had other breeds on his farm, in which case the likeliest would have been Southdowns from Sussex, since their neighbour Mr Bramston at Oakley had a ewe flock of Southdowns. Just as all the longwool breeds can be traced back to Robert Bakewell and his Dishley Leicester flock in the mid-eighteenth century, so at the same time John Ellman of Glynde in East Sussex was selectively breeding his native short-wool sheep of the Sussex downlands and created the Southdown; it was a small stocky hornless animal with a dense fleece of high quality, that produced a small fast-growing lamb in October ready for the butcher by Christmas, and by the late eighteenth century it was recognized as a distinctive breed. The keen-eyed naturalist Revd Gilbert White noticed

Two Prize Border Leicester Rams in a Landscape, *by Thomas Weaver, 1800.*

when travelling from his native Selborne in Hampshire to visit relatives in Sussex that on the western side of the county, up to the River Adur, 'all the flocks have horns, and smooth white faces, and white legs; and a hornless sheep is rarely to be seen; but as soon as you pass that river eastward, and mount Beeding-hill, all the flocks at once become hornless, or, as they call them, poll-sheep; and have moreover black faces with a white tuft of wool on their foreheads, and speckled and spotted legs . . . the black faced poll-sheep have the shortest legs and the finest wool.' These black-faced sheep in the east were Southdowns, the white-faced in the west Dorset Horns.

What sheep do Mr Knightley and Robert Martin keep on their farms on the Donwell Abbey estate in Surrey? Jane does not tell us, but it would seem likely that two such progressive farmers would not be content with any

173

poor-quality miscellaneous beasts, but would buy in ewes for their flocks from what were now recognized breeds such as these Leicesters or Southdowns; and as Surrey is adjacent to Sussex, it would seem probable that they chose Southdowns – which would account in turn for Robert Martin's wool crop fetching such a high price, as Harriet proudly tells Emma. Nor do we know what kind of sheep were at Kellynch in Somerset, which Admiral and Mrs Croft drove out to inspect as soon as they were settled in at the Hall – farming matters that Sir Walter Elliot had no doubt considered beneath his notice. There were small, hardy and half-wild animals roaming on Exmoor and the Mendip Hills on the western side of the county, which farmers were crossing with the Leicesters in order to improve the quality of their wool and mutton; and perhaps Sir Walter's lawyer and agent John Shepherd had bought some of these in the Crewkerne markets – it seems Jane had envisaged Kellynch as being fairly near Crewkerne. Other West Country breeds that were becoming standardized at this time were the Wiltshire Horns, the Dorset Horns and the Portland, all originating in flocks of animals that had become best suited to their particular local conditions. The Portland was considered to produce excellent mutton, which was provided for the royal table when George III and his court made visits to Weymouth at the end of the eighteenth century.

Cows

Up to the eighteenth century, free-range grazing on common land led to free-range breeding, and cattle in general were motley and ill-assorted in their herds. They were kept for three purposes: as draught animals, milkers, and finally killed for beef; however, indiscriminate breeding meant they yielded little milk and took too long to fatten for slaughter. The Enclosure Acts increasingly curtailed this free-range grazing and, with cattle more confined and under control, breeding could become selective and directed towards producing either dairy or beef animals; the use of oxen as draught animals, for pulling ploughs or heavy waggons, gradually died out during the nineteenth century. The aim for a beef breed of cattle, as for sheep, was to have animals that were muscular and solidly oblong in shape, with small

A Small Black Cow, *oil on canvas, artist unknown, nineteenth century.*

bones and heads, long straight backs and heavy rumps for maximum meat; dairy cows were required to be wedge shaped, deeper and wider in the rear than the front, hence room for large udders; and draught animals would need heavy shoulders to give them pulling strength, but only a small rump. The industrialization of Britain created ever-higher demands for beef and dairy produce, and Robert Bakewell, who had developed the Leicestershire sheep, turned his attention to Longhorn cattle and made this also one the prime breeds of the time. He wanted a beast with plenty of fat as food energy for active working men, and for tallow to make candles, while the long horns themselves had commercial value, fulfilling some of the roles which plastic now occupies in our century. Soon cattle breeding became a fashionable pastime amongst the aristocracy – the Duke of Bedford and the Earl of Leicester were noted agriculturalists.

At this date Hampshire farmers had large flocks of sheep and herds of pigs, but very few cows, which seem to have been kept in a more domesticated manner just to provide milk to individual households; these were usually 'Norman' cows, a general name which covered the dairy cattle from the Channel Islands – the Alderneys, Jerseys, and Guernseys – which had already evolved into specialized breeds by the late eighteenth century thanks to their isolation on these small outcrops of land. They were dainty and decorative animals, small in size and golden-brown in colour, very suited for gentlemen's parks and pleasure grounds, easy to keep in domestic circumstances, and known for the richness of their milk and the quantity of butter that could be made from it – witness Mrs Austen's letters to Mrs Walter around the time of Jane's birth. For countrywomen like Bet Littleworth, who could only afford to buy one cow, that cow would probably have been an Alderney, as she could graze it on common land and it would provide her with the maximum returns of milk, cream, clotted cream and butter for sale locally. It was probably her own experience of having Alderneys as the domestic cows which led Jane to add them to the livestock at Abbey Mill Farm. At the beginning of their friendship, Harriet tells Emma of the Martins 'having eight cows, two of them Alderneys, and one a little Welch cow, a very pretty little Welch cow, indeed; and of Mrs Martin's saying, as she was so fond of it, it should be called *her* cow'. The Welsh cattle, being small like the Channel Island breeds, were suitable as domestic cows, and were dual purpose, kept for meat as well as milk. However, as Harriet is so fond of this particular little cow, presumably it will be kept as a milker and not end up in later years on her plate at table. When Edward Ferrars and Elinor Dashwood are married and settling down at Delaford parsonage, they 'could chuse papers, project shrubberies and invent a sweep . . . nothing to wish for, but the marriage of Colonel Brandon and Marianne, and rather better pasturage for their cows'; and Mansfield Park of course has its own dairy, where Mrs Whitaker the housekeeper oversees the production of 'a famous cream cheese', and gives one of them to Mrs Norris along with the recipe for it.

Oxen

For centuries past young bulls not wanted for breeding had been castrated into oxen, and used as draught animals, for ploughing and pulling large waggons; they were worked from the ages of about three years to about six, when they were fattened and slaughtered for beef. They were very slow but strong and could provide a steadier pull on the plough, especially in heavy soils; it was agreed that horses were quicker and their working life longer, but in this country horse has never been used for meat at the end. The discussion as to whether oxen or horses were better for plough beasts continued all through the nineteenth century and even in the early years of the twentieth there were a few ox teams still at work in Hampshire.

The Durham Ox, *etching by John Boultbee, 1802.*

Once the idea of selective breeding of livestock had taken root, at the end of the eighteenth century a passion arose amongst farmers for creating ever bigger and bigger oxen, until in fact they became so large that they could not actually do any work and so were kept for curiosity value only, touring the country to earn money by being exhibited at agricultural fairs and having their portraits painted and engraved for further sales and publicity. The most famous of these beasts was perhaps the Durham Ox, bred in the North of England in 1796, and slaughtered in 1807 after it had sustained an injury to its leg. From 1801–7 it toured England and Scotland, in its own special carriage drawn by four horses, and for most of 1802 was on show in London. Its portrait painted at that time gave details of its dimensions – the most important one being its height, measured to the top of the shoulder in the old rural unit of *hands* [that is, the width of a man's hand, taken to be four inches]. The Durham Ox stood 16 hands high, otherwise 5 feet 4 inches. This fashion for exhibiting huge beasts, and the method of measuring horses and cattle in *hands* enabled Jane to create Emma's punning conversation with Mr Knightley, as he tells her that Robert Martin proposed again to Harriet Smith when they were both together in London, in a family party with the John Knightleys visiting Astley's Amphitheatre, and this time she has accepted his suit. 'But, Mr Knightley, are you perfectly sure that she has absolutely and downright *accepted* him. – I could suppose she might in time – but can she already? – Did not you misunderstand him? – You were both talking of other things; of business, shows of cattle, or new drills – and might not you, in the confusion of so many subjects, mistake him? – It was not Harriet's hand that he was certain of – it was the dimensions of some famous ox.'

Pigs

The Old English hog had been still very much the wild boar type found throughout northern Europe – a tall hairy long-legged beast, usually yellow-brown in colour, with a narrow razor back, low shoulders, flat slab sides, large flopping ears and a long rooting snout. Pigs are omnivorous, and under the eye of the village swineherd the hogs of medieval times could roam on commons, on stubble fields and in woodlands, finding what food they could in plant roots, tree mast, berries, fruit, vegetables and grain, and also rootling for worms, grubs, carrion and any unwary small animals. Feeding them was therefore cheap, but it took at least sixteen months to reach slaughter weight. Over the centuries regional types had developed – the Hampshire, Berkshire, Essex, Oxford and Shropshire were some of them – but in the early eighteenth century small numbers of Asian pigs were first imported and by 1770 importation was on a large scale. These Chinese pigs, as they were loosely termed, were small, black and plump; they developed a thick layer of fat much more quickly and could be killed before the age of nine months. Contemporary agriculturists noted that '. . . they are very prolific, are sooner made fat than the larger kind, upon less provisions, and cut up, when killed, to more useful and convenient portions . . . they are smaller, have

A Leicester Sow, 2 years old, *lithograph by W.H. Davis, nineteenth century.*

shorter legs, and their flesh is whiter and sweeter than the common kind.' The Chinese were crossed with the local breeds, and this led to the development of three basic types of English pig: a large-framed one to provide much fat, a medium-sized one for bacon, and the smallest for pork joints.

As in the case of the prize oxen, pig-breeders soon started to vie with each other to produce ever bigger beasts, and Jane may well have heard of two local heroes: Mr Charles Butler's hog at Tidmarsh Farm near Pangbourne in Berkshire, which was bred in 1794 and when killed in 1797 stood 3 feet 8 inches high, was 8 feet long and 9 feet in girth, with 11 inches of fat on the shoulder; and Mr William White's hog at Kingston in Surrey, even bigger when killed at age of three in 1798: 4 feet high, 8 feet 9 inches long, 9 feet 2 inches in girth and with 5 inches thickness of fat all over, and weighing over 70 stone. 'It was generally allowed that this pigg would have fatted nearly as much again.' Another huge beast was the Yorkshire Hog, 10 feet long, bred at Doncaster in 1809, which toured the country and earned its owner nearly £3,000 in admission fees in three years.

In November 1798, when Cassandra was away from home and staying with brother Edward at Godmersham in Kent, Jane passed on the domestic information that 'We are to kill a pig soon' and also the request that Mr Austen would like to have some news of Edward's pigs. The following week Jane was able to say: 'My father is glad to hear so good an account of Edward's pigs, and desires he may be told, as encouragement to his taste for them, that Lord Bolton is particularly curious in his pigs, has had pigstyes of a most elegant construction built for them, and visits them every morning as soon as he rises.' Lord Bolton lived at Hackwood Park, a mansion near Basingstoke; it was originally built in the late seventeenth century but remodelled in the 1760s into something like the shape of an E: the main house was a large central block of nine bays width, and curving quadrant colonnades on each side led round to smaller east and west service wings. The pigstyes were indeed 'most elegant' and Lord Bolton was evidently a man with a sense of

ABOVE The north front of the remodelled Hackwood Park, *aquatint*, c.*1830*.

BELOW Hackwood Park, *oil on canvas, by Paul Sandby, c.1764. The landscape shows the earlier house on the site.*

humour, because he had built them as a miniature version of his mansion – the curving colonnades were divided up into separate styes for the pigs, and the mansion and its wings were diminished to a large central cottage and four smaller ones, two at each end of the runs of styes, to house the farm workers tending the pigs. This pigstye block still exists, re-named 'Roundtown' and adapted recently for housing humans far wealthier than farm workers, and is now listed by English Heritage.

In January 1799 pigs still entered into Jane's home news to Cassandra: 'My father furnishes him [Edward] with a pig from Cheesedown; it is already killed and cut up, but it is not to weigh more than nine stone; the season is too far advanced to get him a larger one. My mother means to pay herself for the salt and the trouble of ordering it to be cured by the sparibs, the souse, and the lard.' Although Jane did not write *Emma* till nearly twenty years later, these practicalities of killing pigs and consuming the pork reappear in detail in the dialogue one day at Hartfield, when Mr Woodhouse tells Mr Knightley:

'Now we have killed a porker, and Emma thinks of send-ing them [the Bates family] a loin or a leg; it is very small and delicate – Hartfield pork is not like any other pork – but still it is pork – and, my dear Emma, unless one could be sure of their making it into steaks, nicely fried, as our's are fried, without the smallest grease, and not roast it, for no stomach can bear roast pork – I think we had better send the leg – do not you think so, my dear?'

'My dear papa, I sent the whole hind-quarter. I knew you would wish it. There will be the leg to be salted, you know, which is so very nice, and the loin to be dressed directly in any manner they like.'

'That's right my dear, very right. I had not thought of it before, but that was the best way. They must not over-salt the leg; and then, if it is not over-salted, and if it is very thoroughly boiled, just as Serle boils our's, and eaten very moderately of, with a boiled turnip, and a little carrot or parsnip, I do not con-sider it unwholesome.'

The Hartfield pigs were no doubt kept under control and in excellent order by Mr Knightley, treating them as part of his Donwell Abbey farm; but those at Longbourn House evidently suffered from a lack of attention on the part of Mr Bennet's employees, just as he himself paid little attention to his family. Elizabeth had just recently arrived at Mr Collins's rectory at Hunsford, when

> . . . a sudden noise below seemed to speak the whole house in confusion; and after listening a moment, she heard some-body running upstairs in a violent hurry, and calling loudly after her . . . Maria would tell her nothing more, and down they ran into the dining-room, which fronted the lane, in quest of this wonder; it was two ladies stopping in a low phaeton at the garden gate. 'And is this all?' cried Elizabeth. 'I expected at least that the pigs were got into the garden, and here is nothing but Lady Catherine and her daughter!'

Drove roads and drovers

In pre-railway days, when there were no such things as cattle-trucks for mass movement of beasts, all farm animals had to be moved from place to place on their own legs, and some came from very far away indeed. When Jane and her family drove to any of the towns in the vicinity of Steventon, they might well find themselves held up on the road by the passage of large flocks of sheep and herds of cattle, and sometimes pigs as well, numbering into the hundreds, *en route* to fairs and markets, and moving on average at no more than two miles an hour. The animals were herded on their way by profes-sional drovers aided by their large and cunning dogs, and in order to avoid highways with toll-gates used unenclosed lanes, some of which are still called 'the drove' or 'drove roads' today. Common land was also sought, as places where the animals could rest and graze while the drovers went off to inns that specialized in their custom. Experienced drovers who could conduct a flock of sheep skilfully through all the difficulties of lanes and commons, streets and highroads, and deliver them punctually and in good condition, were held in high repute by farmers and dealers, and their services were much sought after. There is no documentary evidence that Jane ever went to or through the little village of Stockbridge on the River Test south of Andover, but if she did, she would have seen a large cottage, once an inn, which still exists. It has the name 'Drovers House' painted on the front, and above it, in Welsh, 'Gwair tymherus porfa flasus cwrw da a gwal cycurus', which can be translated as 'Seasoned hay, rich grass, good beer, sound sleep', and it also has a paddock behind it where animals could safely stay overnight. Welsh cows from Pembrokeshire, such as the one at Abbey Mill Farm of which Harriet is so fond, would have to be ferried across the River Severn and then walk from Bristol via Bath, Salisbury and Stockbridge to Farnham, Guildford and Dorking and so continuing eastwards into Kent, where there were large cattle markets at Canterbury, Maidstone and Chilham. Another line of drove roads came through Oxfordshire and Berkshire to Reading, then on to Farnborough and Farnham to cross the Welsh route and turned south to go to fairs in Sussex. From Somerset fat oxen were driven to Bristol, Salisbury and the great Smithfield market in London, the latter journey taking nine days to cover 130 miles.

Horses and carriages

It seems that Mr Austen usually kept three riding-horses at his Steventon rectory, and apart from these, everywhere that Jane went she would have seen horses, whether grazing in fields, tied up for sale at fairs and markets, or drawing every variety of wheeled carriage, both domestic and agricultural. In one of the comic short stories in her Juvenilia, the 'Memoirs of Mr Clifford', written in 1788 when she was only thirteen, Jane gives a list of the carriages her hero is said to own: coach, chariot, chaise, landau, landaulet, phaeton, gig, whiskey, Italian chair, buggy, curricle, and a wheelbarrow – to think in modern terms, in the United Kingdom this would be everything from a Rolls Royce to a Reliant Robin and, in America, from an Escalade to an Eon – and in order to draw all of them, Jane adds that he has an amazing fine stud of horses, six greys, four bays, eight blacks and a pony.

Eclipse at Newmarket, with a groom and a jockey, *oil on canvas, by George Stubbs, 1770.*

At the top of the equine tree was the racehorse, always a descendant of one of the three great stallions brought into England at the beginning of the eighteenth century: the Byerley Turk (1684–1706), the Darley Arabian (1700–30), and the Godolphin Arabian (1724–53), named after their original owners. By the end of the century a contemporary writer could say: 'By great attention to the improvement of this noble animal, by a judicious mixture of several kinds, and by superior skill in management, the English Race Horse is allowed to excel those of the rest of Europe, or perhaps the whole world.' There was a racecourse laid out on Basingstoke Down, which Jane and her family would have seen as they drove into the town from Steventon; the race meetings ceased to be held after 1788, but perhaps it was watching the motley crowds assembling round the course which inspired Jane to list all the carriages she saw and bestow them upon Mr Clifford. The meetings were revived in September 1811, and though Jane had by then left Steventon, her brother James and his family attended and her nephew James-Edward, also aged only thirteen, wrote some little verses about this new event:

Of horses they've twenty, & jockeys in plenty
And the turf only wants a good wetting
The rain comes with speed, many fine days succeed
The course will look wonderous gay
There are booths in a row, which make a great show,
To the race let us hasten away.

Apart from the specialized racehorse, the two most usual riding horses for gentlemen to own were the Hunter '. . . a happy combination of the Race-Horse with others of superior strength, but inferior in swiftness; and may be considered as the most useful breed of Horses in Europe. Their speed and activity in the field are well known . . .' and the 'Old English Road-Horse [which was] a strong, vigorous, and active kind, capable of enduring great hardship; its stature rather low, seldom exceeding fifteen hands; the body round and compact, its limbs strong, and its head thick.' Ladies naturally would need smaller and quieter animals, perhaps galloways – ponies or small horses measuring 13–15 hands high [52–60 inches], so called from their origin in Scotland – or, in Hampshire, the nimble and sure-footed New Forest ponies, the 'Foresters'. Jane's great-grandfather, Theophilus Leigh of Adlestrop in Gloucestershire (c.1643–1725) was renowned in his neighbourhood for breeding excellent grey galloways with Turkish or Arabian blood crossed into the Scottish stock.

As far as draught animals were concerned, Robert Bakewell of Dishley had made improvements in breeding horses as well as sheep and cows, and had produced the Black Horse for use in carriages – the best specimens of his work being reared in Leicestershire and Lincolnshire. There were of course many strong but less well-bred animals being used as cart horses, pulling all sorts of specialized vehicles, the biggest of which was probably the common stage waggon with its huge roller wheels. The wheels were deliberately made very wide, on the theory that they would actually improve the road by levelling out the ruts and potholes as they rumbled along at three miles an hour.

A hunter, with a groom and a greyhound, at Creswell Crags, Derbyshire, *oil on canvas by George Stubbs*, c.*1762*.

Another contemporary writer commented admiringly:

> These waggons will contain a vast quantity of luggage; considerable attention and skill is requisite in the lading of them; and accidents rarely occur, although immense property is conveyed by their means from one great town to another throughout England. No country but England exhibits such ponderous machines drawn by horses; neither do any other people devote equal attention to the breed of cattle for this purpose. A broad-wheeled waggon, upon a fine road, with eight or ten horses bearing an equal share in the draught, is an object that excites no inconsiderable degree of admiration.

In May 1799 Jane travelled to Bath with her brother Edward and his family, and as they were planning upon a month's holiday in the city, had to take a

A waggon, *from W.H. Pyne*, British Costumes, *1805*.

trunkful of clothes with her. This trunk created a problem, 'for it was too heavy to go by the Coach which brought Thomas & Rebecca [Edward's servants] from Devizes, there was reason to suppose that it might be too heavy likewise for any other Coach, & for a long time we could hear of no Waggon to convey it.' Edward did eventually find a waggon on the point of setting out for Bath, but the trunk's arrival was delayed by a day if not longer, and Jane would be without her best gown until such time as the maidservant could finish unpacking the contents.

When Jane Austen introduces her characters into the storyline, she usually slips in a reference to the carriages and horses which they own, as this would immediately have given her contemporary readership an insight into their social standing without any need on her part to provide long detailed descriptions. Mrs Dashwood and her daughters are reduced to an income of only £500 a year, thanks to her stepson's refusal to give them any financial assistance, and therefore cannot afford to keep a carriage and horses. When Willoughby offers to give Marianne a horse, called Queen Mab, which he has bred himself on his Somerset estate at Combe Magna, Elinor points out to her that she must refuse the gift since their mother could not afford the extra expense: they would have to build a stable and provide for Queen Mab's keep, as well as engaging a groom to care for her and accompany Marianne when she rode out, which would mean buying a horse for the man as well. Willoughby himself has a curricle – two-wheeler, two-seater, owner-driven, drawn by a matching pair of horses, very smart and consequently expensive – and keeps hunters; he also wants to sell a brown mare, and is annoyed because Colonel Brandon does not wish to buy it. Mrs Jennings has a chaise, and can afford to hire the four horses managed by two postilions which are necessary to draw it – though as it can only accommodate three people, the maidservant Betty has to be sent on ahead by the public stage coach in order to leave room for the Dashwood sisters to travel up to London with Mrs Jennings when she invites them to stay with her in Berkeley Street, near Portman Square.

The largest private carriage was a closed coach, which could seat about six people; Mr Musgrove senior has a coach, but as it would take three and a half hours to do the seventeen miles from Uppercross to Lyme Regis, hence seven hours if his family party went there and back on the same day, for the sake of his horses he would not consent to its being used in this way; and the plans for a trip to Lyme have to be altered to include an overnight stay so that the horses can rest. The difficulty in travelling in Dorset and Somerset, even on main roads, was well-known: in real life, in September 1804, it took the Mackie family four hours to travel the sixteen miles from Blandford to Dorchester, 'for the hills are immensely high, and in great number', and by the time they reached Dorchester the horses were too tired to go on to Weymouth. The extravagant Sir Walter Elliot buys his horses at Tattersall's Repository in London: 'It is the grand mart for everything connected with the sports of the field, the business of the turf, and equestrian recreations' – but is now obliged to sell his four carriage-horses, and their last office is to take him, his daughter Elizabeth and her friend Mrs Clay, from Kellynch to Bath. Mrs Norris fishes for compliments upon her kind-heartedness, when she loudly recalls how she travelled with Maria Bertram from Mansfield Park to Sotherton Court in the middle of winter, in Lady Bertram's chaise with its four horses, and the difficulty they had in negotiating

> . . . the rough lanes about Stoke . . . And then the poor horses too! To see them straining away! You know how I always feel for the horses. And when we got to the bottom of Sandcroft Hill, what do you think I did? You will laugh at me but I got out and walked up. I did indeed. It might not be saving them

much, but it was something, and I could not bear to sit at my ease, and be dragged up at the expense of those noble animals. I caught a dreadful cold, but *that* I did not regard . . .

In Highbury, as Emma stands at the door of Mrs Ford's shop and looks out at the High Street while Harriet dithers over choosing muslins, she sees Mr Cole's carriage horses returning from exercise, and a stray letter boy on an obstinate mule – the only time mules are mentioned in Jane's novels. The importance of horses for transport is pointed up later in the year, when the trip to Box Hill has to be delayed because a carriage horse has gone lame – Jane does not tell us who owns it, but 'It might be weeks, it might be only a few days, before the horse were useable, but no preparations could be ventured on, and it was all melancholy stagnation.' Mr Knightley, 'keeping no horses, having little spare money and a great deal of health, activity, and independence, was too apt, in Emma's opinion, to get about as he could, and not use his carriage so often as became the owner of Donwell Abbey.' He would certainly need to have horses for work on his farm, but these presumably are not the elegant beasts usually expected to draw a gentleman's carriage. However, when the Coles give their dinner party in February, he shows his thoughtful kindness by hiring a pair of horses so that he can use his carriage to convey Miss Bates and Jane Fairfax to and from the party on a chilly spring evening, as Emma and Mrs Weston notice and comment approvingly.

Mr Bennet's carriage horses work on his farm as well, and careless of his property though he is, he admits that the farmwork has to take precedence. He does send his coach, with Kitty and Lydia in it, to meet Lizzy, Jane, and Maria Lucas at the George inn in Ware upon their return from Kent. After lunch at the inn, 'the carriage was ordered; and after some contrivance, the whole party, with all their boxes, workbags, and parcels, and the unwelcome addition of Kitty's and Lydia's purchases, were seated in it'. Lydia later tells her disapproving elder sister Mary: 'I thought we never should have got into the coach. I was ready to die of laughter. And then we were so merry all the way home! we talked and laughed so loud, that any body might have heard us ten miles off' – though one suspects it was Kitty, Lydia and Maria who were making all the noise rather than Jane and Lizzy. A few months later, when Lydia returns to Longbourn following her elopement with Wickham and forced marriage thereafter, she uses her ride home in the family coach as a means of spreading the news in the neighbourhood: 'Oh! mamma, do the people here abouts know I am married today? I was afraid they might not; and we overtook William Goulding in his curricle, so I was determined he should know it, and so I let down the side glass next to him, and took off my glove, and let my hand just rest upon the window frame, so that he might see the ring, and then I bowed and smiled like any thing.'

When Catherine Morland goes with the Tilney family from Bath to Northanger Abbey, she and Eleanor and the maidservant occupy the General's fashionable chaise-and-four, and 'they set off at the sober pace in which the handsome, highly-fed four horses of a gentleman usually perform a journey of thirty miles . . .' – but after fifteen miles they have to wait for two hours at the inn at Petty France while the horses rest and feed. The General himself has been travelling with Henry in the latter's curricle, and now suggests that he and Catherine should change places, much to her relief: '. . . the chaise-and-four wheeled off with some grandeur, to be sure, but it was a heavy and troublesome business . . .

Lady and gentleman in a phaeton, *oil on panel, by George Stubbs, 1787.*

half the time would have been enough for the curricle, and so nimbly were the light horses disposed to move, that, had not the General chosen to have his own carriage lead the way, they could have passed it with ease in half a minute.'

Chaises were useful for small families, or perhaps for conveying the ladies of a family while the gentlemen rode separately beside the carriage. Sir William Lucas has a chaise, as does Bingley; and the Parkers wreck their chaise when driving into Sussex in search of a surgeon for Sanditon. Single men in possession of a good, or at least a reasonable fortune, would usually drive curricles – like Willoughby and Henry Tilney, so do Darcy, William Elliot, and Charles Musgrove junior – the equivalent of a modern sports car. Another very dashing carriage was the phaeton, a two-seater with a light-weight body perched above four huge wheels and drawn by either two, four, or six horses; due to its extreme height it was consequently very dangerous to drive, and therefore was popular with daring sportsmen such as the Prince of Wales in his younger days before he became Prince Regent and then George IV. Other versions of the phaeton were developed, lower and safer, suitable for ladies to ride in – hence Mrs Gardiner looks forward to driving round the Pemberley estate in a 'low phaeton, with a nice little pair of ponies', and Miss de Bourgh and her companion Mrs Jenkinson are in a low phaeton when they stop at Mr Collins's garden gate. Lady Catherine de Bourgh of course keeps several carriages, as Mr Collins hastens to inform Elizabeth.

A gig was viewed as a useful little carriage for both business and pleasure: owner-driven, two-wheeler, two-seater, but only one horse. As it was so much less expensive to acquire and maintain than a curricle, to drive a gig immediately betrayed the fact the owner had only a moderate fortune and so affected his social standing in the eyes of the world. The cheerful and unpretentious Admiral and Mrs Croft have no hesitation in acquiring a gig in which to drive about the Somerset countryside around Kellynch Hall; but at Sanditon, Sir Edward Denham, baronet though he may be, is too poor to own anything better, to the annoyance of his sister: 'Miss Denham was a fine young woman, but cold and reserved, giving the idea of one who felt her consequence with pride and her poverty with discontent, and who was immediately gnawed by the want of an handsomer equipage than the simple gig in which they travelled, and which their groom was leading about still in her sight.'

The coarse-minded vulgar undergraduate John Thorpe can only afford a gig, and a second-hand one at that, hence does his boastful best to tell Catherine Morland how marvellous it is, nearly as good as a curricle: 'Well hung; town built; . . . curricle-hung you see; seat, trunk, sword-case, splashing-board, lamps, silver moulding, all you see complete; the iron-work as good as new, or better.' In this gig Thorpe cruelly over-drives his horse, pretending again it can maintain a speed of ten miles an hour for hours on end, and that he will drive it for four hours every day if he so chooses. The truth of the matter is that when the four young people set off for a trip to Blaise Castle near Bristol – John Thorpe driving Catherine, and James Morland with Isabella Thorpe in a hired gig – it takes them one hour just to travel seven miles from Bath and they get no further then Keynsham before running out of time and having to turn back. On a second trip – James and Isabella together again, but this time John taking his sister Maria since Catherine has refused to be of the party – they succeed in reaching the York House Hotel at Clifton on the outskirts of Bristol, about sixteen miles away; and '. . . then had a delightful drive back, only the moon was not up, and it rained a little, and Mr Morland's horse was so tired he could hardly get it along' – which meant, of course, he had to keep whipping it; but that was the usual fate of cheap hired horses, which were sometimes quite literally worked to death.

Of the other types of carriages mentioned here and there in the novels, Captain Wentworth buys 'a very pretty landaulette' for Anne Elliot after their marriage – a small four-wheeled low-slung open four-seater with folding hoods over both seats, drawn by a pair of horses and coachman-driven. Henry Crawford's barouche, also with four wheels and folding hoods, and capable of carrying five people in addition to the driver, was a new design which came into use about 1800 and was always a very impressive vehicle, demanding to be drawn by big, upstanding horses, a pair, four, or six being used. A variant of this, the barouche-landau, was developed later in the nineteenth century, and Mrs Elton constantly boasts that her rich brother-in-law, Mr Suckling of Maple Grove near Bristol, owns a barouche-landau as well as a chaise and that he will come to visit her in Highbury travelling in the former – but somehow it never actually appears on the scene. Finally, the ailing Revd Mr Watson can afford nothing better than an old chair – the smallest form of two-wheeled vehicle – for his eldest daughter to drive into Dorking on shopping trips, with one old mare to draw it.

Individual horses also appear occasionally in the background of the novels, though usually unnamed. When Bingley first calls at Longbourn, the Bennet girls see from an upper window that he wears a blue coat and rides a black horse; but when he and Darcy ride into Meryton some weeks later, Jane Austen does not tell us anything about the latter's horse. Tom Bertram has a horse which he has entered to run at the B_____ races; this racecourse, tactfully unidentified by Jane, might perhaps be at Banbury, Bedford or Buckingham, all of which towns are not too far away from Northampton. Thereafter Tom probably takes his horse with him when he goes to Newmarket, the home of English bloodstock breeding and flat racing; a typical newspaper report of the period reads: 'On 25th of March 1799, a match for 3,000 guineas was run at Newmarket, by Sir H. Vane Tempest's Hambletonian, and Mr Cookson's Diamond, and won by the former. It was supposed that wagers to the amount of nearly two hundred thousand pounds were betted on the event of this severe race.' It is here that Tom's riotous life of gambling, riding and drinking with a party of other young men, brings on a fever after a neglected fall – and makes Mary Crawford think that Edmund stands a good chance of inheriting the baronetcy. Edmund himself keeps two hunters and a useful road-horse at Mansfield Park, and exchanges the latter for a quiet mare, which Fanny could ride. Henry Crawford has his hunters brought over to Mansfield from his estate at Everingham in Norfolk, and hopes to please Fanny Price by lending one of them to her brother William to ride while he is staying at the Park on leave from the navy; but Fanny, timid as ever, 'feared for William; by no means convinced by all that he could relate of his own horsemanship in various countries . . . [meant] that he was at all equal to the management of a high-fed hunter in an English fox-chase'. She herself had learned to ride on the 'old grey poney', now deceased, though Wilcox the old coachman is tactless enough to remind her how nervous she had been: 'Lord bless me! how you did tremble when Sir Thomas first had you put on!' Apart from the horse he drives in his gig, John Thorpe claims to own three hunters and tells Catherine that he and his friend Sam Fletcher intend to rent a house in Leicestershire for the next hunting season; but as his deceased father had been only a village lawyer in Putney, west of London, and his mother was now a not very rich widow, contemporary readers would have soon realized that the horses and the hunting box were probably all figments of John's boastful imagination, and accordingly begun to suspect his intentions towards Catherine.

When Frank Churchill is late arriving at Mr Knightley's strawberry party at Donwell Abbey, 'Mrs Weston looked, and looked in vain. His father would not own himself uneasy, and laughed at her fears; but she could not be cured of wishing that he would part with his black mare.' In real life, uncontrollable horses could indeed lead to fatal accidents, and in 1814 Mrs Austen was worrying about her grand-daughter Anna's horse: 'The first thing I have to say is, that I am truly glad to find that you do not intend to take any more rides on that high spirited Mare; I hope you will keep your resolution, and not be persuaded by any body, ever to get up on her back again; it always made me unhappy when I thought of you in that situation.' James Austen and his family were all good riders and 'never thought any horse or pony could do wrong'; and James's younger daughter Caroline, not yet in her teens, recalled:

Our stable establishment [at Steventon] consisted of three horses – two of them could carry a lady – they were useful animals, and were expected to take their turn as hunters besides. My father kept one horse in exercise; if he did not hunt, he rode. I think very few days passed all through the year, that he was not on horseback. But in the winter two of them had to be exercised daily, and I was delighted to get often an hour's ride, with the groom, in a large meadow near the house. . . . I rode though very often with my father and my brother, and I think riding was my greatest pleasure.

From time to time in her letters to Cassandra, Jane mentions the horses her brothers owned. When Edward Knight was holidaying in Bath in June 1799, he bought a pair of black coach horses for sixty guineas; and in October 1800 Jane wrote that James had just bought a new horse at Winchester Fair: '. . . about five years old, used to draw, & thought very pretty'. When Mr Austen retired and left Steventon in 1801, his brown mare and black mare were taken over by James, to replace old Hugh Capet and Mr Skipsey, both of whom had had to be put down. Brother Henry, when running his banking partnership of Austen Maunde & Tilson at No. 10 Henrietta Street, in London's Covent Garden, kept a road horse called High-diddle; and Jane thought that as the bank's profits were increasing, she hoped he would not work poor Highdiddle so hard as he used to do – presumably by either buying a second horse or travelling more by hackney or stage-coaches.

Asses and donkeys

Donkeys, being traditionally quiet, patient and slow, were considered very suitable as transport for ladies, providing just enough speed for shopping trips around villages if driven in a little cart, and keeping ladies' feet out of dust or mud in lanes when ridden side-saddle. They were also popular at seaside or spa resorts, where to ride a donkey formed part of the amenities female visitors would expect; in 1802 a teenager visiting Tunbridge Wells recorded in her journal: '. . . as it was the fashion there, hired a Donkey on which I took some very pleasant rides . . . I with a Donkey & a girl to lead it when necessary, went to the Rocks which are about 3 miles from Tunbridge Wells.' Mrs Elton utters one of her usual self-centred monologues when the Donwell Abbey strawberry party is being planned:

> I wish we had a donkey. The thing would be for us all to come on donkies, Jane, Miss Bates, and me – and my caro sposo walking by. I really must talk to him about purchasing a donkey. In a country life I conceive it to be a sort of necessary; for, let a woman have ever so many resources, it is not possible for her to be always shut up at home; – and very long walks, you know – in summer there is dust, and in winter there is dirt.

To this Mr Knightley replies: 'You will not find either, between Donwell and Highbury. Donwell-lane is never dusty, and now it is perfectly dry. Come on a donkey, however, if you prefer it. You can borrow Mrs Cole's.'

Asses' milk is in fact very close in its composition to that of humans, and so was considered excellent nourishment for invalids. Lady Denham, the Sanditon equivalent of Kent's Lady Catherine de Bourgh, is constantly planning how to combine the growth of the seaside resort, in which she has a financial interest, with the advancement of her nephew Sir Edward Denham; and confides in Charlotte Heywood: 'Now, if we could get a young Heiress to be sent here for her health – (and if she was ordered to drink asses milk I could supply her) – and as soon as she got well, have her fall in love with Sir Edward! –' Lady Denham is therefore delighted when Mrs Griffiths, who keeps a seminary for young ladies in Camberwell, arrives at Sanditon with three of her pupils, one of whom is Miss Lambe, half-mulatto, chilly and tender; and

'Flo and Peggy going abroad', *drawing by Hilary Bonham Carter of her cousin Florence Nightingale riding a donkey, c.1830.*

instantly moves into action: 'In Miss Lambe, here was the very young Lady, sickly and rich, whom she had been asking for; and she made the acquaintance for Sir Edward's sake, and the sake of her Milch asses . . . [but] as to the Animals, she soon found that all her calculations of Profit would be vain. Mrs Griffiths would not allow Miss Lambe to have the smallest symptom of a Decline, or any complaint which Asses milk could possibly releive . . .'

Dogs

As might be expected, the dogs Jane mentions, either in her novels or in her letters, are all sporting breeds – foxhounds, terriers or gundogs – with only two exceptions: the two curs which Emma sees quarrelling over a dirty bone in the middle of the street in Highbury; and Lady Bertram's pug. This pug has always presented a small puzzle to careful readers: which sex is it? When Fanny Price's adoption is first being discussed at Mansfield Park, Lady Bertram says: 'I hope she will not tease my poor pug . . . I have but just got Julia to leave it alone' – so apparently neutral and unnamed; but then in the hot midsummer seven years later she murmurs helplessly: 'Sitting and calling to Pug, and trying to keep him from the flower-beds, was almost too much for me.' There is another reference in the masculine a few days after this – 'the barking of pug in his mistress's arms' – but the last we hear of him is some six months afterwards, when Lady

Bertram says with unwonted enthusiasm: 'And I will tell you what, Fanny . . . the next time pug has a litter you shall have a puppy' – which would seem to imply Pug is now female. It may be that Jane made a mistake in composition; but it may also be that she deliberately created this confusion to demonstrate again Lady Bertram's mental laziness – it could be that the hot summer weather proved too much for a wheezing middle-aged lapdog and Pug-the-male had to be replaced by Pug-the-female, but

Princess Ekaterina Dmitrievna Golitsyna, *by Louis-Michel van Loo, 1759.*

Lady Bertram cannot be bothered to think of a name for the replacement – he or she, is just Pug.

Jane's first reference to a specific breed of dog occurs in her short and unfinished story 'The Generous Curate' in Volume the First of the Juvenilia, and was probably written about 1793. After the title, the Generous Curate himself in fact hardly appears, and we hear instead of his friend the Revd Mr Williams and the latter's six very fine children:

> The eldest had been placed at the Royal Academy for Seamen at Portsmouth when about thirteen years old, and from thence had been discharged on board of one of the Vessels of a small fleet destined for Newfoundland, where his promising and amiable disposition had procured him many friends among the Natives, and from whence he regularly sent home a large Newfoundland Dog every Month to his family.

The island of Newfoundland had been under British rule since the Treaty of Paris in 1763, and since its fisheries were very valuable the Royal Navy kept an active presence there during Britain's frequent wars with France, Spain and Holland. The huge dogs that had been bred by the settlers were used by them as draught animals, since three or four of them yoked to a sledge were able to draw two or three hundredweight of wood or other goods. They had webbed paws and were therefore very good swimmers, their thick oily coats protecting them from cold water, so were also used by the fishermen as retrievers for nets and equipment as well as helping save any man who had fallen overboard. Devon fishermen trading transatlantic with Newfoundland from the late seventeenth century onwards had brought back some of these dogs to England, where by Jane's time they were used as gun-dogs to retrieve ducks and geese shot by wildfowlers.

When Catherine Morland goes with General Tilney and Eleanor to visit Henry at Woodston, she sees that: 'At the further end of the village, and tolerably disengaged from the rest of it, stood the Parsonage, a new-built substantial stone house, with its semi-circular sweep and green gates; and, as they drove up to the door, Henry, with the friends of his solitude, a large

Newfoundland puppy and two or three terriers, was ready to receive and make much of them.' The mention of a Newfoundland dog, together with the previous reference to the 'dark little room' in Northanger Abbey, 'owning Henry's authority, and strewed with his litter of books, guns, and great coats' – shows that he goes out wildfowling on the Gloucestershire marshes. During this dinner visit, Catherine also enjoys 'A saunter into other meadows, and through part of the village, with a visit to the stables to examine some improvements, and a charming game of play with a litter of puppies just able to roll about, brought them to four o'clock . . .' The puppies are presumably more terriers, the progeny of the two or three who stood beside Henry on his doorstep to greet Catherine. Terriers were especially needed to live in stable yards, in order to keep down the rats and mice that would inevitably also live there to avail themselves of such good food supplies; they were used in fox-hunting as well, being sent down fox-earths to drive out any fox which had gone to ground. John Thorpe rudely keeps Catherine waiting in the ballroom, because he is busy discussing horses and dogs with a friend, and the 'proposed exchange of terriers between them' – which, since John has no house and stable yard of his own, are likely to be for use in fox-hunting.

Foxhounds and fox-hunting as such are mentioned only briefly in Jane's letters and novels, although of course all the young men whose horses are described as hunters would be using them for this purpose. A landowner would keep a pack of hounds for his own amusement and for that of his friends in the neighbourhood, and at his own expense, and during the

LEFT The Newfoundland
Dog; CENTRE The Harrier;
RIGHT The Terrier; *wood
engravings by Bewick.*

hunting season would take them out as and when he saw fit without any prior public advertisement, the field usually consisting of those few near neighbours whom he chose to invite. Emma Watson has already told young Lord Osborne that her family is too poor to own riding horses, so his suggestion that she should come to watch his hounds meet at Stanton Wood the following week, was therefore a compliment indeed. When the Lucas ladies call upon Mrs Bennet after the Meryton assembly ball and talk over Mr Darcy's rude behaviour: "'If I were as rich as Mr Darcy,' cried a young Lucas who came with his sisters, 'I should not care how proud I was. I would keep a pack of foxhounds, and drink a bottle of wine every day.'" Other breeds of hounds, harriers and beagles, were kept to catch hares, harriers being able to run as fast as their prey while beagles, though slower, pursued very skillfully by scent. The Steventon neighbours – the Harwoods at Deane and the Terrys at Dummer – each had their own harrier packs, and the Digweeds had a few couples of beagles. James Austen himself had kept a pack of harriers for a time in the 1790s, after his first marriage, but found the expense was too great.

Nowadays game-bird shooting is highly organized, with many guns present supported by their loaders and shooting fast at the pheasants rocketing overhead when driven up by teams of beaters. In past years fast shooting could not happen, since flint-lock guns took a long time to reload – the percussion cap was not invented till 1807 – nor were there any teams of beaters and loaders to keep the guns in action. A sportsman would go out alone or perhaps with a friend or two, early in the morning, accompanied by his pair of pointers whose

A Couple of Foxhounds, *oil on canvas, by George Stubbs, 1792.*

training he had personally superintended, and watching the intelligent way they worked was in itself one of the pleasures of the day. He would bring down enough birds to carry home, plenty for the larder and some for friends. This is how the Dashwood sisters meet Willoughby, carrying a gun, with two pointers playing round him. Sir John Middleton later tells Marianne that Willoughby is a 'very decent shot, and there is not a bolder rider in England', also that he 'has got the nicest little black bitch of a pointer I ever saw. Was she out with him today?' Sir John himself owns a pointer bitch called Folly, and had offered to give Willoughby one of her puppies – a promise he almost retracts upon hearing how badly Willoughby has treated Marianne.

Cats

Unfortunately for the cat lovers amongst us, there are no references to cats in the novels, and only two in Jane's letters. In May 1799 when she went to Bath and stayed in Queen Square, she wrote to Cassandra: 'Mrs Bromley [the landlady] is a fat woman in mourning, & a little black kitten runs about the Staircase', amused by the comparison; and some years later she said of herself: 'I am still a Cat if I see a Mouse.' When James Austen and his family were living at Steventon following Mr Austen's retirement, little Caroline had a tabby cat called Tyger, about which James wrote two sets of verses regarding her misbehaviour: firstly, sleeping on the warm bread-dough which Harriet the cook had set aside for it to rise, and secondly, stealing the piece of meat reserved for James's own lunch. At the end of the eighteenth century small fat spaniels on cushions and shrieking parrots on a perch in the drawing room are mentioned in memoirs as being the pets often kept by elderly ladies; but it does not seem that either Mrs Austen, Cassandra or Jane herself was interested in having any kind of pet – no lapdogs, cats, parrots or canaries – though no doubt some cats lived in the backyards at Steventon and Chawton, engaged in practical mouse-hunting business.

Rats

There is one mention of rats in the novels – in *Persuasion*, at the Musgrove farm at Winthrop. Young Charles Musgrove is somewhat puzzled by his sister Louisa's choice of Captain Benwick for her husband, and finds him too reserved and too bookish; but admits naively to Anne: 'His reading has done him no harm, for he has fought as well as read. He is a brave fellow. I got more acquainted with him last Monday than ever I did before. We had a famous set-to at rat-hunting all the morning, in my father's great barns; and he played his part so well, that I have liked him the better ever since.'

JANE AUSTEN'S COUNTRY LIFE

Poultry

As so much of the meat from cattle, sheep and pigs slaughtered in the autumn had to be salted or otherwise preserved to ensure it could be safely kept over the winter, and as not everyone was able to acquire game-birds, a poultry yard was a necessity in order to provide fresh meat and eggs until such time as early lambs appeared on dinner tables once again. Some farmhouses might also have a dovecote in the yard, where semi-wild pigeons were encouraged to roost so that their squabs could be collected from the nesting-holes and turned into squab pie. Geese were able to find sufficient grazing in rough areas that would otherwise be wasted, and a farmer would turn his flock out on common land until they could be finally fattened on stubble after harvest and sold at goose fairs in September. The Martins keep geese at Abbey Mill Farm, and when Harriet returns to Mrs Goddard's school in Highbury after her visit there, Mrs Martin sends her home with '. . . a beautiful goose, the finest goose Mrs Goddard had ever seen. Mrs Goddard had dressed it on a Sunday, and asked all the three teachers, Miss Nash, and Miss Prince, and Miss Richardson, to sup with her.'

Mrs Austen's poultry yard at Steventon contained turkeys, ducks, chickens and guinea fowl, and she was evidently keen to share her expertise in rearing these birds with her children, for when Cassandra was staying at Godmersham in December 1798, Jane passed on the message: 'My Mother wants to know whether Edward has ever made the Hen House which they planned together.' Other ladies kept poultry more for their decorative qualities than for their practicality as table-birds, and the several breeds of brightly-coloured pheasants were very popular in this respect. At Mansfield parsonage, '. . . Mrs Grant having by this time run through the usual resources of ladies residing in the country without a family of children; having more than filled her favourite sitting-room with pretty furniture, and made a choice collection of plants and poultry, was very much in want of some variety at home . . .' and so was very pleased, therefore, at the idea of Mary and Henry Crawford coming to stay with her. At Sotherton Court, old Mrs Rushworth wants to show her plants and 'curious pheasants' to the Mansfield Park party; and when the Bertrams are returning from their visit, Mrs Norris sits in the barouche surrounded by baskets and packages, and rattles on greedily about the various gifts she has wheedled from Mrs Whitaker the housekeeper during the afternoon. These include

> ... four of these beautiful pheasant's eggs, which Mrs Whitaker would quite force upon me; she would not take a denial. She said it must be such an amusement to me, as she understood I lived quite alone, to have a few living creatures of that sort; and so to be sure it will. I shall get the dairy maid to set them under the first spare hen, and if they come to good I can have them moved to my own house and borrow a coop; and it will be a great delight to me in my lonely hours to attend to them. And if I have good luck, your mother shall have some.

As always, Mrs Norris's enjoyment is at the expense of the Bertram family – it is Sir Thomas's dairymaid who is to tend the eggs in the Mansfield farmyard, and then lend a coop when the chicks are old enough to move to Mrs Norris's White House in the village on the other side of the park.

Orchards and pleasure grounds

Apart from the crops growing and the animals grazing in the farmers' fields, Jane would also have seen the more domestic forms of cultivation – the orchards and kitchen gardens, flower gardens, wildernesses and shrubberies that formed part of the estates of the houses she knew and visited in both Hampshire and Kent, including her own home in Steventon. Beyond the walled garden on the south side of the rectory, there were two footpaths, one going straight up the hill to St Nicholas's church and therefore called by the Austens simply the Church Walk; the other, overhung by tall elm trees and winding through clumps of underwood, was a westward continuation of the turf terrace and formed the southern boundary of the meadow in which the rectory stood, and in later years the Austens developed this into a decorative shrubbery with rustic seats placed therein. Jane referred to it as the Elm Walk, and in October 1800, when Cassandra was away from home

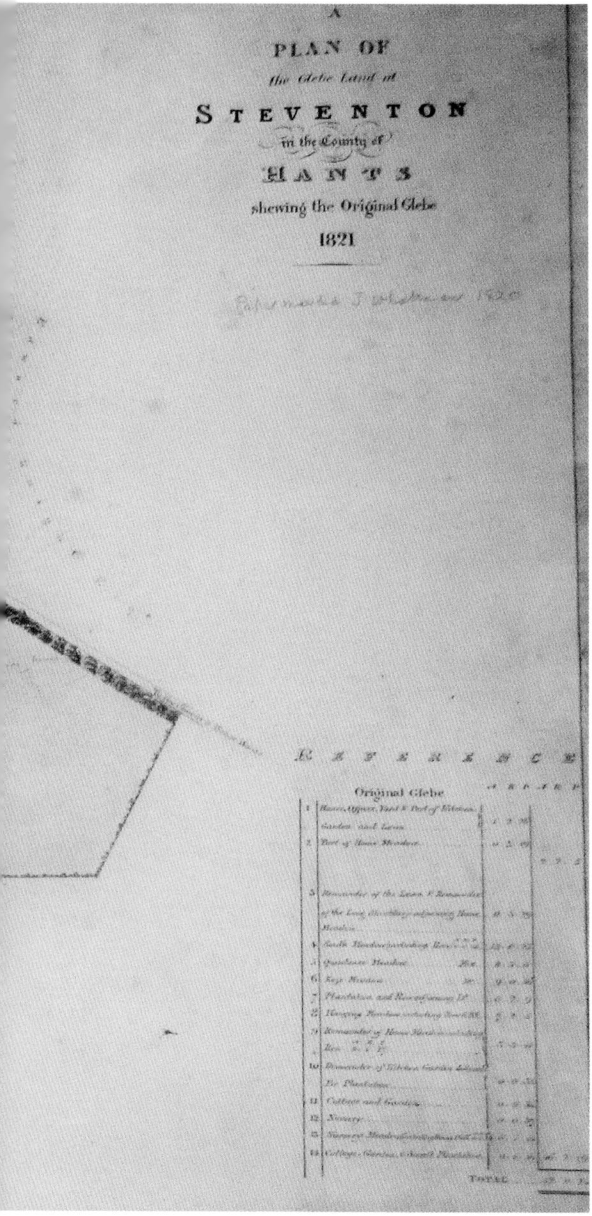

A
PLAN OF
the Glebe Land at
S T E V E N T O N
in the County of
H A N T S
shewing the Original Glebe
1821

REFERENCE

Original Glebe

Plan of the glebe land at Steventon, 1821 – *showing the rectory at the road junction, with its carriage sweep in front and kitchen-yard on the west side.*

and staying at Godmersham, wrote to tell her that: 'Our Improvements have advanced very well; – the Bank along the Elm Walk is sloped down for the reception of Thorns & Lilacs; it is settled that the other side of the path is to continue turf'd & be planted with Beech, Ash, & Larch.' Three weeks later she wrote again: 'Hacker [the local nursery-man] has been here to day, putting in the fruit trees. – A new plan has been suggested concerning the plantation of the new inclosure on the right hand side of the Elm Walk – the doubt is whether it would be better to make a little orchard of it, by planting apples, pears & cherries, or whether it should be larch, Mountain-ash & acacia.'

A Moor Park apricot, *chromolithograph by James Anderson, 1875.*

As soon as Mrs Dashwood and her daughters arrive at Barton Cottage, hospitable Sir John Middleton sends over 'a large basket full of garden-stuff and fruit' from his own grounds at Barton Park, and follows this up with a present of game. Later on, Mrs Jennings tells Elinor Dashwood that Colonel Brandon's manor house at Delaford is a 'nice old-fashioned place' – which probably means it was built in the seventeenth century – and that it is 'quite shut in with great garden walls that are covered with the best fruit-trees in the country; and such a mulberry tree in one corner!' At Mansfield, Mrs Norris quarrels with Dr Grant about the apricot tree which she and her late husband put in against the stable wall at the rectory:

> 'The tree thrives well beyond a doubt, madam,' replied Dr Grant. 'The soil is good; and I never pass it without regretting, that the fruit should be so little worth the trouble of gathering.'

'Sir, it is a moor park, we bought it as a moor park, and it cost us – that is, it was a present from Sir Thomas, but I saw the bill, and I know it cost seven shillings, and was charged as a moor park.'

'You were imposed on, ma'am,' replied Dr. Grant; 'these potatoes have as much the flavour of a moor park apricot, as the fruit from that tree.'

A true Moor Park apricot bears a large bright golden fruit, smooth-skinned and of excellent flavour; so perhaps Sir Thomas was indeed imposed upon by the nurseryman.

As usual, it is in *Emma*, the most agriculturally based of all the novels, that we hear about the fruit as well as the crops grown in Highbury. At midsummer Emma notices at a distance the orchard at Abbey Mill Farm; and when she takes Harriet there to call on her friends the Martin sisters, she sees that a white gate opened on to a broad, neat gravel walk, which led between espalier apple trees to the front door. These apple trees might have been the old dessert cultivar called Margil, in season from October to January; the fruits are sweet with a rich flavour, but as the trees are small and of weak growth, they are well suited to be trained espalier-fashion. From Miss Bates's stream-of-consciousness chatter to Emma about Jane Fairfax's liking for baked apples, we learn that Mr Knightley has just recently given the Bates family some more of the particular culinary cultivars which he has grown in his own orchard:

The apples themselves are the very finest sort for baking, beyond a doubt; all from Donwell – some of Mr Knightley's most liberal supply. He sends us a sack every year; and certainly there never was such a keeping apple any where as one of his trees – I believe there is two of them. My mother says the orchard was always famous in her younger days. . . . William Larkins came over with a large basket of apples, the same sort of apples, a bushel at least. . . . William said it was all the apples of *that sort* his master had; he had brought them all – and now his master had not one left to bake or boil.

Apples: TOP ROW Harvey *and* Catshead; MIDDLE ROW Warner's King *and* Blenheim Orange; BOTTOM Nonpareil; *drawings by Rosanne Sanders, 1988.*

As every supermarket now stocks apples all the year round, imported from New Zealand, South Africa or France when they are out of season in the United Kingdom, it is easy to forget that in Jane Austen's day orchards had to be carefully planned to ensure that they included different types of apple trees which could provide fruit for as long as possible from late summer until the following spring. Early cultivars will not keep and cannot be stored; those which ripen in mid-season will only keep for a short period, but the late cultivars need time to mature after picking and have to be stored before they reach their full flavour. Miss Bates appreciates that the apples Mr Knightley gives them keep very well; and as William Larkins's basketful arrives in late February, the apples therefore might have been Lemon Pippins, Harveys, Catsheads, or Warner's Kings. Miss Bates also knows that Mr Knightley has just two trees of these late-fruiting culinary cultivars in his orchard; and as Mrs Bates confirms that the Donwell Abbey orchard has been famous for years, it must contain as well a good selection of other trees to provide dessert apples over several months. These might have included the very old Nonpareil, Wheeler's Russet, the Blenheim Orange which originated in Oxfordshire, or Duchess's Favourite, the more recent creation of a Surrey nurseryman.

Donwell Abbey is famous locally not only for its orchard, but also for its strawberry beds; and Mr Knightley's casual comment in June that his strawberries are ripening fast leads to Mrs Elton's insistence that he should organize a 'gipsy party' [the contemporary term for a picnic] for his Highbury friends 'We are to walk about your gardens, and gather the strawberries ourselves, and sit under trees . . .' When the picking is in full swing we hear Mrs Elton's half-hour-long opinionated monologue about strawberries, mentioning in particular Hautboys, Chili (*sic*) and White Wood. The latter is the original wild strawberry of the Northern Hemisphere, very small but strongly flavoured; the Hautboys [anglicized from *hautbois*] is as its name suggests the French version of the species, also known as the musk strawberry; and Chile strawberries were an early imported species which produced larger fruit but only a sparse crop and with not so good a flavour. These and other imported species, when crossbred with the smaller more flavoursome varieties, were the ancestors of today's strawberries.

At Sanditon, young Mr Parker, the enthusiastic modernizer, is delighted to have moved out of his old family house in the valley, where in his opinion the kitchen garden was too close for comfort, with '. . . the yearly nuisance of its decaying vegetation. – Who can endure a cabbage bed in October?' – and thinks instead of how fast his plantations around his new house on the clifftop are growing. General Tilney's kitchen garden, by contrast, is a separate building in the park at Northanger, and Catherine is amazed at the size of it: 'The walls seemed countless in number, endless in length; a village of hot-houses seemed to arise among them, and a whole parish to be at work within the inclosure.' The General has a dedicated hothouse for growing pineapples, and boasts with mock modesty that even 'the utmost care could not always secure the most valuable fruits. The pinery had yielded only one hundred in the last year.' Hothouses were used for growing melons and cucumbers, as well as the grapes, nectarines and peaches which Georgiana Darcy offers to Elizabeth and the Gardiners when they call at Pemberley, and for forcing other out-of-season fruits and vegetables – to eat green peas at Christmas was a luxury indeed.

Greenhouses were not kept so warm as hothouses, and were used more for growing and protecting flowers, or over-wintering tub-planted orange trees. The Palmers have a greenhouse at Cleveland, though the negligence of their gardener or gardener's boy in leaving the door or window open means Charlotte's favourite plants are killed by frost. John Dashwood tells Elinor that he is planning to build a greenhouse at Norland, '. . . upon the knoll behind the house. The old walnut trees are all come down to make room for it. It will be a very fine object from many parts of the park, and the flower-garden will slope down just before it, and be exceedingly pretty. We have cleared away all the old thorns that grew in patches over the brow.' When Sir Walter and Elizabeth Elliot give a card party in their Bath house, Anne and Captain Wentworth can seize a few minutes private conversation together in short meetings, '. . . each apparently occupied in admiring a fine display of green-house plants . . .' which would have been hired for the evening from a nurseryman to grace the drawing rooms in Camden Crescent. A greenhouse might be a separate building, as in the case of John Dashwood's new creation, but could also be part of the main house and used as we would a modern conservatory, as an extra room; in real life, in Jane's earliest letter, that of 9–10 January 1796, she tells Cassandra about the ball at Manydown the previous night, when she had flirted with Tom Lefroy and adding, perhaps in an unconscious giveaway: 'We had a very good supper, and the greenhouse was illuminated in a very elegant manner.' This greenhouse can be seen in old pictures and photographs, on the right of the front door of the now-demolished mansion.

Sweet-scented flowers and herbs such as violets, pinks, thyme, marjoram, lavender and roses were naturally the main ingredients in jars of pot pourri, but roses in particular were used in various other ways: they could be eaten – pulped with sugar into a long-lasting conserve or small sweetmeats – or mixed with fats and wax into cosmetics. At Mansfield Park the flower garden is full of roses at midsummer, and one evening Lady Bertram explains to Edmund why Fanny has a headache: 'I sat three quarters of an hour in the flower garden, while Fanny cut the roses, and very pleasant it was I assure you, but very hot. It was shady enough in the alcove, but I declare I quite dreaded the coming home again. . . . *She* found it hot enough, but they were so full blown, that one could not wait. . . . [and] when the roses were gathered, your aunt wished to have them, and then you know they must be taken home . . .' so Fanny has to walk twice across the open park in the hot sun to Mrs Norris's White House to put them in the

Manydown House.

213

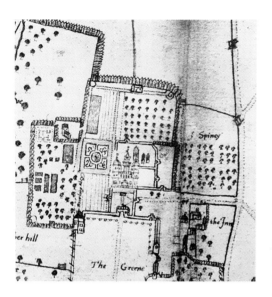

Plan of Holdenby, Northamptonshire, 1587, *showing the formally planted gardens and wildernesses around the newly-built mansion; the Sotherton grounds would have been laid out like this.*

spare room to dry, and is now suffering for this by the end of the day. Mrs Norris, as always, is availing herself of her brother-in-law's property, perhaps to make Rose Drops: 'The roses and sugar must be beat separately into a very fine powder, and both sifted; to a pound of sugar an ounce of red roses; they must be mixed together, and then wet with as much juice of lemon as will make it into a stiff paste; set it on a slow fire in a silver porringer, and stir it well, and when it is scalding hot quite through, take it off and drop it on a paper; set them near the fire, the next day they will come off.' Or else Rose Pomatum: 'To a pound of Roses finely pounded one pound of Lard, mixed well together, & let stand three days. A small quantity of white Wax, melt it altogether & keep it stirring when it has boiled a few minutes strain it into your pots.' Other flowers might also be used for culinary purposes: nowadays we use only about a dozen herbs – mint, sage, thyme and parsley being the most common – but in Jane's time practically every flower or berry that grew, wild or cultivated, would be used somewhere in the household for flavouring or colouring food, or for medicinal purposes, such as Mrs Austen's dandelion tea. Marigold petals would colour cheese rind yellow, spinach juice would colour jellies, creams and cheesecakes green, and sage would not only colour cheese green but add a herbal tang as well.

Apart from orchards, kitchen gardens and flower gardens, the other out-of-door locations in which Jane and her heroines might find themselves, were wildernesses – which in fact were carefully planted and cultivated mini-woodlands – and shrubberies. When Lady Catherine de Bourgh visits

Longbourn, she notices that there is a 'prettyish kind of a little wilderness' at one side of the lawn in front of the house; it has a summer house fashionably designed as a hermitage, in the romantic taste of the mid-eighteenth century, and Lady Catherine sits with Elizabeth in this hermitage and tries to bully her into agreeing to give up any idea of marrying Darcy. Sotherton Court is a sixteenth-century Elizabethan mansion, its gardens and grounds still laid out in stiffly geometric sections, and young Mr Rushworth is anxious to improve at least the grounds of it into the modern style of 1810. On a hot August afternoon the Mansfield Park party wander out from the house onto the bowling green, and from there 'a considerable flight of steps landed them in the wilderness, which was a planted wood of about two acres, and though chiefly of larch and laurel, and beech cut down, and though laid out with too much regularity, was darkness and shade, and natural beauty, compared with the bowling-green and the terrace.'

By the end of the eighteenth century, these formally planted wildernesses, with wide open paths running straight through from one end to the other, were going out of fashion, and shrubberies were created instead. These aimed to be secluded, sheltered, and with a slight air of mystery about them, since there were no clear-cut sightlines and the gravel paths were planned to twist and turn round clumps of shrubs such as syringa, laburnum, lilac, and evergreen laurel, with a few taller trees to make a contrast. At Cleveland the Palmers have erected a Grecian temple on a hill in their grounds, reached by walking through winding shrubberies; at Northanger Abbey Miss Tilney wishes to walk to the tea house in the park along a narrow winding path through a thick grove of old Scotch firs, and in years to come, when Henry Tilney's newly planted shrubbery at Woodston has grown to a respectable height, Catherine will be able to sit there with her children and – no doubt – puppies around her. Mansfield parsonage likewise has a new shrubbery, planted by Mrs Grant upon Dr Grant's arrival in the parish three years ago, in which Fanny sits reluctantly when in company with Mary Crawford, but which will in due course be part of her thoroughly perfect home there with Edmund; and Hartfield's shrubbery is sufficiently well-grown for it to provide shelter enough for Mr Woodhouse to walk for quarter of an hour even on a winter's day. Elizabeth Elliot has a flower garden at Kellynch, with an expensive Scottish gardener, Mackenzie, to tend it, and there are of course shrubberies as well, though Sir Walter is not sure whether he will allow the Crofts to walk in them: 'I am not particularly disposed to favour a tenant. I am not fond of the idea of my shrubberies being always approachable; and I should recommend Miss Elliot to be on her guard with respect to her flower-garden.'

In real life, the ideas for replanting the Elm Walk shrubbery at Steventon rectory, which Jane was discussing with Cassandra in late November 1800, never materialized, for a week or two later Mr Austen suddenly decided to retire to Bath. His plans matured very rapidly: the remainder of the lease of Cheesedown Farm was to be taken over by Mr Holder of Ashe Park, and John Bond was to continue working there and become Mr Holder's bailiff; the auctioneer came in early January to prepare the sale catalogue; and a few days later 'a party of fine Ladies' – Mrs Heathcote, Miss Bigg, Miss Jane Blachford, Mrs Harwood and Mary Lloyd – all arrived in a coach together to buy up Mrs Austen's poultry yard between them. The sale of the contents of the rectory was advertised in the *Reading Mercury* during April 1801 and lasted for three days early in May, and although no complete catalogue has survived, the newspaper advertisement gives a general impression of the interior of Jane's earliest home:

> The neat Household Furniture, well made Chariot (with box to take off) and Harness, 200 volumes of Books, Stump of Hay, Fowling Pieces, three Norman Cows & Calves, one Horse, and other Effects. The furniture comprises four-post and field-bedsteads, with dimity, moreen and other furnitures, fine feather-beds and bedding, mattresses, pier- and dressing-glasses, floor and bedside carpets, handsome mahogany sideboard, modern set of circular dining tables on pillar and claws, Pembroke and card ditto, bureaus, chests of drawers and chairs, a piano forte in a handsome case (by Ganer), a large collection of music by the most celebrated composers, an 18-inch terrestrial globe (by Adams), and microscope,

The Grass Roller, *from W.H. Pyne*, British Costumes, *1805*.

mahogany library table with drawers; bookcase with six doors, eight feet by eight feet; a smaller ditto; tea china, a table set of Wedgwood ware; eight-day clock; side of bacon; kitchen, dairy and brewing utensils, 13 ironbound casks, an end of hops, set of theatrical scenes &c &c. The cows, nag horse, carriage and hay will be sold on the first day.

A separate sale was held on 18 September to dispose of Mr Austen's farm stock and implements, again being advertised in the *Reading Mercury*:

All the Valuable Live and Dead Farming Stock, and Fine Meadow Hay Rick about Ten Tons . . . comprising five capital cart horses, three sows, 22 pigs, and seven stores, three market waggons, two four-inch-wheel dung-carts, two narrow-wheel ditto, one grass cart, four ploughs, eight harrows, two drags, two rollers, troughs, timber-bob, shovels, prongs, useful plough timber and iron, &c. May be viewed any time previous to the sale.

James Austen became his father's curate and he and his family moved from Deane into Steventon rectory; Mr and Mrs Austen rented a house in Bath; and Jane was no longer a farmer's daughter.

CHAPTER 6
URBAN INTERLUDE

'another stupid party'

MR AUSTEN'S DECISION TO RETIRE was quite unexpected, taken while Jane was away staying with Martha Lloyd and her old mother at Ibthorpe, about five miles to the north of Andover, close to the county boundaries with Berkshire and Wiltshire. Ibthorpe was a hamlet of flint and thatched cottages with prosperous farmsteads and some larger houses of warm red brick with red tiled roofs, such as the one in which the Lloyds had lived since 1792, and where James Austen's marriage to Mary Lloyd took place five years later. An offshoot of the village of Hurstbourne Tarrant, it lay in a deep dale which provided a great thoroughfare for flocks of sheep and herds of pigs being driven from Wiltshire and Dorset into Berkshire and Oxfordshire and still further afield; the windy chalk downland hills rose up steeply behind the village, with cornlands sweeping round their feet like waves round a cliff and then pasture, woods and common-land at the top. The Revd Peter Debary was vicar of Hurstbourne Tarrant, and his four daughters were more anxious to brave walking in a dirty lane from the parsonage to call upon the Lloyds, than Jane and Martha were to return their visits; on one occasion Jane commented acidly: 'I was as civil to them as their bad breath would allow me.'

While Jane was at Ibthorpe, Cassandra was at Godmersham staying with Edward and his family; and Jane wrote to her cheerfully on 30 November 1800: 'Martha has promised to return with me, & our plan is to have a nice black frost for walking to Whitchurch, & there throw ourselves into a postchaise, one upon the other, our heads hanging out at one door, & our feet at the opposite.' But according to Austen family tradition, when Jane returned home a few days later accompanied by Martha Lloyd, the news was abruptly announced by Mrs Austen the moment they walked through the front door: 'Well, girls, it is all settled; we have decided to leave Steventon in such a week, and go to Bath – '; and that the shock of the intelligence was so great to Jane that she fainted away. Mary Lloyd, who was also present in the rectory hall to greet her sister, remembered afterwards that Jane was 'greatly distressed' and that she was very sorry to leave her native home.

None of Jane's letters to Cassandra during December 1800 has been preserved; and as Cassandra too seems to have been kept in the dark about their parents' plans for leaving Steventon, it would seem likely that the sisters' correspondence at this time contained their feelings of grief and perhaps resentment at not being consulted about such a major change in their lives. By January 1801, however, Jane was able to put on a brave face, telling Cassandra: 'I get more & more reconciled to the idea of our removal. We have lived long enough in this Neighbourhood, the Basingstoke Balls are certainly on the decline, there is something interesting in the bustle of going away, & the prospect of spending future summers by the Sea or in Wales is very delightful. – For a time we shall now possess many of the advantages which I have often thought of with Envy in the wives of Sailors or Soldiers.'

When the time came to leave Steventon for good, at the end of April 1801, Mr Austen went to London to check on his financial affairs while his wife and daughters stayed for a few days at Ibthorpe. From there Mrs Austen and Jane set off for Bath on 4 May, in a hired post chaise, leaving Cassandra and Mr Austen to follow on later. They joined the main coach road at Andover, and then travelled through Ludgershall, Everleigh, Devizes, Melksham and so to Bath, where they planned to stay with Mr and Mrs Leigh-Perrot in Paragon Buildings while house-hunting for themselves. This route took them for twenty miles across Salisbury Plain, a great undulating area of grassy chalk downland covering most of the county of Wiltshire. Some of it is now under cultivation, and some of it is held by the War Office for military training purposes, but the scarcity of streams and villages, coupled with the numerous remains of prehistoric sites such as Stonehenge and Avebury, distinguish it from any other part of southern England.

Stonehenge at Daybreak, *mezzotint from watercolour by J.M.W. Turner, 1816.*

In the eighteenth century Arthur Young, the agricultural journalist, described Salisbury Plain as being a vast tract of dreary open country, where the farms were very large, up to 800 acres of arable land. Other travellers called it real down country: hills and steep little valleys, pale stubble lands and lonely farms, lost amongst miles and miles square of open grassland without a tree or hedge or bush, its roads only bare chalky lines across the turf which in rain became milk-white rivers. Hundreds of sheep lived out in their folds all the year round, providing a constant undertone of bleating and tinkling sheep-bells. Catherine Morland would have taken a different road across another part of the Plain when accompanying Mr and Mrs Allen for their holiday in Bath, but as she had lived all her life in a village near Salisbury, such countryside would not have seemed remarkable to her.

In real life, in the summer of 1793 a tall gaunt young man walked for three
days across the Plain – William Wordsworth aged twenty-three, penniless
and starting out on his chosen career as a poet – and one evening found himself hopelessly lost:

> And scarce could any trace of man descry,
> Save wastes of corn that stretched without a bound,
> But where the sower dwelt was nowhere to be found . . .
> Huge piles of corn-stack here and there were seen
> But thence no smoke upwreathed his sight to cheer;
> And see the homeward shepherd dim appear
> Far off – He stops his feeble voice to strain;
> No sound replies but winds that whistling near
> Sweep the thin grass . . .
> On as he passed more wild and more forlorn
> And vacant the huge plain around him spread; . . .
> No watch-dog howled from shepherd's homely shed. . . .
> Along the moor no line of mournful light
> From lamp of lonely toll-gate streamed athwart the night . . .

In later years, when Edward Knight and his daughter Fanny drove from
Winchester to Bath in 1814, she too referred to it in her diary as frightful,
open dreary country. As Jane herself had visited Bath on at least two occasions in the recent past, the bleakness of the Plain would come as no surprise
to her, and on this occasion she told Cassandra: 'Our Journey here was perfectly free from accident or Event; we changed Horses at the end of every
stage, & paid at almost every Turnpike; – we had charming weather, hardly
any Dust, & were exceedingly agreeable, as we did not speak above once
in three miles.' The silence of the journey, which Jane mentions with quiet
irony, is not surprising, originating as it did from a source of sadness – however much Mr and Mrs Austen may have wanted to retire to Bath, the day
had now come when Mrs Austen was finally leaving behind her the house and
village in which she had spent her entire married life. And, as Mary Lloyd
recalled, Jane was very sorry to leave the only home she had ever known;

when she was writing *Elinor and Marianne* (the first version of *Sense and Sensibility*) in 1795, she had imagined how Marianne Dashwood would have felt: '"Dear, dear Norland!" said Marianne, as she wandered alone before the house, on the last evening of their being there; "when shall I cease to regret you! – when learn to feel a home elsewhere!"' – and she now found herself in the same situation in real life and experiencing the same regrets.

Mrs Austen and Jane arrived at No. 1 Paragon in the early evening, and Jane told Cassandra: 'The first veiw of Bath in fine weather does not answer my expectations; I think I see more distinctly thro' Rain. – The Sun was got behind everything, and the appearance of the place from the top of Kingsdown, was all vapour, shadow, smoke & confusion.' During the next five years her life in Bath was similarly insubstantial and uncertain, the family moving to different addresses several times as circumstances dictated. Her previous visits had been purely holidays – strolling in the fashionable Pump Room, going to the theatre, shopping for family commissions – but to live permanently in the city was a different matter, especially as her father's income was diminished by his retirement. Did she perhaps experience the feelings which she later on ascribed to Anne Elliot? 'She disliked Bath, and did not think it agreed with her – and Bath was to be her home . . . caught the first dim view of the extensive buildings, smoking in rain, without any wish of seeing them better . . .'

For the first few weeks the Austens stayed with Mr and Mrs Leigh-Perrot; Jane found the house too hot and stuffy, and her aunt's card parties appallingly dull: 'Another stupid party last night; perhaps if larger they might be less intolerable, but here there were only just enough to make one card table, with six people to look over, & talk nonsense to each other.' She was anxious to have news of the Steventon sale, which might have augmented the family's finances, but this was not entirely satisfactory: 'Sixty one Guineas & a half for the three Cows gives one some support under the blow of only Eleven Guineas for the Tables. – Eight for my Pianoforte, is about what I really expected to get; I am more anxious to know the amount of my books, especially as they are said to have sold well . . . we have heard the price of nothing but the Cows, Bacon, Hay, Hops, Tables, & my father's Chest of Drawers & Study Table.'

After viewing various small houses in less fashionable streets, Mr Austen was at last able to acquire a short lease on No. 4 Sydney Place, a terrace house only a few yards away from the exclusive pleasure grounds of Sydney Gardens, at the end of Great Pulteney-street. The publicity for the Gardens promised that: 'Groves, vistas, lawns, serpentine walks, shady bowers, waterfalls, alcoves, bowling-greens, Merlin swings, grottoes, and labyrinths, are all crowded into this fairy realm' – and Jane suggested rather wryly to Cassandra that they might go into the labyrinth every day. Her letters show her as full of restless energy: instead of walking to Ashe, Deane and Oakley with Cassandra to call on the neighbours, or round Hurstbourne Tarrant with Martha, she now had to find companions to walk with her to the villages surrounding Bath – Charlcombe, King's Weston, Twerton, Lyncombe and Widcombe.

> Our grand walk to Weston was again fixed for Yesterday & was accomplished in a very striking manner . . . we went up by Sion Hill & returned across the fields; in climbing a hill Mrs Chamberlayne is very capital; I could with difficulty keep pace with her – yet would not flinch for the World – on plain ground I was quite her equal – and so we posted away under a fine hot sun, <u>She</u> without any parasol or any shade to her hat, stopping for nothing, & crossing the Church Yard at Weston with as much expedition as if we were afraid of being buried alive.

'future summers by the sea'

While based in Bath, for the next four years the Austens escaped from the summertime heat in the city by making the seaside trips for which Jane had hoped, visiting several of the small quiet resorts in South Devon. Precise dates are lacking, but in 1801 it seems likely they went to Colyton and Sidmouth; in 1802 they certainly visited Dawlish and probably nearby Teignmouth; and family memories recalled a trip to Wales as well – Tenby and perhaps Barmouth – that same year. In the autumn of 1803 they went to Lyme Regis, on the Dorset coast, and were so well pleased with the place as to return there in the late summer of 1804. If Jane, like Fanny Price, was interested in 'observing the appearance of the country, the bearings of the roads, the difference of soil . . .' she would have been struck by the West Country's lush green pastures, and its red soil which produced first-class wheat and barley and immense oak trees, and dropped sharply into cliffs at the coastline. If Mr Austen by force of habit studied the state of the local agriculture, he might have pointed out to his daughter the Dorset Horn sheep, and the Red Devon and Sheeted Somerset cows, so different from the livestock which he and Mrs Austen had owned at Steventon.

Sidmouth, situated where the little River Sid cut through the red cliffs to the sea, had a climate so mild that sub-tropical vegetation could grow there; Dawlish made a landscaped feature of the stream which ran through the little town to a sandy beach, and Teignmouth was built on a broad spit of land where the River Teign joined the sea and so was almost surrounded by water. All these small seaside towns had a local fishing trade, but Lyme Regis was in addition a thriving port, with its famous quay, the Cobb, stretching 600 feet out to sea to provide protection for vessels from the frequent south-westerly gales. During the long years of war with France, the isles of Guernsey and Jersey had to be supplied from Lyme, as being the nearest port to them and convenient for the supply of Devonshire cattle, and Jane may have witnessed a scene on the Cobb such as she could never have dreamed of when living in Hampshire. As a resident of Lyme remembered: 'These cattle were driven along the wall and the craft was moored close to the wall seaward, and then these large animals had a belt swathed round their body having a loop at the back to which a hook was inserted, the crane then raised them and the animals were let down into the transport full fifty feet below.' Callous little boys were amused by the struggles of the unfortunate beasts, 'for indeed not infrequently an ox would make a complete somersault'. For more civilised visitors, there was a beautiful cliff-top walk leading from Lyme to Charmouth; the grass was 'verdant velvet . . . unequalled for its even close growth and soft texture . . . and the ample walk was most attractive, being above 100 feet in height and of a good width and seats were placed at suitable distances, it was a promenade few towns can boast.' Unfortunately, the cliffs at Lyme are notoriously unstable, and this walk was swept away by a landslide in the 1820s.

A Beautiful fat Devon Heifer, *coloured engraving by George Garrard, 1805.*

Five Dorset Horn Sheep, *oil on canvas, by Richard Whitford, 1865.*

In *Persuasion*, Jane Austen speaks for herself, not in the guise of any character, when she praises Lyme and the surrounding countryside:

> . . . the Cobb itself, its old wonders and new improvements, with the very beautiful line of cliffs stretching out to the east of the town, are what the stranger's eye will seek; and a very strange stranger it must be, who does not see charms in the immediate environs of Lyme, to make him wish to know it better. The scenes in its neighbourhood, Charmouth, with its high grounds and extensive sweeps of country, and still more its sweet retired bay, backed by dark cliffs, where fragments of low rock among the sands make it the happiest spot for watching the flow of the tide, for sitting in unwearied contemplation; – the woody varieties of the cheerful village of Up Lyme, and, above all, Pinny, with its green chasms between romantic rocks, where the scattered forest trees and orchards of luxuriant growth declare that many a generation must have passed away since the first partial falling of the cliff prepared the ground for such a state, where a scene so wonderful and so lovely is exhibited, as may more than equal any of the resembling scenes of the far-famed Isle of Wight: these places must be visited, and visited again, to make the worth of Lyme understood.

Nowhere else in her novels does Jane describe scenery with such obviously personal enthusiasm; there was a family legend that it was at some West Country seaside resort she briefly met the only man whom she could seriously have wished to marry and whom Cassandra thought would have been worthy of her love; and it may be that these words of praise for Lyme and its environs had a deeper private meaning for her sister than we can now understand.

When the lease of No. 4 Sydney Place expired, the Austens moved to the cheaper No. 3 Green Park Buildings, even though they had previously rejected houses in this low-lying unhealthy area of the city. It was

Lyme Regis from Charmouth, Dorset, *drawing by William Daniell, 1822–3.*

here that Mr Austen died rather unexpectedly in January 1805, and the prospect of further lengthy seaside tours died with him. For the next few months Mrs Austen and her daughters lived in lodging houses, until a family plan was made that they should move to Southampton. Jane's fifth brother, Francis, was now a Captain in the Navy, had recently married, and would soon be sent off on another voyage; hence he felt his young wife, Mary Gibson, would be better off living with his family than on her own, and Southampton was conveniently near the great naval dockyard at Portsmouth. With this plan in view, the Austen ladies left Bath for good

in the summer of 1806 – and as Jane reminded Cassandra two years later:
'. . . with what happy feelings of Escape!'

'*a watering place of elegant and fashionable resort*'

Young Mr Moy Thomas, visiting Southampton as part of his walking tour in
the summer of 1810, was very much impressed by the town:

> We reached Southampton about three O'Clock, crossing the
> Itchen Ferry, & entering the Town by the Gate at the lower
> end. From this gate to the Ferry, is a very pleasing walk or
> promenade; there is a double row of Trees all the way, &
> on the right you look direct upon the Southampton Water
> which is an arm of the Sea, about 9 Miles in length & nearly
> three in breadth, the Country on each side is finely wooded
> & very Picturesque. . . . The Bar Gate at the upper end of
> the Town has a good Effect & in this part the High Street is
> handsome & Spacious but at the lower end it is very narrow
> & confined. About a Mile beyond the Bar Gate, a noble
> Avenue of lofty Elms, forms the entrance into the Town.
> Upon the whole Southampton is a large & respectable Town,
> very clean and of a pleasing appearance . . . The Assembly
> Room is large & handsome, there is also a good Billiard
> Room & commodious Bathing Rooms & a very pretty
> Theatre. . . . The Rank & Fashion which adorn the Environs
> of Southampton (& sweeter Spots for elegant Residence but
> few places in England can boast of) will always give peculiar
> Life & animation to the place & even if these were want-
> ing, yet its contiguity to the Sea, the beautiful Walks & rides
> about it, the Vicinity of the New Forest & above all the Isle
> of Wight, contribute to throw a charm around this Spot,
> which will ever secure to it a high reputation as a Watering
> Place of Elegant and Fashionable resort.

Mrs Austen and her daughters, together with Martha Lloyd who had joined forces with them following her mother's death, lived for a few months in lodgings while Frank looked for a house which he could afford to rent on his naval pay. Even though Jane was glad to have left Bath, and life in Southampton would undoubtedly have been much more to her taste, the family's calculations regarding their future living expenses in the town seem to have depressed her greatly: '[Mrs Lance] was civil and chatty enough, and offered to introduce us to some acquaintance in Southampton, which we gratefully declined. . . . They live in a handsome style and are rich and she seemed to like to be rich, and we gave her to understand that we were far from being so; she will soon feel therefore that we are not worth her acquaintance.' The 'commodious old-fashioned house in a corner of Castle Square' which Frank chose lay in the shadow of the Gothic-folly castle just newly-built by the eccentric Marquess of Lansdowne on the site of the original medieval castle keep. Moy Thomas walked specifically to see this new castle, and was disappointed: 'The Tower & upper part of the Building have a very fine appearance as you view it from Itchen Ferry & other places without the Town, but when you approach near, the tout-ensemble has a poor appearance, the lower part is not nearly finished, it is situated in the worst part of the Town, very confined, & surrounded with mean little hovels, occupied by the lowest description of poor people. The view, however, from the Upper Rooms & especially from the Top of the Tower is most picturesque & beautiful & perhaps in the judgment of its noble Proprietor amply compensates for the disadvantages I have alluded to.'

The Gothic-style castle built by the Marquess of Lansdowne; *early nineteenth century drawing.*

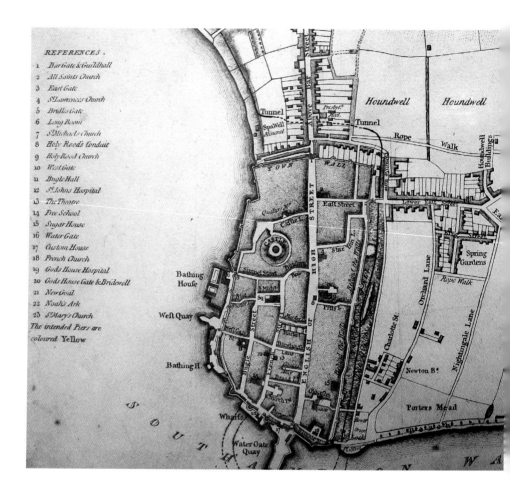

No doubt the rent of the house was low due to the fact that Castle Square had now become so run-down; Jane as always put a brave face on things: 'We hear that we are envied our House by many people, & that the Garden is the best in the Town.' Mrs Austen was planning to replace some old shrubs with roses, syringa and laburnum, and to plant currants, gooseberries and raspberries in a border under the terrace wall. After a few months' residence, however, it became clear that the house was not only old-fashioned but in poor condition: 'The Masons are now repairing the Chimney, which they

OPPOSITE Detail of map of Southampton, *by Milne, 1791. The circular mound of the castle is shown in the centre of the map, and the Austens' house was just to the north of it.*

ABOVE Blue Anchor Lane, Southampton, *a late nineteenth century engraving. This squalid lane was one of the approaches to Castle Square.*

found in such a state as to make it wonderful that it shd have stood so long, & next to impossible that another violent wind should not blow it down' – and faulty gutters meant the roof leaked into the store closet whenever it rained. In spite of these defects, it seemed likely that the rent would be increased; hence when Edward's bailiff for his Hampshire estates died in 1808 and his house in the village of Chawton became vacant, Mrs Austen was delighted to accept her son's offer that she should leave Southampton and live rent-free in Chawton instead.

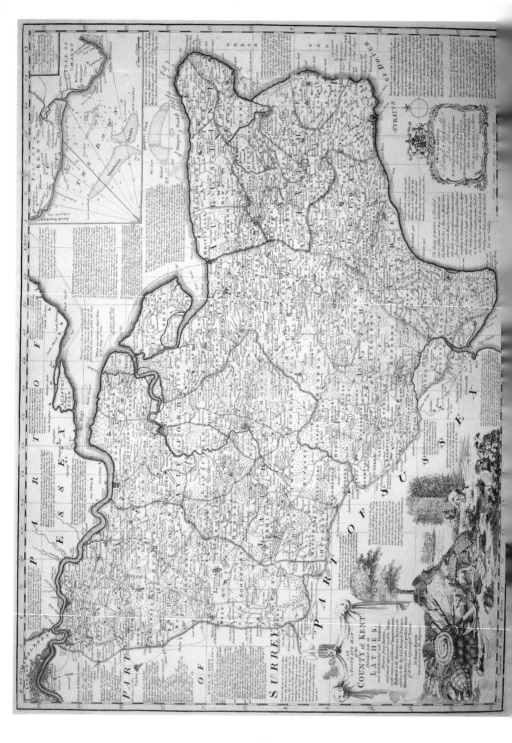

232

CHAPTER 7
LIFE AT GODMERSHAM
AND CHAWTON

I T WAS PROBABLY IN 1788 that Jane wrote one of the short stories of
her Juvenilia, 'Sir William Mountague', in which she composed the
following succinct biography for her hero: 'Sir William was about 17
when his Father died, & left him a handsome fortune, an ancient House & a
Park well stocked with Deer.' All her Juvenilia pieces were written as jokes
to be read aloud for the Austen family's enjoyment; and while 'Sir William
Mountague' is no exception to this rule, it does also contain some overtones
of the genuine situation in which her third brother Edward then found himself. Edward was born in 1767, and by 1783 it had become accepted that he
would be made the heir of Mr Austen's distant cousin Thomas Knight II, and
thereby eventually inherit three estates with their respective incomes, mansions, parks and livestock: Godmersham not far from Canterbury in Kent,
Steventon and Chawton in Hampshire. During the 1780s Edward spent more
and more time with the Knights at Godmersham, learning how to manage a
large property, until they sent him on a Grand Tour in 1786 which lasted for
four years. He was a serious and conscientious young man, and kept jour-
nals during this Grand Tour in which he made notes on the topography and
produce of the various countries through which he travelled; and in later
years included in his library about thirty treatises, many in several volumes,
dealing with agriculture, horticulture, and local Kentish history. Upon his

Map of Kent, *hand-coloured engraving by Emanuel Bowen, c.1780.*

The Hop Garden, *by W.F. Witherington, nineteenth century.*

return to England in 1790, Edward soon married Elizabeth, one of the many children of Sir Brook Bridges, Bt., of Goodnestone, a few miles to the east of Godmersham. For the first few years of their married life the young couple lived at Rowling, near Goodnestone, until the widowed Mrs Knight handed over the Godmersham estate to Edward in 1797; and following her death in 1812 he took the name of Knight by deed-poll.

Kent was a rich county, including as it did seaside resorts, fishing fleets, cross-Channel ports, quarries for the building stone Kentish Rag, large arable farms, sheep flocks, market gardens and orchards to provide vegetables and soft fruit for Londoners, and concentrations of hop gardens to serve the brewing industry. The area around Mereworth and Maidstone in particular was proudly called by the people of Kent the Garden of Eden – a district of meadows, cornfields, hop-gardens and orchards of apples, pears, cherries and filberts, interspersed with plantations of chestnut and ash trees

Godmersham Park, *engraving from E. Hasted, The History and Topographical Survey of the County of Kent, 1799.*

to provide the poles necessary for use in the hop-gardens. Sheep could also be grazed in the orchards, and the white long-woolled Romney Marsh breed were hardy and adaptable, very fine and large, and it was from this wool that Jane's clothier ancestors had made their money, enabling them to buy the small estates of Broadford and Grovehurst near Tonbridge in West Kent. As Jane wrote at the time of Edward's accession to his inheritance: 'Kent is the only place for happiness, Everybody is rich there.'

When Edward took over Godmersham, he became the owner of a handsome red-brick mansion in the Palladian style, built in the 1730s and enlarged in the 1780s, and which Jane could therefore perhaps describe as 'modern', as she did the Bertram family's Mansfield Park when she came to write that novel a few years later. The church of St Lawrence with its vicarage stood at a small distance from the village itself, where the home farm and some twenty houses clustered around the little River Stour, which flowed on past the mansion house, feeding fishponds as it went and in winter freezing over to fill the ice-house in the park. There were about twenty more houses elsewhere in the parish, with about 240 inhabitants in all.

Jane's first visit to Kent was in 1788, when she and Cassandra were taken by their parents to be introduced to Austen cousins in Sevenoaks and Tonbridge. After Edward's marriage the Austens visited him at Rowling, and once he was installed at Godmersham Jane and Cassandra stayed there frequently, for weeks and months at a time. From Jane's letters we know that Edward had pigs and hens on the farm, and that his cows and large flock of sheep grazed in the enclosed parkland around his mansion; she does not mention their breeds, but the sheep were probably Romney Marsh, and the cattle may have been Sussex Reds or perhaps the small black Welsh, which had been found to thrive in this part of Kent. They shared the parkland with a herd of some 600 fallow deer – very graceful animals which lent elegance to a landscape and also provided excellent venison for feasts and the honouring of guests. When Jane was staying at Rowling in September 1796, venison was on the menu, sent by Mrs Knight from Godmersham for the benefit of Edward and his visitors. The hills in the park were riddled with rabbit holes, and Edward's sons made rabbit nets as an evening pastime.

'the duties and dignities of the resident landholder'

It was remembered by his descendants that Edward never wanted to enter upon a political career and consistently declined any suggestion that he should offer himself as a candidate for Parliament, nor did he encourage any political ambitions in his sons. He was happy to take his share in local government – he was Deputy Lieutenant for Kent in 1792, High Sheriff of the county for the year 1801, and a visiting magistrate – and would have been prepared to fight for his country if need be. In May 1803 the short-lived Peace of Amiens, which had ended the French Revolutionary Wars, broke down and hostilities between Britain and France flared up afresh into the Napoleonic Wars. A cross-Channel invasion was daily expected, and as a result those able-bodied male inhabitants of Kent who were not already enrolled in the county militia formed themselves into Volunteer companies, whose duties, apart from learning basic military drill, consisted mainly of spending some weeks in rotation on guard duty at the Kentish ports and main towns. The East Kent Volunteers were embodied in the summer of 1803, and as Edward was appointed one of their captains, he formed his tenants into the Godmersham & Molash corps of the main company. His eldest daughter Fanny, then aged eleven, was amazed to see her peaceable father suddenly transformed into an army officer; in January 1804 she wrote to her ex-governess Miss Chapman:

> Today the men are to appear in there cloaths [*sic*] for the 1st time. Captain Austen looks very nice in his red coat, blue Breeches, & red Sash, he is now setting opposite to me & I can hardly write my letter for looking at him. The hat is a plain round common one with an oak bough & a Crescent in the middle.

During the next few months the Godmersham corps joined in with all the military exercises, and on Monday 18 June Fanny wrote in her diary: 'Papa went to Ashford early in the morning the men reviewed by Colonel Webb & marched home in the evening they dined or supped here & cheered Papa.' Luckily the Volunteers were never called upon to defend their county, since Admiral Nelson's victory over the French and Spanish fleets at Trafalgar in 1805 destroyed all Napoleon's hopes of invading the United Kingdom.

Edward's greatest interest was to attend to and improve his estates: when he first came to Godmersham the field called Bentigh was ploughland, but he planted it with underwood and made gravel walks through it, with an avenue of lime trees on each side of the principal walk, and added it to the shrubberies as part of the pleasure grounds of the park. The family always walked through the lime tree avenue on their way to church, leaving the shrubberies by a little door in the garden wall of the mansion, which brought them out opposite the church. Just outside the park was a small rounded hill on top of which, within the woods, was a summer house which had been built by the Knights earlier in the eighteenth century as a Grecian temple in the Doric style with a portico entrance of fluted columns and marble steps, and a fine grassy walk leading up to it. Edward planted more trees in this area and also created another plantation on what was called the Canterbury Hill. Fanny mentions in her letters and diaries the Temple Walk, the River Walk, the Serpentine Walk, the Hermitage, the Bathing House and the Gothic Seat – but apart from the Temple itself, it seems these landscape features have all disappeared.

Jane stayed at Godmersham at least seven times during the early years of the nineteenth century, and many of her letters to Cassandra, written during these visits, have survived; they show that even though she was no longer the

Study of Deer: stag in foreground with a group of does and fawns under a tree, *by Robert Hills (1769–1844)*.

daughter of an active hands-on farmer, her interest in the countryside and agriculture continued unabated. One evening in August 1805: '. . . we took a quiet walk round the Farm . . .', and a week later: 'We have also found time to visit all the principal walks of this place, except the walk round the top of the park, which we shall accomplish probably today.' She wrote an amusing pen-picture in verse of one of the Godmersham villagers:

> Happy the Lab'rer in his Sunday Cloathes!
> In light-drab coat, smart waistcoat, well-darn'd Hose
> And hat upon his head to Church he goes,
> As oft with conscious pride he downward throws
> A glance upon the ample Cabbage rose
> Which stuck in Buttonhole regales his nose,
> He envies not the gayest London Beaux.
> In Church he takes his seat among the rows,
> Pays to the Place the reverence he owes,
> Likes best the Prayers whose meaning least he knows,
> Lists to the Sermon in a softening Doze,
> And rouses joyous at the welcome close.

She went there again in the summer of 1808, travelling from London together with her brother James and his wife Mary Lloyd: 'The country is very beautiful. I saw as much as ever to admire in my yesterday's journey . . .', and a day or two afterwards:

> Yesterday passed quite à la Godmersham: the gentlemen rode about Edward's farm, and returned in time to saunter along Bentigh with us; and after dinner we visited the Temple Plantations. . . . James and Mary are much struck with the beauty of the place . . . James & Edward are gone to Sandling to-day; a nice scheme for James, as it will shew him a new & fine Country. Edward certainly excels in doing the Honours to his visitors, & providing for their amusement. . . . Edward began cutting Stfoin [sainfoin, *Onobrychis sativa*, a forage

plant introduced from France in the seventeenth century] on Saturday & I hope is likely to have favourable weather; – the crop is good.

Another rural amusement that summer was to drive to Buckwell, a farmhouse belonging to the Godmersham estate on the Ashford road, and see the fishpond dragged. Saltwater fish could only be obtained if one lived near the coast, and most people never knew its taste unless some kind friend sent a cod or turbot as a present, packed in straw in a basket and taken by the nearest stagecoach. When Jane was living in Southampton, she sent soles to their friends at Kintbury in Berkshire in this way. Freshwater fish – carp, tench, eels, pike, bream and roach – were therefore kept wherever it was feasible to create ponds, and from time to time the ponds would have to be dragged and the water drained off, so that stocks could be checked and replenished or diminished as necessary. For schoolboys it was great fun to splash about in the mud catching the fish with small landing-nets or eel-tongs. Jane did not join the expedition to Buckwell on this occasion, but a memory of it appears later in *Emma*: 'The cold repast was over, and the party were to go out once more to see what had not yet been seen, the old Abbey fish-ponds . . .' Instead she appreciated the summertime luxury that Edward's ice-house could provide: 'I shall eat Ice and drink French wine, & be above Vulgar Economy . . .' and Mrs Raffald's *The Experienced English Housekeeper* shows how ice-cream was made in pre-refrigeration days:

> Peel, stone and scald twelve apricots, beat them fine in a mortar, and put to them six ounces of sugar and a pint of scalding cream. Work it through a fine sieve, put it into a tin that hath a close cover, and set it in a tub of ice broken small and a large quantity of salt put among it. When you see your cream grow thick around the edges, stir it and set it in again until it is all frozen up. Then put on the lid and have ready another tub with ice and salt as before; put your tin in the middle and lay ice over and under it; let it stand four or five hours, and then dip your tin in warm water before you turn

it out. You may use any sort of fruit if you have not apricots, only observe to work it fine.

Jane's last visit to Godmersham was for two months in the autumn of 1813, when she commented to Cassandra: 'How Bentigh has grown! & the Canty.-Hills-Plantation!' She was rather disappointed in her eldest nephew, Edward junior, who had just come back from a trip to Scotland but had been uninterested in its wild romantic scenery. 'Edward is no Enthusiast in the beauties of Nature. His Enthusiasm is for the Sports of the field only. He

Landscape with tourists at Loch Katrine, Scotland, *oil on canvas, by John Knox; early nineteenth century.*

Chilham Castle, the seat of Jas. B. Wildman, Esq.; *lithograph from a drawing by G. Rymer, 1838. The Wildman family were close friends of Edward Knight, and their grounds at Chilham adjoined his at Godmersham.*

is a very promising & pleasing young Man however upon the whole. . . . & we must forgive his thinking more of Growse & Partridges than Lakes & Mountains.' He and his next brother, George, were out every day, either foxhunting or shooting game-birds, and getting very wet in the process, as October seems to have been constantly stormy.

Edward junior had his twenty-first birthday on 10 May 1815, and Fanny told Miss Chapman all about the celebrations:

[That was] the day Edward came of age – we had grand doings on the occasion – at least very pleasant doings, for it is always delightful to see a number of people happy & I believe that was most thoroughly the case. We had a ball for the servants and tenants, & as the Laundry was not thought large

Chawton House, Hampshire, *by Mellichamp, English School, c.1740.*

enough, the beds were taken down in the Nursery for them to dance there & the servants ornamented the room very prettily with handfuls of Lavender and Lilacs & at the upper end E.K. in gold letters surrounded with boughs & lamps. I had the honour of opening the Ball . . . and I believe they danced till 1 o'clock, & then supped in the Servants' Hall & Lobby . . . The next day the poor people danced before the Servants' Hall door, & afterwards danced on the green in front of the house – we counted above 200 people, & I never witnessed a more gratifying sight, than the glimpses of dancers & smokers . . . they gave several rounds of cheers, & I think their hurrahs might almost have been heard at Chilham . . . & we had also 'God Save the King' in fine style.

Godmersham was the Knights' principal estate, and Steventon and Chawton in Hampshire were always leased out to provide income. The Digweed family had been the tenants of Steventon since 1758 and were still farming there when the estate was sold in 1854; and of course that village had been Jane Austen's home for – as it turned out – more than half her lifespan. Chawton lay to the south-east of Steventon, about fifteen miles away by cross-country winding lanes, and until Edward offered a house there to his mother, it seems that the rest of the Austens did not know much about the village. The manor house was Elizabethan, similar in age to that at Steventon and like it built of local flints and stone; over the years it had been altered by succeeding generations of Knights and was now an awkward rambling old mansion, very unlike the planned Georgian elegance of Godmersham. The Knights usually rented this house out on short-term five- or seven-year leases; in 1807 it was empty in between tenancies, and as Godmersham needed to be redecorated, it was very convenient for Edward to move his family to Chawton for a few weeks during the summer. James Austen and his family came over from Steventon, and Mrs Austen and her daughters likewise travelled up from Southampton, and the family gathering lasted for about a fortnight. It was the first time Fanny had seen Chawton Great House (as the family came to call it) and she wrote to Miss Chapman in late August 1807:

> This is a fine large <u>old</u> house, built long before Queen Elizabeth I believe & here are such a number of old irregular passages &c &c that it is very entertaining to explore them, & often when I think myself miles away from one part of the house I find a passage or entrance close to it, & I don't know when I shall be quite mistress of the intricate, & different ways. . . . There are quantities of Trees about the house (especially Beech) which always makes a place pretty, I think.

The Austens would also then have seen the large cottage on the outskirts of Chawton village, where Edward's steward of the manor Bridger Seward was the tenant; it was about a hundred years old, L-shaped, built of red brick throughout and with red roof tiles as well, and contained quite a number of rooms though none of any great size. It was situated just at the junction of two main coach roads as they approached the little town of Alton about a mile further on – one road coming from Winchester and Southampton, and the other from Fareham and Gosport – and a wide but shallow pond filled in the triangle between the roads. The property had been briefly used as an inn from 1769–87, and was still referred to in documents as 'Late Inn' for decades thereafter, despite its return to private occupation. When Bridger Seward died in 1808, Edward offered the cottage to his mother, and as Mrs Austen and her daughters were glad to leave Southampton behind them they moved in during July 1809; and this was Jane's last home, until her death eight years later.

'The many comforts that await our Chawton home'

James Austen and his family were now able to keep in much closer touch with the inhabitants of the Cottage, and many years later his younger daughter Caroline wrote down her very clear memories of the house and the lifestyle of her grandmother and aunts:

> The front door opened on the road, a very narrow enclosure of each side, protected the house from the possible shock of any runaway vehicle. A good-sized entrance, and two parlours, called dining and drawing room, made the <u>length</u> of the house; all intended originally to look on the road – but the large drawing room window was blocked-up and turned into a bookcase when Mrs Austen took possession and another was opened at the side, which gave to view only turf and trees. A high wooden fence shut out the road (the Winchester road it was) all the length of the little domain, and trees were planted inside to form a shrubbery walk – which carried round the enclosure, gave a very sufficient space for exercise – you did not feel cramped for room; and there was a pleasant irregular

Chawton Cottage, Hampshire, *drawing by A.H. Hallam Murray, 1897.*

mixture of hedgerow, and grass, and gravel walk and long grass for mowing, and orchard – which I imagine arose from two or three little enclosures having been thrown together, and arranged as best might be, for ladies' occupation – There was besides, a good kitchen garden, large court and many out-buildings.

Some of these sheltered the two donkeys and their carriage which Edward had also provided for his mother's convenience.

The census of 1811 showed that Chawton had 347 inhabitants, making it twice as large as either Steventon or Deane, and apart from grazing flocks of sheep much of Edward's land was used to grow wheat, oats, barley,

turnips and peas. Pound Farm, Lower Farm and Manor Farm were all tenanted by an old friend of the Austens, Harry Digweed, second son of the
family farming the Steventon estate, who had married Jane Terry, one of
the huge Terry family at Dummer whom Jane had met at assembly balls in
past years. Not only was Chawton itself a much bigger village, it was not
nearly so isolated as Steventon had been, since it was within walking distance of the market-town of Alton which, with about 2,500 inhabitants, was
much the same size as Basingstoke. A contemporary gazetteer described
Alton as being '. . . a pleasant healthy town, on the great western road from
London through Farnham, to Southampton and the Isle of Wight. It con-
sists of three streets, the principal of which is wide, and modern built. It has
a market on Saturdays and two annual fairs . . . There are two good inns, the
Swan and the Crown. . . . The country round is remarkably fertile and populous, having an excellent neighbourhood.' The town was divided by the
little River Wey which ran through the middle of it and so on northwards to
join the Thames at Weybridge in Surrey; Alton Westbrook held its annual
fair at the end of April, and Alton Eastbrook's was at Michaelmas, and in
years to come Jane would take one or more of her little nieces to enjoy these
festivities. The Alton Book Society, which Mrs Austen and her daughters
promptly joined, held its meetings at the Swan Inn; and Mr William Curtis,
the Quaker apothecary in the High Street, became their local doctor. Austen
Gray & Vincent, a branch of Henry's London bank, also had its premises in
the High Street, and letters to and from Henry could therefore travel conveniently in the bank's parcels. On some occasions Francis and his young
family lived in Chawton or Alton in between his naval duties, and his eldest
daughter Mary-Jane often visited the Cottage as a playmate for her cousins
– James's Caroline, and the three motherless daughters of Jane's youngest
brother Charles while he too was away at sea.

Mrs Austen now settled back into very much the same way of country
life that she had enjoyed in Steventon, though with these urban benefits of
Alton close at hand. During the years of absence in Bath and Southampton,
she had never lost touch with Steventon, pleased to have Mary Lloyd's
news of the villagers: 'I am very glad to have so good an account of Jenny
Smallbones, she is one I have a regard for', the Old Shepherd and the

Windsor Forest with Oxen Drawing Timber, *gouache on paper, by Paul Sandby, 1798.*

Tilburys – and a youthful William, one of the familiar Littleworth clan, was taken on as manservant at the Cottage. Mrs Austen no longer kept any cows but set up a chicken run again, and enjoyed planting her own vegetables – digging potatoes while dressed in a green smock like a labourer, as her grandchildren remembered – as well as tending the soft fruit bushes, including her favourite gooseberries. With Cassandra's aid she filled the flower borders, asking Edward's family to provide her with seeds from his Godmersham gardens, and over the next few years Jane mentions in her letters mignonette, pinks, sweet Williams, columbines and peonies, as well as the orchard trees of Orleans plums, greengages, mulberries and apricots. Indoors, she was happy to hand over all domestic duties to her daughters: it was Jane's task to make the family's breakfast and to take charge of the stores of tea, sugar and wine, and Cassandra did the rest, supervising the manservant and two maids.

Young Caroline recalled: 'After luncheon, my Aunts generally walked out – sometimes they went to Alton for shopping. – Often, one or the other of them, to the Great House – as it was then called – when a brother was inhabiting it, to make a visit – or if the house were standing empty they liked to stroll about the grounds – sometimes to Chawton Park – a noble beech wood, just within a walk –' Jane's letters from now on are full of comments on the weather, the countryside and the agricultural life around her. With a knowledgeable eye she told Cassandra that their neighbour Mr Prowting had opened a gravel pit '. . . just at the mouth of the approach to his House but it looks a little as if he meant to catch all his company. Tolerable Gravel.'

At New Year 1813 Cassandra was staying with James and his family in Steventon and found their old home was wet and muddy; Jane wrote teasingly in response: 'A very sloppy lane last Friday! – What an odd sort of country you must be in! I cannot at all understand it! It was just greasy here on Friday, in consequence of the little snow that had fallen in the night . . . upon the whole, the Weather for Winter-weather is delightful, the walking excellent.' A fortnight later she told Cassandra: 'I walked to Alton, & dirt excepted, found it delightful, – it seemed like an old Feby. come back again' – but soon the month lived up to its country nickname of February Filldyke, and became too wet and windy for Jane to walk again to Alton to post her next letter to Cassandra. At midsummer, Jane wrote to Francis Austen, sailing in the Baltic Ocean: 'July begins unpleasantly with us, cold & showery, but it is often a baddish month. We had some fine dry weather preceding it, which was very acceptable to the Holders of Hay & the Masters of Meadows – In general it must have been a good Haymaking Season. Edward has got in all his, in excellent order . . .' and the wheat harvest too was abundant that year.

Apart from rejoicing in her regained freedom in the country, the settled routine of life in the Cottage enabled Jane at last to concentrate upon writing and publishing her novels. While at Steventon she had written *Sense and Sensibility, Pride and Prejudice* and *Susan* (her original title for *Northanger Abbey*), and during the Chawton years she was finally able to publish the first two, in 1811 and 1813 respectively. Even before *Pride and*

Prejudice appeared in print, Jane was working on *Mansfield Park*, and possibly it was her relief at being back in rural Hampshire which led to her endowing Fanny Price with her own feelings of interest and pleasure in the appearance of the countryside and everything around her. Later in 1813 brother Henry took Jane up to London, and for some of the way they drove along the crest of the long hill called the Hog's Back, part of the North Downs which cross Surrey from east to west. Nowadays all roads are dull grey with tarmac or concrete, but in Jane's time the road at Farnham was bright yellow sand, turning to staring white chalk as it rose up to the Hog's Back where it ran straight for nine miles, with wide grassy verges and thick hedges of dog-rose and privet side by side with holly, elder, hazel and buckthorn, and gnarled yew trees bent over by the prevailing wind. Upon arrival in London Jane wrote to Cassandra: 'I was very much pleased with the Country in general – ; – between Guildford & Ripley I thought it particularly pretty, also about Painshill & every where else; & from a Mr Spicer's Grounds at Esher which we walked into before our dinner, the views were beautiful. I cannot say what we did <u>not</u> see, but I should think there could not be a Wood or a Meadow or a Palace or a remarkable spot in England that was not spread out before us, on one side or the other. . . . I never saw the Country from the Hogsback so advantageously.'

In 1814 Jane started writing *Emma*, a story as happy as that of *Pride and Prejudice* and, with a hero who is a practical landowner managing his own farm, as thoroughly rooted in the soil as one of Mr Knightley's apple-trees. After a cold spring, there was good weather all through the summer months; in mid-June Jane wrote to Cassandra in London: 'This is a delightful day in the Country, & I hope not much too hot for Town.' July continued very hot, and there was brilliant sunshine during August and September which greatly aided harvesting. Jane herself went to London again in late August, and noticed that: 'The wheat looked very well all the way . . .' – and undoubtedly the sunshine around her made its way into the happy ending, where Jane uses the weather as a symbol of the resolution of misunderstandings between Emma and Mr Knightley.

There was a fine summer also in 1815 continuing right up to October; but on the other side of the globe Mount Tambora in Indonesia erupted – the

Summertime, *drawing by Thomas Hearne, 1780–4.*

world's largest eruption for over 1300 years. Just as had happened with the Icelandic eruptions in 1783 in Jane's childhood, ash and sulphur dioxide gas were blasted into the stratosphere; however in this case the result was the opposite – there was no excessively hot summer weather but in the following year all the northern hemisphere suffered under a volcanic winter with unusually low temperatures. In Britain and Ireland it was cold and very wet and 1816 became known as 'the year without a summer.' The effects seem to have reached Chawton in the spring. In mid-March Jane told Caroline: 'Our Pond is brimful & our roads are dirty & our walls are damp, & we sit wishing every bad day may be the last. It is not cold however.' But as the months passed the rain continued, and Jane wrote to her nephew James-Edward at Steventon in July:

> Oh! it rains again; it beats against the window. – Mary Jane & I have been wet through once already today, we set off in the Donkey Carriage for Farringdon as I wanted to see the improvements Mr Woolls is making, but we were obliged to turn back before we got there, but not soon enough to avoid a Pelter all the way home. We met Mr Woolls – I talked of its being bad weather for the Hay – & he returned me the comfort of its being much worse for the Wheat.

There were severe frosts in early September, and the harvest was one of the most disastrous known. Jane was working on *Persuasion* this year, and perhaps the dismal weather had an effect upon the composition of this novel too; when Anne Elliot drives off from Uppercross in Lady Russell's carriage on a wet November day, 'she could not quit the mansion-house, or look an adieu to the cottage, with its black, dripping, and comfortless veranda, or even notice through the misty glasses the last humble tenements of the village, without a saddened heart'.

'. . . an handsome house and large income . . .'

Now that she was living in Chawton, Jane was no longer a farmer's daughter but instead the squire's sister – a difference in status and outlook; and this is subtly reflected in her later novels. The first three, those composed at Steventon, are set in rather lower and poorer ranks of society than the three written at Chawton. Catherine Morland is merely the daughter of a country parson, and her childhood spent running about the countryside and joining in boys' games with her brothers is probably quite similar to what Jane's must have been; in *Sense and Sensibility* Mrs Dashwood and her daughters have been dispossessed of their wealthy life at Norland Park and have become the poor relations of Sir John Middleton, learning how to live in Barton Cottage with its few plain rooms, dark narrow stairs and smoky kitchen – perhaps not unlike Steventon rectory. *Pride and Prejudice* is very much a small-town story: the excitement caused by the arrival of a new family in the neighbourhood, inhabited as it is by Sir William Lucas, the tradesman and former mayor, who earned his knighthood merely by 'an address to the King, during his mayoralty'; Mrs Long, who is too poor to keep her own carriage and has two nieces to marry off; the Bennet girls' Uncle Gardiner the London merchant, and Uncle Phillips the fat stuffy local attorney, with his wife as noisy and gossipy as their own mother – Jane must have seen plenty of such people in Basingstoke and Odiham. When the novel was first published some readers considered Lizzy Bennet's background to be deplorably vulgar and she herself ill-mannered, impertinent and quite unsuitable for Darcy.

After Jane's experience of life at Godmersham, amongst just such rich landowners as her brother and his neighbours, the novels of her maturity – *Mansfield Park*, *Emma* and *Persuasion* – are written much more from the point of view of that rank of society: the domestic lives of the men who have the responsibility of managing large estates and leading their local communities. In the social structure of the time, it was expected that landowners would employ the villagers who lived on their estates, and villagers in turn would expect to be employed by the landowner, either as indoor domestics or outdoor labourers. Such employment could be for life, men and women alike, and a good master would also find light work for the very young and the very old, whether it were weeding paths, cutting the lawns and sweeping up fallen leaves in pleasure-grounds, or simply being allotted a plot of waste ground upon which to grow their own vegetables. Housing might also be provided: it was reported in the agricultural press that Mr Bramston had erected two kinds of cottage at Oakley, 'one for individual families, the other a sort of poor-house cottage for the reception of pauper families, when the pressure of these indigents is so hard on the parish as to preclude the whole from being supplied with single tenements'. The larger cottages were single-storey, with cob walls and thatched roof; in the middle was a common kitchen or living room 15 feet square with a fireplace, separate oven and two pantries, and to left and right of the kitchen were two bedrooms, each 7 feet 6 inches by 15 feet. Two or more pauper families would be placed in these cottages, and expected to care for each other, the old people looking after the children while the parents were out at work. The cottage intended for individual families had a smaller living room, but was otherwise the same plan.

In winter it was expected that the landowner would provide 'broth' for the poorest tenants for several months, though by most accounts this would seem to have been more like a thick soup or stew. The James Austen family's friend, Mrs Chute of the Vyne at Sherborne St John, recorded in her diary buying 36 pounds of beef every month, as well as bushels of onions and peas, and serving out this 'broth' up to sixteen times in one year. Jane shows her readers the best side of Emma Woodhouse's rather domineering nature when she describes her paying a charitable visit in mid-December to some miserable cottagers living on the outskirts of Highbury:

> Emma was very compassionate; and the distresses of the poor were as sure of relief from her personal attention and kindness, her counsel and her patience, as from her purse. She understood their ways, could allow for their ignorance and their temptations, had no romantic expectations of extraordinary virtue from those, for whom education had done so little; entered into their troubles with ready sympathy, and always gave her assistance with as much intelligence as goodwill.

As Emma starts to walk up the muddy lane again on the way home, she was 'overtaken by a child from the cottage, setting out, according to orders, with her pitcher, to fetch broth from Hartfield.'

The female part of the landowner's family would be expected also to buy or make clothes for the poorer cottagers, especially at Christmas-time – rugs or blankets, thick woollen stockings for men and women alike, warm waistcoats for the old men, calico or linen shifts and aprons for the women, and shirts and flannel wrappers for the babies. Before the Austens left Steventon, Jane wrote to Cassandra in October 1798: 'Dame Tilbury's daughter has lain in – Shall I give her any of your Baby Cloathes?' – and at Chawton she visited Dame Garnet in the midst of her children: 'I took her an old Shift & promised her a set of our [baby] Linen.' At Mansfield Park, Mrs Norris is as usual scolding Fanny: 'If you have no work of your own, I can supply you from the poor-basket. There is all the new calico that was bought last week, not touched yet. I am sure I almost broke my back by cutting it out.'

As the nineteenth century progressed, the ladies of the manor began to set up schools for the labourers' children: in 1816 Mrs Chute opened a Sunday School – 'then an almost unheard-of thing' – in Sherborne St John, using two rooms in an empty cottage, one for the boys and one for the girls. Clothing might also be given to those who attended: when the political journalist William Cobbett was riding through East Stratton in Hampshire in 1822 he saw a little girl wearing a woollen gown, with white apron and plaid cloak, and carrying a book, who told him that Lady Baring gave her the clothes and had her taught to read and to sing hymns and spiritual songs. Chawton itself had no proper village school until 1840, and Cassandra did what she could to fill the gap by teaching reading, sewing, and the catechism to some of the little girls.

As might be expected, Edward Knight was a most conscientious landowner and considerate employer; apart from what is known of his life at Godmersham from Jane's letters and his daughter Fanny's diaries, two meticulously kept account books survive relating to his Hampshire estates, the earlier of which is for the years 1808–19. This book shows that up to 1816 Edward's gross income from Chawton and Steventon combined was on average £5,000 per annum; after a rent increase this jumped to £6,000 in 1817, and to £8,000 in 1819. If he had as much again from the Godmersham estate, he was even more wealthy than Mr Darcy with his annual £10,000 at Pemberley. The incomings are rents for main properties – Mr Middleton paid £100 every half-year for the Great House tenancy, and the Digweeds paid £312 half-yearly for the Steventon manor house and lands – other smaller payments from agricultural tenants, and the sales of timber, bark, underwood and faggots. Outgoings are land tax, property tax, parochial rates, repairs to properties, allowances to tenants against rents, payments to his workers and miscellaneous cash payments, such as that to Triggs the gamekeeper who looks after the sporting dogs and is reimbursed for buying their food. Once Mrs Austen and her daughters come to Chawton in 1809, Edward gives £10 to Cassandra every December for distribution amongst the poorer of the cottagers. Rent or audit days were held twice a year, midwinter and midsummer, when the tenant farmers would come

Man holding a staff, *oil on canvas, by Thomas Barker, c.1800.*

to pay their rents and afterwards be entertained to dinner. Edward owned two inns in Alton, the Crown and the George, and on 21 June 1809 the audit day was held at the latter hostelry; fifteen tenants attended, and the bill totalled £5.7s.6d. [£5.37], including wine, punch, grog, cider, tobacco, and extra waiters to serve it all.

In the summer of 1813 Edward brought his whole family to stay at Chawton Great House for four months, and this prolonged holiday evidently inspired one of his Kentish villagers to take the opportunity to follow suit, for Fanny Knight recorded in her diary on 19 June: 'Old W. Amos came from dear Godmersham having walked or rather <u>hopped</u> the whole way.' Old Will enjoyed talking of gardening matters with Cassandra, and after his return to Godmersham sent a message to her via Edward's second daughter, Lizzy, when she wrote to her aunt in October 1813: 'Poor Will Amos hopes your skerrets [a root vegetable of the parsnip family] are doing well; he has left his house in the poor Row, and lives in a barn at Builting. We asked him why he went away, and he said the fleas were so starved when he came back from Chawton that they all flew upon him and <u>eenermost</u> eat him up.' Perhaps in emulation of Will Amos's enterprise, in her turn Bet Littleworth walked to Kent, as Anna Lefroy recalled: '[She] once travelled on foot from Steventon to Godmersham, more than a hundred miles; it was her delight in after life to relate the history of that adventure – and how the Squire [Edward] came out to welcome her arrival, and gave a special charge to his servants to make much of her because she was his old Playfellow.'

'a state of alteration, perhaps of improvement'

When Mr Austen first came to Steventon in the middle of the eighteenth century, the then old Squire Harwood of Deane said to him: 'You know all about these sort of things. Do tell us. Is Paris in France, or France in Paris? – for my wife has been disputing with me about it.' The landowners who appear in Jane's novels are no longer so totally ignorant of life beyond their parish boundaries, but in *Sense and Sensibility* the Middletons are unashamedly bucolic: 'Sir John was a sportsman, Lady Middleton a mother. He hunted and shot, and she humoured her children, and these were their only resources. Lady Middleton had the advantage of being able to spoil her children all the year round, while Sir John's independent employments were in existence only half the time.' Twenty years later, the Musgroves in *Persuasion* remain unmodernised: 'The Mr Musgroves had their own game to guard, and to destroy; their own horses, dogs, and newspapers to engage them; and the females were fully occupied in all the other common subjects of housekeeping, neighbours, dress, dancing, and music.' Their in-laws, the Hayters, who live on the other side of the hill from Uppercross, are even more behind the times: 'Winthrop, without beauty and without dignity, was stretched before them; an indifferent house, standing low, and hemmed in by the barns and buildings of a farm-yard.'

Young Charles Musgrove knows that this estate is not less than two hundred and fifty acres, and that the Hayters also own a farm near Taunton 'which is some of the best land in the country' – and thinks of the future, when his cousin 'will make a different sort of place of it, and live in a very different sort of way . . .'

Mrs Reynolds, the old housekeeper at Pemberley, speaks glowingly of Mr Darcy: 'He is the best landlord, and the best master that ever lived. Not like the wild young men nowadays, who think of nothing but themselves. There is not one of his tenants or servants but what will give him a good name. Some people call him proud; but I am sure I never saw any thing of it. To my fancy, it is only because he does not rattle away like other young men.' In a comically inverted way, this concern for an estate's tenants appears also

Stag at Bay – scene near Taplow, Bucks., *watercolour, by Thomas Rowlandson, between 1795 and 1801.*

in Darcy's aunt, Lady Catherine de Bourgh, for '. . . though this great lady was not in the commission of the peace for the county, she was a most active magistrate in her own parish, the minutest concerns of which were carried to her by Mr Collins; and whenever any of the cottagers were disposed to be quarrelsome, discontented or too poor, she sallied forth into the village to settle their differences, silence their complaints, and scold them into harmony and plenty.'

Sir Walter Elliot is sufficiently proud of his estate to refuse his lawyer's suggestion of selling some of it: 'He had condescended to mortgage as far as he had the power, but he would never condescend to sell. No; he would never disgrace his name so far. The Kellynch estate should be transmitted whole and entire, as he had received it' – but he is not willing to reduce his spending and live in a more modest style; nor does it seem that either he or Elizabeth take any interest in the wellbeing of their tenants, beyond Sir Walter making 'condescending bows for all the afflicted tenantry and cottagers who might have had a hint to shew themselves', when he and

LIFE

Elizabeth, with the ingratiating Mrs Clay in tow, finally drive off to Bath. It is Anne who spends time, as she says, 'going to almost every house in the parish, as a sort of take-leave. I was told that they wished it.' The Kellynch tenants might well have preferred Lady Catherine's well-meaning interference to Sir Walter's neglect and, no doubt, long-standing debts to the local tradesmen.

Sense and Sensibility, Pride and Prejudice and *Persuasion* are abstract qualities, and these titles give clues as to the nature of the story and the way in which the course of the plot may unfold. *Emma* gives the clue that the action must be centred upon the heroine so named. *Northanger Abbey* and *Mansfield Park* are the titles which specify places, and it is the place which shapes the lives of the residents and their visitors. Of all Jane's six novels, *Mansfield Park* has the most references to estates and landowners, their interests and concerns: the action opens at the Bertrams' home, the Park itself, 'a spacious modern-built house, so well placed and well screened as to deserve to be in any collection of engravings of gentlemen's seats in the kingdom . . . set in a park five miles round . . .' and then moves to Sotherton, a few miles away, '. . . built in Elizabeth's time . . . a large, regular, brick building heavy but respectable looking . . .', where its new owner, young Mr Rushworth, now that he has become engaged to Maria Bertram, wants to modernise the pleasure-grounds.

Jane does not tell us precisely how wealthy Sir Thomas Bertram is, but the profits of the Mansfield estate, plus those of his plantation in Antigua – although this has suffered some recent losses – presumably add up to about £10,000 a year, since Mr Rushworth's £12,000 a year means that after her marriage Maria will be richer than her father. Jane gives her readers a pen-picture of the Sotherton property, in Maria's boastful words during the drive there:

> She could not tell Miss Crawford that 'those woods belonged to Sotherton,' she could not carelessly observe that 'she believed it was now all Mr Rushworth's property on each side of the road,' without elation of heart . . .

'Now we shall have no more rough road, Miss Crawford, our difficulties are over. The rest of the way is such as it ought to be. Mr Rushworth has made it since he succeeded to the estate. Here begins the village. Those cottages are really a disgrace. The church spire is reckoned remarkably handsome. I am glad the church is not so close to the Great House as often

Pheasant Shooting, *oil on canvas, by George Morland, 1792.*

happens in old places. The annoyance of the bells must be terrible. There is the parsonage; a tidy-looking house, and I understand the clergyman and his wife are very decent people. Those are alms-houses, built by some of the family. To the right is the steward's house; he is a very respectable man. Now we are coming to the lodge gates; but we have nearly a mile through the park still. It is not ugly, you see, at this end; there is some fine timber, but the situation of the house is dreadful. We go down hill to it for half a mile, and it is a pity, for it would not be an ill-looking place if it had a better approach.'

Henry Crawford's estate is at Everingham, in Norfolk, and worth £4,000 a year; we do not hear anything about the house, but he tells the Bertrams that he has already improved the grounds – started planning when he was at school, altered his ideas a little while at Cambridge, and carried out the work as soon as he came of age – so now he has nothing left to do except advise Mr Rushworth and flirt with Maria during the visit to Sotherton. Later in the story, he tries to impress Fanny Price by taking on the role of a conscientious landowner anxious to supervise his local agent: 'I have half an idea of going into Norfolk again soon. I am not satisfied about Maddison. I am sure he still means to impose on me if possible, and get a cousin of his own into a certain mill, which I design for somebody else. . . . [It would be] worse than simple to let him give me a hard-hearted, griping fellow for a tenant, instead of an honest man, to whom I have given half a promise already.'

Emma is set in a world based upon practical farming rather than landowning, since Mr Knightley's property at Donwell Abbey provides him with a comfortable but by no means unduly large income – he does not keep any carriage-horses, because he has 'little spare money and a great deal of health, activity, and independence', and so walks everywhere instead. He is in fact one of the most cultured of Jane's heroes: although he spends his days out supervising his home farm, in the evenings he reads and studies the 'books of engravings, drawers of medals, cameos, corals, shells, and every other family collection within his cabinets'. Early on the story, when Emma is still puffed up with her own conceit, she looks down upon Harriet's suitor Robert

Martin, Mr Knightley's hardworking tenant at the Abbey Mill Farm: 'He is very plain, undoubtedly – remarkably plain; – but that is nothing, compared with his entire want of gentility . . . I had no idea that he could be so very clownish, so totally without air. . . . He will be a completely gross, vulgar farmer – totally inattentive to appearances, and thinking of nothing but profit and loss.' By the end, however, when her foolish matchmaking plans for Harriet have resulted in only her own embarrassment and unhappiness, and she has actually met Robert Martin, 'she fully acknowledged in him all the appearance of sense and worth which could bid fairest for her little friend'.

Apart from meadows and fields, woodland upon estates provided shelter for the game-birds, deer and foxes which would be pursued by the landowner and his friends in autumn and winter. In his youth James Austen had gone out foxhunting with local Hampshire packs; and Henry enjoyed shooting at Godmersham; but niece Caroline remembered that Edward Knight, who had always had unlimited means to indulge in field sports, cared not for them at all, and never hunted or shot. In fictional life, although Mr Bennet seems to take little interest in his estate, he has presumably been out shooting deer and partridges, since Mrs Bennet congratulates herself upon the dinner she has provided: 'The venison was roasted to a turn – and everybody said, they never saw so fat a haunch . . . and even Mr Darcy acknowledged, that the partridges were remarkably well done; and I suppose he has two or three French cooks at least.' – and she also begs Bingley to come and shoot game-birds at Longbourn whenever he wishes. General Tilney tells Catherine: 'I cannot in decency fail attending the club. . . . They are a set of very worthy men. They have half a buck from Northanger twice a year; and I dine with them whenever I can.' Mansfield Park has plenty of woods to shelter pheasants, and Tom and Edmund have been shooting for several days in October just before Sir Thomas returns home, while Maria is already beginning to regret her engagement: '. . . with only Mr Rushworth to attend to her, and doomed to the repeated details of his day's sport, good or bad, his boast of his dogs, his jealousy of his neighbours, his doubts of their qualification, and his zeal after poachers –' The right to hunt game was restricted to those with the legal qualification of a freehold worth at least £1,000 a year or a leasehold of at least £150 a year; so from his pinnacle of £12,000 a year Mr Rushworth no doubt feels he is entitled to despise his poorer neighbours; and if he is zealous after poachers, he is probably happy to set mantraps and spring-guns in the Sotherton woods. There is a trout stream at Pemberley, hence Darcy is able to invite Mr Gardiner to come and fish as often as he chooses, promising as well to lend him the necessary fishing tackle. Colonel Brandon's relations at Whitwell presumably can fish as well as sail upon their 'noble piece of water' there; and though Mr Knightley's Donwell Abbey estate does not seem to be large enough for him to keep deer, perhaps he and Robert Martin may join in fishing in the mill-stream.

Another advantage landowners might also possess was that of having the advowson of some parish on their estate – that is, the right to present their own clerical candidate to be the parson – which right they naturally exercised in favour of their family and friends. Colonel Brandon has the presentation of Delaford and so is able to benefit his brother-in-law Edward Ferrars; General Tilney has that of Woodston and builds a new parsonage there for his son Henry; Sir Thomas Bertram has Mansfield and Thornton Lacey, and by the end of the book his son Edmund has become the rector of both of them. In real life, the Knight family owned Steventon and Chawton, which is why Jane's father, as a cousin of the Knights, was presented by them to Steventon.

Although Edward Knight was not interested in politics, it was quite usual for landowners to become Members of Parliament: Mr Chute of the Vyne was an MP for Hampshire for many years, though never very active in the House of Commons. In 1813 Jane met at Godmersham Mr Stephen Lushington, the Member for Canterbury, and wrote sardonically to Cassandra: 'I am sure he is clever & a Man of Taste. . . . He is quite an M.P. – very smiling, with an exceeding good address, & readiness of Language. . . . I dare say he is ambitious & Insincere.' Sir Thomas Bertram is definitely an MP, as Jane tells us: 'Lady Bertram, in consequence of a little ill-health, and a great deal of indolence, gave up the house in town, which she had been used to occupy every spring, and remained wholly in the country, leaving Sir Thomas to attend his duty in Parliament, with whatever increase or diminution of comfort might arise from her absence.' It would seem that General Tilney is probably in the House, since he tells Catherine: 'I have many pamphlets to finish . . . before I can close my eyes; and perhaps may be poring over the affairs of the nation

A Country Race Course, *aquatint after William Mann, 1786.*

for hours after you are asleep.' Sir Walter Elliot remembers that he and young William Elliot '. . . must have been seen together . . . once at Tattersal's, and twice in the lobby of the House of Commons.'

After the cold wet year of 1816, January 1817 brought yet more storms and floods but was unusually mild, which was a relief for the inhabitants of Chawton Cottage, as Jane wrote to her friend Alethea Bigg: '. . . & though we have a great many Ponds, & a fine running stream through the Meadows on the other side of the road it is nothing but what beautifies us & does to talk of.' Jane had been inexplicably unwell during 1816 but told Alethea she now thought she was getting better; and on 27 January started writing her next novel, known to us as *Sanditon*. Despite these hopes, her strength continued to ebb away, and though in early March she felt '. . . quite equal to walking about & enjoying the Air; & by sitting down & resting a good while between my Walks, I get exercise enough,' she wrote her last sentence in the manuscript on 18 March. She still wanted 'air & exercise' and managed to take a short ride on one of the Cottage's donkeys, led by Cassandra; but thereafter had to stay in her bedroom, and Mr Curtis the Alton apothecary admitted he could do nothing further to help her. At the end of May James Austen provided his carriage to take his sisters to Winchester so that Jane could consult one of the surgeons there, and she and Cassandra set off together on yet another rainy day, with brother Henry and nephew William Knight becoming wet through as they rode beside the carriage. They took lodgings in College Street; and the surgeon told James and his wife privately that it was now only a question of time.

After a brief hot spell in June, rain set in again and was almost incessant until the end of August. Lying in bed in the lodgings, on 15 July Jane remembered it was St Swithin's Day, when according to popular superstition if it rained upon that day, then it would rain for forty days thereafter. In its issue of Monday 14 July, the *Hampshire Chronicle* had advertised that horse-races would be held on Worthy Down, just outside Winchester, on 29, 30 and 31 July; and Jane amused herself with the idea of old St Swithin arising from his tomb to reproach the race-going inhabitants of the town:

These races and revels and dissolute measures
With which you're debasing a neighbouring Plain
Let them stand – you shall meet with your curse in your pleasures
Set off for your course, I'll pursue with my rain.

These verses were her very last composition, for on the 17th she suddenly became much worse and died in the dawn of Friday 18 July, with Cassandra and Mary Lloyd beside her.

As her niece Anna Lefroy remembered and told her family in later years, Jane's delight in natural scenery was such that she would sometimes say she thought it must form one of the joys of heaven – and being a parson's daughter as well as a farmer's daughter, perhaps in her last conscious moments she may have recalled the comforting words of Psalm 23: 'The Lord is my shepherd, I shall not want. / He maketh me to lie down in green pastures, he leadeth me beside the still waters . . .'

INDEX

Acknowledgments

The Publishers have made every effort to contact holders of copyright works. Any copyright holders we have been unable to reach are invited to contact the Publishers so that a full acknowledgment may be given in subsequent editions. For permission to reproduce the images of the following pages, and for supplying photographs, the Publishers thank those listed below.

BRIDGEMAN ART LIBRARY: 2–3, 24, 40, 49, 70, 89, 92–3, 94–5, 107, 133, 145, 153, 173, 179, 185, 234, 248, 251

BRITISH MUSEUM IMAGES: 76

CHAWTON HOUSE LIBRARY: 243

COMPTON VERNEY HOUSE TRUST: 99

ELMBRIDGE MUSEUM: 151

FITZWILLIAM MUSEUM: 74

HAMPSHIRE ARTS & MUSEUMS SERVICE: 31, 35

HAMPSHIRE RECORD OFFICE: 1, 58, 197

JANE AUSTEN'S HOUSE MUSEUM: 206–7

MUSEUM OF ENGLISH RURAL LIFE: 66, 73 below, 175,

NATIONAL GALLERY, LONDON: 191

NATIONAL GALLERY OF VICTORIA: 103

ORION BOOKS: 110, 134

PUSHKIN MUSEUM OF FINE ARTS, MOSCOW: 198

ROSIE SANDERS: 210

SCOTTISH NATIONAL GALLERY: 241

SOUTHAMPTON CITY COUNCIL: 231

TATE GALLERY, LONDON: 64, 175, 187, 202,

YALE CENTER FOR BRITISH ART: 55, 67, 96–7, 112, 113, 119, 121, 149, 177, 180 BELOW, 220, 227, 238, 256, 258, 260